THE ULSTER AWAKENING

THE ULSTER
AWAKENING

An Account of the 1859 Revival in Ireland

John Weir

THE BANNER OF TRUTH TRUST

THE BANNER OF TRUTH TRUST

3 Murrayfield Road, Edinburgh EH12 6EL, UK

P.O. Box 621, Carlisle, PA 17013, USA

*

First published 1860
This reset edition 2009
© Banner of Truth Trust 2009

ISBN-13: 978 1 84871 037 5

*

Typeset in 10.5/13.5 pt Adobe Caslon Pro at
The Banner of Truth Trust, Edinburgh
Printed in the USA by
Versa Press, Inc.,
East Peoria, IL

CONTENTS

PART TWO
Personal Observations and Inquiries

PART THREE
Matters Arising from the Revival

PREFACE

WHY WE MAY EXPECT A REVIVAL[1]

It being admitted that the real and active agency of the Spirit of God for the conversion of souls may reasonably be expected in the Christian church, the only question which remains to be considered is whether that divine agent will *always act in one uniform method,* quietly and gradually extending the kingdom of Christ by the successive conversion of individual sinners, as he is wont for the most part to do: or whether he may not, for wise reasons, and in the exercise of that sovereignty which belongs to him, *act occasionally in a more extraordinary and remarkable way,* turning multitudes at once, and perhaps suddenly, from darkness to light, and bringing about a general Revival of the power of religion in particular places and congregations? In other words, *may we reasonably believe and expect that the Spirit of God will occasionally produce a remarkable religious Revival?*

That we may proceed to the calm and impartial consideration of this question, it may be useful, first of all, to obviate and remove some prejudices which might either prevent us from entertaining it at all, or unfit us for deciding it aright.

It is of great importance to form a clear and definite idea of what is meant by a 'Revival' of religion. It properly consists in these two things:—a general impartation of new life, and vigour, and power, to those who are already of the number of God's people; and a remarkable awakening and conversion of souls who have hitherto been careless

---

[1] An abridgement of James Buchanan, *The Office and Work of the Holy Spirit* (London: Banner of Truth, (1843), repr. 1966), Chapter IX, 'Revivals, Acts 2:17, 18' (pp. 220-239), taken from the *Banner of Truth* magazine, Issue No. 44, Sept-Oct 1966.

and unbelieving: in other words, it consists in *new spiritual life imparted to the dead,* and in *new spiritual health imparted to the living.*

A Revival properly consists in one or both of these two things—a revived state of religion among the members of the church, and the increase of their number by the addition of souls converted to God. *Can it be doubted by any professing Christian, either such a Revival is possible, or that it is desirable?* Why, what is the end of the gospel ministry? What great design of our Sabbaths and our sanctuaries? What the purport of all gospel promises in reference to the kingdom of grace? Is it not, that such souls as have heretofore been 'dead in trespasses and sins' may be quickened into spiritual life and that such souls as have already been quickened into life may grow in spiritual health and vigour, and be revived and restored when they have fallen into declension and decay? *Do we not all pray for these things?* And is it not our privilege to *expect,* that for these things our prayers *will be heard and answered?*

The simultaneous conversion of many souls, and the increasing power of true religion in the hearts of God's people, are the constituent elements of a religious Revival; and these two effects of the Spirit's grace, while they may be wrought separately, are nevertheless found, when they are wrought together, to exert a powerful reciprocal influence on each other. Sometimes, under a gospel ministry, the faith, and love, and zeal of a Christian church are revived and strengthened, without being immediately accompanied with any remarkable awakening of careless sinners; at other times, many successive conversions are wrought, one after another, while the general tone of Christian piety is not observably raised or strengthened: but when at one and the same time believers are invigorated with new strength, and many careless sinners are converted, there is a powerful reciprocal influence exerted on each by the experience of the other. Decaying and backsliding Christians are aroused and reclaimed, when they see God's power exerted in the conversion of sinners: they feel that there is a reality and a vital energy in God's truth—that Christ lives and reigns—that the Spirit is still present with the church; and they are excited to greater earnestness in prayer, to greater devotedness of heart, to greater holiness of life; while their reawakened zeal, and their fervent prayers, fit them for exerting a holier influence over others, and may be the means of adding many to the church of such as shall be saved. Thus it was on the day of Pentecost.

On that remarkable occasion, it is recorded, that 'fear came upon every soul'; and the result was, that 'the Lord added to the church daily such as should be saved'.

It is of great practical importance to observe, that the work of the Spirit on the soul of every individual convert is *substantially the same* with that which takes place but only on a more extended scale—in a general Revival of religion. When many are suddenly arrested and convinced, when conversions take place in large numbers, and are attended with remarkable circumstances, the work of the Spirit attracts more of public attention, and produces a larger measure of excitement; but, substantially, it is the self-same work, which has often been carried on, in silence, in the secret chamber, in the retired recesses of the heart, when one poor sinner in a congregation has been singled out from a multitude of careless professors, and made the subject of a saving change. It matters not whether a man passes from death unto life in solitude or in society, whether he ventures alone to the mercy-seat, or is accompanied thither by a multitude of earnest suppliants, whether the light of heaven shines in upon his soul, leaving others in darkness, or shines at the same time into the hearts of thousands more. The same change which was wrought on the three thousand converts of Pentecost passed also on the spirit of Lydia, when she worshipped with a few other women by the river side; and on the spirit of the Philippian jailer, when he stood alone with the apostles. *One may be converted at a time, or many; but the work of conversion is the same in all.* Every soul, in a general Revival, must be enlightened by divine truth, and awakened to concern about its salvation, and melted into godly sorrow for sin, and stirred up to lay hold on Christ and his free salvation, and imbued with new views, new affections, new desires, new tastes, new hopes, new habits; in a word, every such soul as passes from death unto life, in a season of general awakening, must pass through the same general experience, which, on other occasions, is realized by the solitary inquirer, when, in his secret chamber, he thinks, and repents, and believes, and prays, and enters into peace with God. No one, therefore, who has experienced that great change in his own soul, who has known what it is to be awakened to concern about his own salvation, who has wept and prayed in secret, and earnestly read his Bible, and has drunk in the precious truths of the gospel, ought to feel any jealousy concerning a general Revival of true religion: on the contrary, he should regard it with such feelings as befit the occasion—the feeling of hope and expectation that some great good will be accomplished; the feeling of gratitude and joy, that new manifestations and proofs of the Saviour's power are vouchsafed; and the feeling of solemn awe, arising from the thought that God is interposing—that immortal souls are being born again and that these souls are now undergoing all that solemn conviction, and feeling all those anxious fears, and impressed with all those awful views of God, and judgment, and eternity, which he himself had experienced, when he first repented, and wept, and prayed, and wrestled for his own salvation.

The Holy Spirit is *not limited to any one mode of operation* in the execution of his glorious work; and his *sovereignty* ought ever to be remembered when we are considering a subject of this nature. It has, unfortunately, been too much overlooked, when, on the one hand, some have insisted, as we think, with undue partiality and confidence, on a general and remarkable Revival, as being in itself the *best manifestation* of the Spirit's grace, and as being, in all cases, a *matter of promise to believing prayer;* and when, on the other hand, not a few have looked to the quiet and gradual success of the gospel ministry, *to the exclusion, or at least disparagement, of any more sudden and remarkable work of grace.* The former have given a too exclusive preference to what is extraordinary and striking; while the latter have fallen into the opposite error, of preferring what is more usual and quiet. We think it were *better to admit of both methods of conversion,* and *to leave the choice to the sovereign wisdom and grace of the Spirit.* It is equally possible for him to convert souls successively or simultaneously; and in adopting either course doubtless he has wise ends in view. We have no sympathy with those who, overlooking the steady progress of the great work of conversion under a stated ministry, make no account of the multitudes who are added, one by one, to the church of the living God, merely because their conversion has not been attended with the outward manifestations of a great religious Revival; nor can we agree with them in thinking, that the church has any sure warrant to expect that the Spirit will be bestowed, in every instance, in that particular way. But as little have we any sympathy with those who, rejecting all Revivals as unscriptural delusions, profess to look exclusively to the gradual progress of divine truth, and the slow advance of individual conversion under stated ministry. *Both methods, the simultaneous and the successive conversion of souls, are equally within the power of the Spirit; and there may exist wise reasons why, in certain cases, the first should be chosen, while, in other cases, the second is preferred.*

Several important purposes may be promoted by the sudden and simultaneous conversion of many souls, and the concurrent Revival of Christian congregations, which either could not be attained at all, or not to the same extent, by the more ordinary and gradual progress of the gospel. A season of general awakening affords, both to believers and unbelievers, a new and very impressive proof of the reality and power of the Spirit's grace—it strengthens the faith and enlarges the hopes of God's people—it awakens those nominal professors who are at ease in Zion, and it alarms and arouses the consciences of the irreligious multitude. For when many are suddenly arrested by the power of the Spirit, and turned from the error of their ways, and made to break off their sins by repentance, and are seen flying to Christ like doves to their windows, the mind of every spectator must be impressed with a sense of the reality and importance of religion, and the most ungodly for a time will tremble.

Such a season of Revival may be designed to manifest, in an extraordinary way, the continued presence and the active agency of the Holy Spirit—to demonstrate the faithfulness of God in fulfilling the promises of his word—to evince the efficacy of believing prayer—to teach the church the weakness of human instruments, and the true source of all spiritual power—to quicken her faith and hope, when, through manifold trials and increasing difficulties, she might be ready to faint and be discouraged, as if the task of regenerating the world were left to be accomplished by inadequate resources—to stir her up to greater efforts in a spirit of lively faith and humble dependence, and to afford new evidence to succeeding generations, that Christ is the exalted Head of the church, and that all power is still given to him in heaven and on earth. These are some of the *important practical lessons* which may be taught by such seasons of Revival in the church—lessons which might be *deduced* from the more ordinary operations of the Spirit under the regular ministry of the word, but which are *more prominently presented,* and *more impressively enforced,* when, in the exercise of his adorable sovereignty, the Spirit of God, instead of descending like 'dew on the grass', comes like 'showers which water the earth', or like 'floods on the dry ground'. And if these or similar ends may be promoted by such means, who will say that they may not be employed by him who is 'wise in counsel, and excellent in working', and of whom it is written, 'There are diversities of gifts, but the same Spirit. And there are differences of administrations, but the same Lord. And there are diversities of operations, but it is the same God which worketh all in all.'—'All these worketh that one and the self-same Spirit, dividing to every man severally as he will.'

That such seasons of general religious Revival as occurred at the feast of Pentecost were *to be expected in subsequent times,* appears from those promises of Scripture which relate to 'times of refreshing from the presence of the Lord', which insure the continued presence of Christ and his Spirit with the church in *all ages,* and which declare that 'when the enemy cometh in like a flood, the Spirit of the Lord *will lift up* a standard against him.' And that such seasons of Revival have occurred at intervals along the whole line of the church's history, is a *fact* which is amply confirmed by *historical evidence,* and sufficient to obviate any prejudice arising from the idea that such an event is novel or unprecedented.

JAMES BUCHANAN
EDINBURGH, 1843

THE ULSTER AWAKENING

PART I
THE ORIGIN, EARLY HISTORY, AND
PROGRESS OF THE AWAKENING

CHAPTER 1
INTRODUCTION

A S a native of the province of Ulster, long familiar with its people, and as one who was a minister for thirteen years of that branch of the Church of Scotland, which, more than two centuries ago, was planted among those who settled as colonists in the North of Ireland, I venture to ask the attention, and to claim the confidence, of my readers. I shall endeavour to lay before them the leading facts and features of that Ulster Revival which is still arresting general attention, and which has provoked much severe animadversion on the one hand, as well as elicited hallowed joy and devout thanksgivings on the other.

I write as a firm believer in the truth of Christianity, and this, both in respect to its great facts, and its distinguishing doctrines. I espouse and hold fast the views common to Evangelical and Protestant Christians; and while differing with many of them on questions of church government and discipline, I am emphatically one with them in faith and sympathy, on all points essential to life and salvation. I believe that Christianity, rightly interpreted, teaches first, that man is guilty before God; and that, in order to deliver him from

I

the everlasting penalties of his sin, there has been provided for him a Saviour, trusting in whose atoning sacrifice and perfect righteousness, a man is 'justified' before God, he is freely forgiven, and he becomes, by adoption and grace, a member of Christ, a child of God, and an heir of the kingdom of heaven. Secondly, I believe that Christianity teaches the entire corruption and moral helplessness of human nature, in consequence of the Fall; and that it also reveals a remedy for this, in a supernatural Agent and agency. In other words, I hold that the Holy Ghost, the third person of the Blessed Trinity, is the 'Lord and Giver of life'; that he imparts, sustains, and consummates this spiritual life in accordance with the Father's eternal purpose, and through the mediation of Jesus Christ. This Spirit, therefore, quickens those who by nature are 'dead in trespasses and sins', and also 'creates anew unto good works', those who are 'very far gone from original righteous-ness': so that thus the sinner saved, is not only 'justified by faith', and 'has peace with God through our Lord Jesus Christ', but he is also sanctified by 'the washing of regeneration and the renewing of the Holy Ghost'.

This Holy Spirit, moreover, I regard, as operating upon the intellect in its spiritual enlightenment; on the conscience in waking it up as a faithful witness and accuser, so as to lead to the conviction of guilt, and of rebellion before God; and acting also upon the affections so as to turn them towards Christ (already trusted in), as their magnet and their cynosure, as the one object of the heart's supreme regard. And while I believe that Baptism and the Lord's Supper are most eloquently expres-sive ordinances, the one, of the grace of the Holy Spirit in cleansing the heart from its filthiness, and the other, of the body and blood of a cruci-fied Saviour,—and while I believe also that these are something more than mere signs, that, to all who believingly receive them, they are also *seals* of Divine favour, and are thus the pledges and assurances of eternal life,—yet I do earnestly reject that Ritualistic theory, which teaches that *ex opere operato* Baptism, administered by priestly hands, is regeneration; and that the Eucharist is a real sacrifice offered on an altar, 'impetratory' in its character, and essential to *the application* of that blood of atone-ment which was offered on Calvary 'once for all'.

Finally, I hold that the Holy Spirit is the sole author of a religious Revival, and this by the instrumentality of *scriptural truth*. Revelation, I regard as completed, in the Canon of the Old and New Testament Scriptures. I reject all pretensions to new revelations, under the names of Swedenborgianism, Mormonism, 'and unwritten tradition'; and also those mistaken applications of Old Testament prophecies, which have been said, by a very few persons, to find their fulfilment, in the alleged 'prophecies', or 'visions', and 'sleeps' (or 'dreams'), of 'young men and maidens' in Ulster. Moreover, with regard to cases of physical agitations and persons 'struck down',—such as I have myself seen,—while treating of these affections more fully afterwards, I wish now to express my conviction, that as an eminent philosopher, the Rev. Dr M'Cosh, regards them, these are but 'the *physiological accidents*' of the Revival in Ulster. He says, 'I do not form my belief that it is a genuine work, on the bodily manifestations'; for 'this would be as contrary to Scripture as to science. Scripture sets no value on "bodily exercise"; and nowhere points to any bodily effect whatever as a proof or test of the presence of the Spirit of God.' And from three weeks' close and constant personal observation and inquiries over the greater part of Ulster, lean also heartily, and with a good conscience, accord with Dr M'Cosh, when he adds: 'Nor have I ever heard anyone who takes an enlightened interest in this work, ever appealing to this evidence.'

By every believer in Divine Revelation, I shall be permitted to speak of the fruits of this Revival as including not only *social* results and a great moral reformation, but also those spiritual fruits which are indicated by a holy apostle (*Gal.* 5:22), and which, if Christianity be a reality, are the primary and essential results of the presence and in-dwelling of the Holy Spirit. I know that many persons speak of 'Christian experience' with scorn, and consider the language employed with regard to it, even though it be scriptural, as 'conventionalism and cant'. But, notwithstanding this, and cheerfully admitting that there is often a use made of Scripture terms, which, as Foster indicates, is a stumbling-block to 'men of taste',—yet still it is never to be forgotten that the New Testament *does* speak of a Divine and supernatural change as 'conversion', as 'turning to the Lord', as being 'born again', as receiving the gospel, 'not in word only, but in power and in the Holy Ghost, and with much assurance' of 'love, joy, meekness, gentleness, long-suffering, goodness, faith'; as well as of 'joy and peace in believing', of 'abounding in hope through the power of the Holy Ghost', and 'singing and making melody in our hearts to the Lord', of 'praying in the Holy Ghost', of a 'life of faith in the Son of God', and of 'holiness without which no man shall see the Lord'. If, therefore, our tests, when applied in due time, shall bring out illustrations of all these spiritual exercises, and graces, in connection with the movement in Ireland,—then we may logically and fairly claim, that without controversy and without scorn, its Divine origin shall be at once admitted by everyone, who would not class himself amongst those who virtually reject the inspiration of the Bible, and who treat the language of Christ and his apostles, as well as the recorded experience of the early Church, as the jargon of imposture, or the ravings of fanatical folly.[1]

We do not, then, expect sympathy with our views and feelings from those who adopt and maintain ritualistic and sacramentarian views on the one hand, nor from the sceptic and unbeliever on the other. But from all who are willing that the Ulster Awakening should be tried by what prophets have taught us to expect in the last days, by what began to be realized on the day of Pentecost, we *do* claim a candid consideration of those facts, and those scriptural 'fruits', which, in all truthfulness of statement, and honesty of purpose, we shall in subsequent chapters place before them.

---

[1] 'Christian experience may be regarded as genuine—1st. When it accords with the Revelation of God's mind and will, or what he has revealed in his word. Anything contrary to this, however pleasing, cannot be sound, or produced by Divine Agency. 2nd. When its tendency is to promote humility in us; that experience which produces humility in us, and subdues pride, must be good. 3rd. When it teaches us to bear with others, and to do them good. 4th. When it operates so as to excite us to be ardent in our devotion, and sincere in our regard to God. A powerful experience of the Divine favour will lead us to acknowledge the same, and to manifest our gratitude by constant praise and genuine piety.'—BUCK's *Theological Dictionary* by Henderson.

CHAPTER 2

The model and conditions of a genuine Revival—Pentecost and the early church—periodical outpourings of the Spirit—historical illustrations of Revivals—Bishop McIlvaine of Ohio, and the Ulster Awakening.

REVIVAL, strictly speaking, implies that spiritual life is already possessed. And just as the fading flower, the drooping plant, the parched cereals, by the gentle shower and the gladsome sunshine, are resuscitated into fresh life—so, by the fresh communications of his heavenly grace, the Holy Ghost restores from a languishing condition that inner life which he had previously bestowed. But, as commonly understood, Revival means not only the enlargement and advancement of the work of grace in the regenerate, but the impartation, by the quickening Spirit, of a divine life to those hitherto dead in trespasses and sins.

It was thus that Christianity itself, was ushered in by a mighty outpouring of the Spirit of God, in connection with the preaching of the gospel,—not by the gospel without the Spirit, nor by the Spirit without the word, nor yet by the gifts of tongues, otherwise as attestations of the divinity of the work, and especially as essential to the *universal* proclamation of the truth by its appointed heralds. The apostles, and those with them who were already Christ's true disciples, were commanded to tarry at Jerusalem till they should receive 'the promise of the Father', and 'power from on high'. They were taught that, without the promised Spirit, they must remain powerless; but for this, they were encouraged to pray with confidence. Accordingly, we find that in answer to their *united prayers* the Divine energy was vouchsafed, and when it came, it operated irresistibly and mightily on the hearts of multitudes.

Thus it was that on the Day of Pentecost, not a few, but a great number, and these, as Bunyan has it, 'the biggest sinners'—'Jerusalem sinners'—were suddenly brought under the most awful convictions of their guiltiness in having 'killed the Prince of life'; and that these men at once, *in numbers*, earnestly asked as to what must be done, in order to escape the Divine wrath and curse, which they felt they had incurred. More than this, when they were informed of what they must do to be saved, they joyfully and at once, complied with the terms. They 'gladly received the word', which assured them that Jesus, the despised Nazarene, was the long predicted Messiah, was David's Son, and David's Lord; and that having died and been laid in the tomb, the soul was brought back from the state of separate spirits (*Hades*)—reunited to the body ere it had 'seen corruption'— and that this same Jesus whom they—the house of Israel—had with wicked hands crucified and slain, was now enthroned at the right hand of God, as 'both Lord and Christ', was invested with universal supremacy, and exalted to give repentance and remission of sins to all who should believe on his name.

Thus three thousand, by one sermon, were suddenly 'converted', and their sins were immediately 'blotted out', because the Spirit accompanied the scriptural testimony borne to Jesus as the Christ, with convincing, illuminating, and quickening power. Thus the New Testament dispensation was ushered in by a Revival, by a mighty Awakening, by a glorious outburst of spiritual life.

Here, then, we have the conditions, and here also the primitive and apostolic type and model of a genuine Revival. First, on the part of Christ's true disciples, there was the offering up of continued, united, and believing supplications for the outpouring of the Holy Spirit, that so God might be glorified, and men in multitudes might be saved. Secondly, there was the simple, earnest preaching of the truth that Jesus was the Christ. Thirdly, this was accompanied by such a divine energy, that multitudes were 'pricked to the heart', and embraced the message of salvation with gladness. Fourthly, there was on the part of the three thousand—thus arrested, penitent and believing—an open espousal of the cause of Christ, and an open profession of their faith in, and love to him, by their being publicly baptized in his name. Fifthly, these converts formed themselves into a visible society, distinguished by firm adhesion to the teaching and society of Christ's apostles, by frequent commemoration of the death of Jesus in the Lord's Supper, by fervent and united prayers, by ardent and self-sacrificing brotherly love, by 'singleness of heart', and thorough uprightness of purpose, and by an exulting gladness, which found expression in songs of praise. More than this, a solemn awe fell upon the unconverted around ('fear fell upon every soul'); and in these new-born children of God such a marvellous, glorious, convincing and genuine change had been wrought, that they 'had favour with all the people'.

The apostolic age thus inaugurated, was marked, and rendered ever memorable and glorious, by a *series* of mighty awakenings. Thus, after the first results among the people of Jerusalem, we find, that 'the Lord added *daily* to the church such as should be saved'; that 'many thousands (Greek, *myriads*) believed'; we read also of 'multitudes of both men and women', and that 'a great company of the priests were obedient to the faith.'

In like manner, when the door of faith was opened to the Gentiles, the life-giving wave swept over every part of the Roman empire. In Rome itself was formed a church, so prominent in zeal, and so sound in doctrine and knowledge, that its 'faith was spoken of throughout the whole world'; and even in 'Caesar's household' its spirit-taught members were to be found.

Over Asia Minor the fertilizing flood of truth passed on, and the moral desert rejoiced and blossomed as the rose. At Ephesus, in spite of the persecuting fury of those whose 'craft' was imperilled, and of the blind superstition of a mob, the 'great goddess Diana' was abased, and Jesus was exalted. In a word, wherever the gospel was preached, men 'turned from dumb idols to serve the living God, and to wait for his Son from heaven'.

In spite of persecution, nay, by means of it—its angry winds sweeping over the church's garden, and bearing upon their wings the seeds of holy truth, to deposit them wide and far over new fields, there to germinate and bring forth fresh harvests—the religion of the Cross was for the first three centuries one continued manifestation of spiritual life and power. No wonder, then, that as a heathen historian records, the temples of the gods were almost deserted, and that the animals intended for sacrifice could scarcely find a purchaser. It was the victory of the two-edged sword of the Spirit. It was the spiritual world-wide conquest which found jubilant utterance in the 'Great Heart' of primitive times, who himself a marvellous trophy of the quickening and transforming grace of the Holy Ghost—like a general addressing his brave captains and companions in arms after a long series of triumphs, exclaimed, 'Now thanks be unto God, who always causeth us to triumph in Christ, and maketh manifest the savour of his knowledge by us in every place' (2 *Cor.* 2:14).

Now, both by the analogies of nature, as well as by the peculiar character of the gospel dispensation, we are warranted to expect that what took place in apostolic times, and in connection with the first successes of Christianity, shall again and again be realized in the history of the church; and this by periodic, special, and abundant visitations of heavenly influence, until Christianity shall become the dominant power in the world. Do we not see the analogy in the kingdom of nature? 'If now winter holds fast the earth in its icy fetters, does not spring clothe it with its flowers, summer quicken it with its heats, and autumn crown it with its fruits? Yes; and even in winter, when death *seems* to reign, life unseen is all the while still busy; great powers are at work, with silent, secret energy, preparing for a glorious resurrection and revival.'

The analogy, too, is strengthened by the consideration that it is that same blessed Spirit who revives the Church, and who gives life to the spiritually dead, who also accomplishes the periodical renovation of the earth. 'Thou sendest forth thy Spirit, they are created; and thou renewest the face of the earth.' And so there is more than poetry in the apostrophe—

> To Him, ye vocal gales,
> Breathe soft, whose Spirit in your freshness, breathes.

When, therefore, we can trace the periodic working of the Divine Spirit in one department of his operations, why may it not exist in another? 'The history of the world', also, as has been well said, 'a world whose great epochs are divinely determined, and all whose tendencies are guided and overruled for a supremely beneficent issue, indicates periodical onward movement. What rapid starts will science sometimes take! Commerce, literature, now, will lay slumbering, and then suddenly awake and draw all minds into the vortex of their influence.'

So has it been in the past, and so Scripture prophecy warrants us to expect it shall be in the history of that divinely constituted society, of which Christ is the head, and for whose sake he reigns over the universe. The wondrous past, reveals a series of mighty manifestations of the quickening Spirit, each of which has advanced the church in her onward march to supremacy and triumph. As God acts, grandly, majestically, like himself, in renewing the face of the earth—parched up, and 'as iron', by reason of the long-continued drought of tropical lands—pouring out from his exhaustless 'river' (*Psa.* 65:9) the copious and long-continued rains—and thus the seed having been sown, the warmth of the earth on which it fell, co-operating with the rains and the unclouded sun-burst that follows, all nature is green and gladsome, and plenty crowns the plains—so in the spiritual world we find him acting in might and majesty in the bestowment of a divine life. It was so even under the Old Testament dispensation, when religion would otherwise have perished. In the prophet Samuel, the Reformer of his age; in King Hezekiah's days, when a whole people were recalled to pristine faith and devotedness, and 'the thing was done suddenly'; in the time of Jehoshaphat, when 'all Judah rejoiced because of the oath'; in the reclaiming of apostate Israel by Elijah on Mount Carmel; in the penitential weeping of Judah's captives; in the great awakenings of life in the days of Ezra and Nehemiah;—we see periodical seasons of Revival. The Spirit of life was there. And so above all has it been under the present dispensation. 'What was the secret of the first and marvellous success of Succath—the traditional 'St Patrick'—when he began to preach a pure and primitive gospel among the pagans of Ireland? What else than the Spirit's teaching and quickening power can explain the raising up of men like Columba and Columbkill, and the monks of Iona, who, owning no homage to Rome, and abjuring her yoke, were the apostles of Christianity in Britain? How do we explain that Ireland herself was once the seat both of religion and learning, and that thither, in the seventh century, 'the Saxon youth', as Lord

9

Coke expresses it, 'did resort as to a fair?' What is it that explains the existence and mighty influence of Wycliffe and the Lollards in England—men who were 'Reformers before the Reformation'? Whence came the zeal and intense earnestness which, in connection with the study of the Scriptures, early showed itself in the English universities, preparing the way for the bold confession of truth before kings and people, and the precursors of a host of martyrs, in the days of 'bloody Mary'?

In the successes of the preaching of honest Latimer at Paul's Cross; in the labours of John Knox for a time as an evangelist in an English diocese, and afterwards as the Reformer of Scotland; in the successive translations of the Bible by Tyndale, Coverdale, and others, and in the eager delight with which the people flocked to drink from the pure well of everlasting truth; as well as in the great religious awakenings of the Puritan age, as also in those during the last century in New England, under President Edwards, Whitefield, and the Tennents; in the rise of the Methodists in England; in the marvellous power attending the ministry of a Berridge, a Romaine, and a Venn (a man before whom 'men fell like slaked lime'), all ministers of the English Church; in the wondrous results of the ministry of Charles, and Rowland, and Griffiths, in Wales; and in the outpourings of the Spirit at the Kirk of Shotts, Kilsyth, Cambuslang, and other parishes in the west of Scotland,—we behold but the fulfilment of those prophecies, which lead us to expect *periodical* visitations of the Spirit.[2]

When we compare and collate such predictions,—embracing as they do the day of Pentecost, and pointing onwards to the glories of the millennial age,—we have the true solution of those periodical visitations of the Spirit enjoyed in the past, and to be expected in the future. It is thus we explain the Revivals in Scotland, in 1809, at Kilsyth and Dundee, in connection with the ministrations of William Burns and Robert M'Cheyne; as well as the remarkable awakenings in the United States in the beginning of the present century, in 1831, and finally in 1858,— the last, a marvellous awakening, which (as will be seen in the sequel) was largely instrumental in stirring up Christians in Ulster to pray for a

---

[2] *Joel* 2:28-29; *Isa.* 32:13, 15-16; 44:3; *Ezek.* 37:1; 47:2.

kindred blessing. And thus, as a religious writer in America last year expresses it—while observing, with just and sober discrimination, that mere animal excitement, the stirring of the emotions upon the pure principle of sympathy, not infrequently passes current for the work of the Spirit—we believe that 'this gift is periodically bestowed. We have in grace, as well as in nature, our dry and wet seasons—the time of drought and the time of showers. *The rain comes by spells.*'

'I cannot', says Bishop McIlvaine, 'doubt that Revivals are the work of God; forty-nine years ago I myself was made a subject of the gospel of the Son of God in the awakening of 1809, and some of my dearest and best friends who are gone home to glory, were the fruits of these manifestations of the Holy Ghost.'

And so the same excellent and judicious prelate, addressing the Bishop of Down and Connor, on August 2nd, 1859, while using words of loving caution and counsel, yet fully recognising with glowing gratitude the reality of a Divine agency in the Ulster Awakening, and a longing for a *general* Revival, the fullness of the heavenly rain, thus writes:—

My dear Bishop,—Why should it be thought a thing incredible that God should raise the dead? Why more incredible that he should raise the spiritually dead to newness of life by hundreds in a day than, as we are too much contented to see, by one or two now and then, the little gift to our great unbelief? Why more incredible that he should so raise the dead as that they should come forth at once, decidedly, manifestly, exhibiting immediately the most striking evidences of newness of life, rejoicing in the change, not doubting its reality, full of the joy of life, than if the work were so unmarked and apparently gradual that it excited no notice, and could hardly be seen? Why more incredible that such rising from the dead should extend over all Ireland, and Scotland, and England, than that it should shake the dry bones of a few valleys of death in one of them? Oh! let us pray—let us pray expectingly. Let us believe more in the Holy Ghost. Let us escape more from our traditionary ideas of what we may hope for, from what we have been accustomed to see and receive; and let us gauge our desires, and hopes, and prayers by the promises—by the office of the Holy Ghost—by the fullness and mightiness of the grace of God. Be sure, my dear Bishop, you and all your clergy, and all the churches of every name in Ireland, and all that love our Lord—all that have recently been called out of darkness into his marvellous light—and all that are yet in spiritual death, have the prayers of a great multitude in this country of the people of God. We pray that God will abound with you more and more, and THAT THE RIVER OF GOD WHICH IS NOW SO GLORIOUSLY MAKING YOU GLAD IN IRE-LAND, may revive the whole land, and all Great Britain, till there shall everywhere be seen the resurrection and the life.'

CHAPTER 3

The two Revivals in Ulster—the Scottish ministers and Archbishop Ussher—the early colonists and the outpouring of the Spirit—physical agitations—remarkable parallel—a line of witnesses—the old field and a fresh harvest.

OF the settlers and colonists in Ulster, in the seventeenth century, some were Episcopalians from England; others—much greater in numbers—were Presbyterians from Scotland. It is well worthy of remembrance, in connection with the theme of this volume, that a great revival of religion, attended by marvellous spiritual and social results, marked the early history of the Ulster colonists. Special care had been taken by James I, to provide for the spread of true religion by the repairing of churches and the provision of glebes for the ministers, as well as by restoring the ecclesiastical possessions, and endowing schools for the revival of learning.

We are not writing the history of Ulster, but it is important to remark that this province—now the stronghold of Irish Protestant-ism, and which in the stormy times of the 'Repeal' agitation, was the great link of British connection—is described by Dupin, a Roman Catholic historian, as having once been 'the most constant in main-taining its liberty and preserving the Catholic religion'.

The Reformation, as such, was a failure in Ireland. Few Protestant ministers were settled in the country, and these, for the most part, were ill qualified for the discharge of their duties. The government aimed at the extirpation of the Irish tongue, because it was the language of rebels. Books might not be printed in it. No man might preach to the people in it. It was commanded that, even in those parishes where English was not understood, the church service should be conducted in Latin.

In Ulster, therefore, Romanism maintained an unbroken sway over the popular mind; and by intestine wars, during the latter part of the reign of Elizabeth, it had been reduced almost to a state of depopulation. But in the purpose of him who is wonderful in counsel and excellent in working, this unpromising field was yet destined to wave with golden harvests. Early, too, were the first sheaves gathered; for, under the auspices of the illustrious Ussher, intolerance was banished from the Church of Ireland, so that many of the English Puritans and Scottish Presbyterian ministers were promoted to posts of honour and usefulness within its pale.

Among the most eminent of those ministers of the Church of Scotland who followed their countrymen to Ulster, the names of Brice, Bruce, Livingston, Blair, and Cunningham are household words in the north of Ireland to this day.[3] Before their arrival the early colonists were in a sadly demoralized condition. 'From Scotland came many, and from England not a few', writes the minister of Donaghadee, in 1645,

> yet all of them generally the scum of both nations, who from debt, or breaking, and fleeing from justice, came to a land where there was little or nothing as yet of the fear of God. And in a few years there flocked such a multitude of people from Scotland, that these northern counties of Down, Antrim, and Londonderry, &c., were in a good measure planted, which were waste before . . . Yet most of the people were void of godliness; they seemed rather to flee from God in this enterprise, than to follow their own mercy. *Yet God followed them when they fled from him.*[4]

[3] See *Scottish Puritans: Select Biographies* 2-vol set, ed. W. K. Tweedie (Edinburgh: Banner of Truth, 2008) for more details of this period, especially John Livingston's ministry in Ulster, *Ed.*.

[4] Stewart's MSS., as quoted by Dr Reid, in his *History of the Presbyterian Church in Ireland*, vol. 1.

One of those eminent and holy Scottish ministers who were settled over Ulster parishes, was the Rev. John Livingston, chaplain to
the Countess of Wigton. When quite a young man, he had preached
on the Monday after the Communion in the churchyard of Shotts, in
Lanarkshire, a sermon on Ezekiel 36:25-26, which was attended with
marvellous power. Of the results of this one discourse, Mr Fleming,
then minister of Cambuslang, writes—

> I can speak on sure grounds, that about *five hundred* had at that time
> a discernible change wrought in them, of whom most proved lively
> Christians. It was the sowing of a seed through Clydesdale, so as many
> of the most eminent Christians in that country could date either their
> conversion or some remarkable confirmation from it. *And the night before
> being spent in prayer,* the Monday's work *might be discerned as a convincing
> return to prayer.*

Of this great sermon at the Kirk of Shotts, coupled with the labours
of the Rev. Robert Bruce,—who, like Livingston, afterwards settled in
Ulster,—Mr Gray of Chryston, a gentleman of rank, thus wrote:—

> At the sermon at Shotts, a goodly number of people were by grace made
> acquainted with the life and power of religion. Many of them became
> eminently good men, and remarkable not only for a pious, inoffensive
> behaviour, but also for abounding in all the good fruits which pure and
> undefiled religion enables its sincere followers to perform. Among other
> good fruits, a principal one was *a strong inclination to promote the spirit-
> ual good of others.* As the labourers were then few in this part of God's
> vineyard, he seemed to have inspired these private Christians with an
> uncommon degree of love to the souls of men—inciting them to labour
> by all proper methods to bring others to the knowledge of that grace
> which had produced such blessed effects on themselves; and their labours
> were not without considerable effect.[5]

In the general awakening that followed the settlement of the
Scottish ministers in Ulster, Livingston's spiritual success[6] was very

---

[5] Letter in Gillies' *Historical Collections of Religious Revivals* (Edinburgh: Banner of Truth,
1981, reprint), *Ed.*.

[6] 'Being a man of a gracious, melting spirit, he did much good, and the Lord was pleased
greatly to bless his ministry.'—STEWART.

remarkable in the parish of Killinchy, where, as will afterwards appear, 'floods' have been recently 'poured' afresh 'on the dry ground'. All over the country a spirit of religious inquiry was excited; ignorance began to be dispelled; the careless and secure were aroused to a sense of their spiritual peril, and the immoral were reclaimed. But it was at Oldstone, in the neighbourhood of the town of Antrim, that a *great* awakening occurred, under the ministry of Mr Glendinning, of which Mr Stewart in his MSS. thus writes:

> Seeing the great lewdness and ungodly sinfulness of the people, he preached to them nothing but law-wrath and the terrors of God for sin. And in very deed for this only was he fitted; for hardly could he preach any other thing. But behold the success! For the hearers, finding themselves condemned by the wrath of God speaking in his word, fell into such anxiety and terror of conscience, that they looked on themselves as altogether lost and damned; and this work appeared not in one single person or two, but *multitudes* were brought to understand their way, and to ask—'Men and brethren, what shall we do?'

This writer also bears testimony to physical agitations as accompanying this early awakening in Ulster, similar to those which have excited such notice in 1859; strong men being thus struck down under the terrors of the Almighty. 'I have seen them myself', says Mr Stewart,

> stricken into a swoon with the word: yea, a dozen in one day carried out as dead; so marvellous was the power of God striking their hearts for sin, condemning and killing. And of these were none of the weaker sex or spirit; but, indeed, some of the boldest spirits, who formerly feared not with their swords to put a whole market-town in a fray; yea, in defence of their stubbornness, cared not to lie in prison and in the stocks; and being incorrigible, were as ready to do the like the next day.
>
> I have heard one of them—a mighty strong man, now a mighty Christian—say, that his end in coming to church was to consult with his companions how to work some mischief. And yet at one of these sermons he was so caught that he was fully subdued. But why do I speak of *him?* We knew, and yet know, *multitudes of such men,* who sinned and gloried in it, because they feared no man, yet are now patterns of sobriety,

fearing to sin because they fear God. And this *spread through the country*, especially to that river commonly called the Six Mile Water, for there this work began at first.

I have been thus particular in referring to this early Ulster Awakening because it is little known, and especially because of the remarkable parallels which it suggests in connection with the recent Revival of 1859. Both were preceded by great religious declension, and abounding immorality; both were ushered in by fervent and united prayer, and godly conference among ministers and other pious persons, as well as by the full and faithful preaching of the truth—especially of the terrors of that law which is 'a school-master' to lead men to a Saviour, that so they may be 'justified by faith'. Both awakenings, moreover, affected *large numbers*, who at the same time were brought under apprehensions of Divine wrath, so overpowering as to affect the bodily frame; and both were followed by a general reformation of manners, the subjects of them becoming 'patterns of sobriety, and fearing to sin because they feared God'. The work also in both cases *spread through the country*, to the glad surprise even of Christians themselves. Finally, the birthplace and the early home of both were in Antrim, in the same districts of that county. And now, at the end of more than two hundred years, we see a second spiritual harvest reaped from the same field, as if in answer to the prayers *then* poured out before God.

Persecution speedily followed that early Revival. Ministers were charged with encouraging bodily prostrations, just as others are wrongly accused now. But, in spite of the actual deposition and banishment of ministers (whom Ussher sought in vain to shelter, and whom James I only restored for a time), although under the oppressive regime of Strafford many of them were compelled to flee to Scotland, and thus to leave their flocks to the tender mercies of the cruel,—and while, also, in the Popish massacre of 1641, not less than thirty Presbyterian ministers perished in the general massacre of the Protestants of Ireland,—yet the effects of that early development of spiritual life are felt in Ulster to this day. And while also, in the last century, the Arian heresy came in like a flood, and a Moderator of the Synod of Ulster could be heard in his official capacity reviling the Confession and Catechisms of the Church of his fathers, yet the people of one district at least—that where the Revival of 1859 burst forth—still held fast the 'old way', and 'walked therein'; and for more than two hundred years, their descendants there, have never wanted a faithful and evangelical ministry.

To one who, as a licentiate of the Presbyterian Synod of Ireland, preached in early days in that particular district, this fact has been particularly suggestive, and it specially impressed my mind, when I was permitted personally to visit some of those scenes in Antrim, where more than two centuries ago, by a plenteous rain, the Lord refreshed his heritage when it was weary.

CHAPTER 4

Origin and birthplace of the Revival—early history—parish of Connor—first-fruits.

WE now proceed to trace the dawn of that spiritual spring-time which already is passing rapidly into the glory of summer at its noon. The origin of the Awakening in Ulster has been ascribed to different instrumentalities, and all are not agreed as to the particular district in which it first manifested its power.

The Rev. S. M. Dill, of Ballymena, states definitely that it originated in the parish of Connor, and thus indicated his convictions with regard to its birthplace and earlier developments in a speech recently delivered by him in the city of Philadelphia, in the United States, as one of a missionary deputation pleading for help in the evangelization of Roman Catholic Ireland:—

> It commenced in the parish next to my own. There was a long work of preparation. The pastor noticed his congregation increasing in numbers. He felt an impulse to speak the word with greater power. The Sabbath schools increased. Sabbath-school unions took the form of prayer-meetings. The Sabbath was better observed. Family prayer was resumed by many who had neglected it, and new altars were erected

in many households. The prayer-meetings were multiplied, and more numerously attended. The Catechism was more generally attended to. Conversions began to take place, and thus the seed which had long been sown began to spring up.

The Rev. Dr Edgar thus gives, in a letter to the *British Banner*, the leading features and facts of the Awakening at Connor:—

I shall not take a wide range—I shall not deal in hearsay, but confine myself entirely to my own knowledge of one congregation in a country district of Ulster, that from a single example a judgment may be readily formed of the whole.

I. The congregation is one of the old, stern, Calvinistic school, long in unbroken enjoyment of an evangelical ministry, yet often lifeless and cold, with many mere formal professors, and many more not having even a name to live.

II. Its present minister is no Whitefield nor Irish Kirwan, whose oratory might be supposed to effect wondrous changes by its own power; but he is plain, honest, direct—meaning somebody going right to the understanding and heart—in doctrinal, practical preaching of the truth which alone can save.

III. The means which he employs are:—

1. Two discourses each Sabbath, such as M'Culloch preached before the great Awakening at Cambuslang.

2. A system of Sunday schools over the districts, the pupils of which he assembles and catechises in his church every Sabbath; and, to enable their teachers to carry forward a successful course, he has printed for them each week a suitable exposition of Scripture, or of doctrine.

3. Pastoral visitation from house to house, so that he knows every one of his people, and can meet every case.

4. He has covered the whole district with a net-work of prayer-meetings, at some five or six of which he officiates weekly (there are a hundred weekly), the people themselves keeping up the religious services.

5. Religious services in the open air. Two years since, when there was no public talk of Revivals, he usually had audiences of two or three thousand.

IV. The means I thus specify particularly, because I wish to give prominence to the fact that God's Holy Spirit is not working by any strange or miraculous means, but by the means of his own appointment. The truth as it is in Jesus—the truth in love—God's Spirit always used, and he still uses, for the conversion of souls. On the reading, but especially the hearing of the word, in the spirit of humility and prayer, God pours out his Spirit's gracious influence, and souls are saved.

V. The agents assisting the minister in his work are:—

1. Ruling elders, Sunday-school teachers, &c.; the old staff before the Revival began. One of these I heard leading in prayer, and most primitive and patriarchal it was. Long might he have sung, with the Psalmist,—

'I waited for the Lord my God,
And patiently did bear'—

because many a long year he and an aged female maintained a prayer-meeting when the members uniting with them seemed hopelessly few; but against hope they hoped and prayed; and now they can continue the psalm, and sing—

'At length to me he did incline,
My voice and cry to hear.'

2. Fresh young hands which the Revival has raised. Many of these are working at home; nine of these are travelling around, on invitations from many parties anxious for their help.

A meeting of such is held each Saturday, specially to ask for God's blessing on the Sabbath services. I lately attended. The place was a butcher's shop. The butcher, two years since, did not know A from B; God converted him; he taught himself to read, and he is now a large tract distributor at his own cost, and a chief hand in the Revival work.

The secretary was a working shoemaker—another Carey. Others present were day-labourers, a stone-breaker, and a blacksmith's boy. The stone-breaker, who still sits on the road-side breaking stones to earn his bread, is one of four brothers lately converted. Their mother was sister to a blackguard pugilist, to whom she used to be bottle-holder, and when she entered a shop she was watched as a noted thief. Her sons were pests, but God's grace has made them vessels of mercy, overflowing with goodness for not a few. I have heard them, and others like them, speak and pray in public. I do not defend their pronunciation, grammar, style, or delivery; but I say fearlessly that their addresses and prayers are scriptural, wise, and powerful, and, as their effects show, most wonderfully adapted to do great and permanent good to persons in humble life like themselves.

3. Let no disgust be raised when I name, as another class of new assistants, females; for these females know their sphere, and keep it, being gratefully sensible of God's goodness in having assigned to woman a sphere of unbounded usefulness and honour. They conduct, for example, female prayer-meetings, where, if a single male be admitted, he is brother to some one present, and asked to impart religious instruction. One such told me that, passing the door of a prayer-meeting, he found a number of young girls engaged in prayer, over one in deep distress for sins; and a more suitable or deeply interesting prayer he had seldom heard than from one of these young, earnest creatures over her distressed sister.

There is another sphere of female agency, and I illustrate it thus:— A gentleman called to me a young girl weeding his garden. Among other questions I asked her, 'Were you with us at the prayer-meeting, last night?' 'No', said she, 'I was at —.' 'Why', I replied, with surprise, 'what took you away through the rain five miles to an open-air prayer-meeting?' 'I was invited', she said, 'by friends, who thought that the Lord might have something for me to do.' Had I heard no more than this I might have deemed it vanity or fanaticism; but the explanation is this. At such meetings females, as well as males, become so deeply affected by the truth, that it is necessary to remove them, and it is most suitable that some experienced, wise, Christian female, should be with such to teach, advise, and pray, and comfort with the consolation wherewith she herself is comforted of God.

The Rev. S. J. Moore, in his *History and Prominent Characteristics of the Present Revival in Ballymena*, writes as follows:—

In September, 1857, was commenced, in a little school-house near to Connor, County Antrim, *The Believers' Fellowship Meeting*. The society consisted at first of four young men—John Wallace, James M'Quilkin, Robert Carlisle, and J. Meneely. The two first-mentioned had lately removed from Ballymena, where, some short time previously, they had seen themselves, and been found by their Saviour. The special object of their society was prayer that God would bless the preaching of the gospel in the Connor congregation, and their own labours, and those of others, in connection with the prayer-meetings and Sabbath schools throughout the district. The society soon ceased to be a secret one; and slowly one kindred spirit after another was introduced, on the recommendation of some of the original members. For a few months they had to walk by faith. The seed, however, was not long cast upon the waters till the tide ebbed, and the tender blade sprung up. They wrestled on. They prevailed. Surely when God's set time is come—when he intends signally to answer prayer, he disposes the supplicant to plead, and, with growing anxiety, to plead on till the blessing is secured.

The first observable instance of conversion occurred in December following. A young man became greatly alarmed. After some time, in answer to earnest prayer by himself and others, he found peace and confidence. Early in January a youth in the Sabbath-school class taught by one of those young men, was brought to the saving knowledge of Christ as his Saviour. Special prayer, about the same period, was frequently offered in the Fellowship Meeting in behalf of two persons who, some three months afterwards, joyfully professed their faith in the Lord Jesus. Faith grew; hope brightened. 'The power of prayer' began to be known, and felt, and seen. The Spring Communion came on. Throughout the extensive parish, consisting of some thousand families, it was generally known that, lately, persons had been turned to the Lord among them, some moral, and some wildly immoral. A few had heard of a similar triumph of Divine grace beyond the Atlantic. The services were peculiarly solemn. The Master's presence seemed to be recognized, and his call heard. A great impulse was given to consideration and seriousness, intensifying and extending these general precursors of conviction and revival. The old prayer-meetings began to be thronged, and many new ones established. No difficulty now to find persons to take part in them. The winter was past; the time of the singing of birds had come. Humble, grateful, loving, joyous converts multiplied. They, with the children of God, who in that district have been revived—greatly refreshed by this Divine Spirit—are now very numerous. There are on an average sixteen prayer-meetings every night in the week, throughout the bounds of that one congregation—*i.e.,* about one hundred weekly. The awakening to a sight of sin, the conviction of its sinfulness, the illumination of the soul in the knowledge of a glorious Saviour, and conversion to him—all this operation, carried on by the life-giving Spirit, was in the Connor district for more than eighteen months, a calm, quiet, gradual, in some cases a lengthened process, not commencing in, or accompanied by, a 'smiting down' of the body, or any extraordinary physical prostration more than what might be expected to result from great anxiety and deep sorrow. Thus, it is worthy of being noticed and remembered, that the present American Revival began in 1857; so did the Revival in Connor: the one began in the month of September, so did the other: one youth in each of the movements dates his conversion, November, 1856: prayer—fervent, confiding, and unceasing—was, and continues to be, the prominent characteristic of the one and of the other: laymen, one or six, in the one case, and four in the other, were the prominent agents, in commencing, as they continue to be in carrying on, the work in the one country as well as in the other. Oh, that it may become as extensive in the Old as it is in the New World!

In the beginning of this year a convert from Connor visited his friends near Ahoghill; and, through his urgency and prayers, the Holy Spirit awakened nearly all the family to a deep sense of their sins. These became missionaries to their neighbours and friends; and about the middle of February hundreds through the parishes of Drummaul and Ahoghill were overwhelmed with convictions of sin, its dangers and demerits; and during the month of March, in private houses, and barns, and school-houses, and churches, prayer-meetings were conducted and addressed by recent converts, attended by multitudes *in* the houses, and *around* them. In their own private homes, as well as at these meetings, many persons were violently convicted. I say *violently,* for in the great majority of cases known to the public in the Ahoghill and Ballymena districts, the process of conviction has been altogether of a different type from that known in the adjoining parish of Connor up till that time.

From another authentic source we have the following:—

This gracious Revival has extended from the parish of Connor to that of Ahoghill; then to Portglenone, and round by Tully, Largey, Grange, Strand, Slatt, Galgorm Park, Killalers, Cloughwater, Clough, and Rasharkin; nor is it yet showing any symptoms of decline—on the contrary, it is moving on with amazing power. Every day, and almost every hour, is bringing tidings of conviction. The interest is more and more awakening and extending.

The means by which this blessed work is carried on are in no way extraordinary. Prayer and praise, the reading of the word, and plain, pointed, solemn, and earnest appeals to the conscience and the heart, with the Holy Ghost sent down from heaven, are the only means that are resorted to. These are within the reach of every congregation and every religious community.

As to the human agency by which this Revival has been begun, and continues to be extended, it is not through the ministers of the churches alone, or even chiefly. The earnest and faithful preaching of the word may have been the preparation in some degree; but the chief and honoured agents in the work are the converted themselves. Not, indeed, schooled in human learning, but taught of God, very many of them have gifts of utterance, in prayer and in exhortation that are powerful instruments for good. Speaking from what they feel, they have great power in awakening slumbering souls. This humble agency can be multiplied to any extent, and in any locality. Their honour and success lie in this, that they are fellow-workers with God.

The Rev. William Arthur,—himself a native of Kells, in the parish of Connor,—in his *Beginnings of a Great Revival: The Awakening in Ulster, Connor,* after observing that the traces of the Antrim Revival, in the 17th century, 'lasted long, spread far, raised up a race of true believers who bore long witness to the power of godliness, and left a luminous trace upon the history of Ulster, never effaced', refers to the 'dark days' that succeeded. He next states, that 'for many years past a very blessed change had been passing over the Ulster churches; and by many faithful labourers the way of the Lord was being prepared.' He then proceeds to describe 'the beginnings' of the present Ulster Awakening, as follows:—

> The origin of the present movement is clearly traced to Connor, a parish seven miles long, peopled by small farmers, weavers, and linen manu-facturers, nearly all Presbyterians, mixed with only a handful of Church people, and scarcely any Roman Catholics. In the centre of the parish stand two villages, Connor and Kells. For many years the Rev. John H.

Moore had laboured among them and not fainted. He had formed Sunday schools on a new plan; not attempting to gather the children into one or two places, but at (I think) thirteen different points of the parish, he had formed rather a class than a school. Here scriptural instruction, real exercises in the word of God, was carefully given. On the training of his teachers he bestowed great labour. Among the topics of his preaching, the revival of God's work had often borne a prominent part. He feared not to speak of hell, or to tell sinners that a God of love was sure to punish sin. Prayer-meetings had been established at different times, but gradually died away, till one only remained, and that was sometimes attended by but one man and one woman.

A young man belonging to this congregation was residing in the town of Ballymena, a few miles away. He was, like many, zealous for religion after his manner, and stood in his own eyes as a Christian. But he heard a lady from England, said to be a Baptist, conversing with some young women, and describing true conversion. She told them that they were strangers to it, and still 'in the gall of bitterness, and the bond of iniquity'. This word reached the heart of the young man. He sought the inward and holy power of religion, the true and mighty regenerating grace, 'the love of God, shed abroad in our hearts by the Holy Ghost which is given to us'. He found clear and joyful acceptance with his Father in heaven. Full of this new happiness, he returned to his own parish.

In the month of September, 1857,—the very same month in which the first noon-day prayer-meeting, the harbinger of the great Revival, was held in New York,—he and three other young men joined together, in secret fellowship, to pray for God's special blessing on the people around them. They met in a little school-house, which stands alone by the way side. For three months their prayers seemed to rise to an unheeding heaven. In December one conversion revived their hearts. In the course of the next month one of the Sabbath-school classes had the unwonted joy of a true and clear conversion. Three months later two persons, who had been frequently prayed for, were brought to know the Lord. Thus slowly, silently, did the Lord at first work; thus steadily did these disciples continue to wait till his Spirit was poured out from on high.

Among the Presbyterian churches the Lord's Supper is administered but twice a-year; and, being thus rare, is made a great solemnity. What is called 'The Spring Communion' (1858) came. The parish had been more or less filled with tidings of the prayers that were being offered, and of the strange, clear, happy conversions which had taken place—conversions which made the person changed go on his way, 'walking, and leaping, and praising God'. Their faithful minister had been preaching on the subject of a great Revival, and telling what the Lord was doing for his vineyard in America, with a strong desire for the like at home. The solemn services of the Communion were crowned with an unwonted influence. Life, inquiry, deep convictions, strong crying and tears, nights spent in wrestling prayer, hearts heavy, and faces mournful with the burden of sin, and others, formerly as reserved upon religion as if it was a life and death secret, telling as simply as babes, and as happily as primitive Christians, of God's pardoning love—these became the familiar tidings of that favoured parish. Prayer-meetings sprang up on every hand, and wonderful was it to the staid Presbyterian folk to hear out of the lips of the unlearned and ignorant, of babes and sucklings, prayers of deep interest and heavenly power, which God must have taught, and that his own hand seemed manifestly to answer.

And then he adds emphatically,—

The conversions were of that marked Bible type, which fail when the power of the Spirit is low in the church, but ever re-appear in seasons of heavenly influence.

It is also worthy of notice—as Mr Arthur says—that 'everywhere faith in prayer, mighty prayer, seemed the first and deepest lesson of the Revival.' 'The impression', it is added, 'was very solemn when one told me that two young men from America had come to see if any good work was going on in the same neighbourhood; for *they had heard Connor and Kells named, at meetings in their own country, as places for which some one had specially requested prayer to be made.*'

Mr Arthur gives an equally authentic and interesting account of the way in which the Revival spread beyond Connor:—

One who had felt the joy of pardoning love filling his own soul, and opening in his breast a little heaven,[7] longed to see his mother, who lived in a neighbouring parish, across the 'Maine Water' as the River Maine is called, as happy as grace had made him. He got one of his comrades to join him in earnest prayer for her conversion. They had seen prayer wonderfully answered in the case of those around them, and why not at a distance? After this he went home to see if prayer had had any effect, and, to his joy and wonder, found that just while they had been praying, deep conviction had fallen upon his mother's soul; she had sought mercy, and was now rejoicing in hope of the glory of God. This triumph of prayer was no sooner won, than came the question, Where was his brother? Away at a cock-fight. Thither he followed him: there he found him, and, seizing him, he said, 'I have a message for you from the Lord Jesus.' This went to his heart; he, too, felt the pangs of deep repentance; he, too, soon fled for refuge to the open arms of the crucified Redeemer. His burden fell off, joy and peace in believing took possession of his soul, and, warm and simple, he rushed away to his minister, exclaiming, 'I am saved! I am saved!' The minister, at first, feared that he was only heated with some passing fervour for, oh how slow we all have been to believe that we live in a world wherein the saving of men is a work committed to an all-willing and Almighty hand, and that, therefore, we should expect to see it going on upon all sides, and at all times. But when he had fully investigated the case, the minister said, 'I wish we had some of those young men over here to hold prayer-meetings.'

This wish led to converts from Connor coming to tell the people of Ahoghill what the Lord had done for their souls. The Awakening also spread to Brougshane, a neighbouring parish teeming with a Presbyterian population. Thence it was conveyed to the town of Ballyclare, in an opposite direction to Ahoghill. On a fair day in that town a man from the neighbourhood of Brougshane, was brought under very awful convictions. He cried aloud for mercy in the presence of the wondering people. A poor slater among others heard him, and he was directed to Connor and Kells for light and consolation—there he found both.

---

[7] When the writer visited Belfast, in August, a minister told him of a young man so happy in Christ that he said, 'Formerly I used to think of heaven as a *future* state. I think less about that now, I have so much [putting his hand on his breast as he spake] of heaven *here*.'

At Belfast the writer conversed with a man who knew well the people of Ballyclare and its neighbourhood, and who told him of the marvellous and mighty operations of the Holy Spirit among them. It was a lad from Ballyclare, to whose instrumentality is to be traced a wonderful work of revival at Hyde Park, a village a few miles from Belfast. He publicly declared at a meeting how he had been converted, and seeing a boy impressed by it, fell upon his neck, and 'the affection of this boy seemed to break down the hearts of the people'. Thus, by unlikely instrumentality, by slight causes, yet powerfully and irresistibly, because the Spirit was at work, did the Divine flame spread wide and far from the spot where first it burst forth.

The sovereignty of Divine grace is, in truth, most marked in this Revival of 1859. It had, indeed, its precursors and pioneers, both in the great increase of light and zeal in the Irish Established Church, and in the faithful and self-denying missionary labours of both Wesleyan and Independent ministers. The Scriptures had been widely diffused, and Sunday schools everywhere established. And, especially in Ulster, such a zeal had been awakened for the 'old paths' of doctrinal truth, and such fidelity was exercised as to the application of discipline and the excision of the unworthy, that the two bodies—the Synod of Ulster and the Secession Synod—so long apart, were united into one General Assembly in 1841. Among the fruits of that union were—the rapid increase of churches in Ulster, and also in the Romish provinces— the establishment of Foreign, Jewish, and Colonial Missions—and a successful effort to provide manses for ministers. There was a great increase of intelligent piety also. Nevertheless, formalism prevailed, immorality began to spread afresh, and good men mourned. Then it was that the Lord the Spirit appeared in his glory.

The following is a record of spiritual and social results, as they came under the notice of the Rev. Dr Edgar, during his visit to Connor.

> The minister's wife told me that a woman had complained of the brutality of her husband. He gave as his apology his *wife's drunkenness*. The good minister's wife laboured for her reform, and one day received a pressing invitation to attend a prayer-meeting, which this woman, once

drunken, had opened. She went; and when the numbers became too great she brought them to the manse, and a joyous manse it was; for of the woman once drunken it could now be said, 'Behold, she prays.' Another woman in prayer said, 'O God, thou knowest, and all here know, how wicked a wretch I have been'; and true, indeed, it was; for, being mother of four illegitimate children, she was deemed a woman exceedingly vile: and yet, to show the exceeding riches of God's grace, He has had mercy both upon her and on one of the hapless daughters, to whom, in her wickedness, she has given birth. A son of that minister's helpmeet was thoughtless, like too many of his age, but God's Spirit moved upon his heart; and in the struggles of the new birth he vowed that if God would give him peace, he would devote himself to the ministry of the gospel. To the ministry of the gospel he is devoted now.

General effects throughout the district are, decrease of Sabbath-breaking, profanity, party spirit, drunkenness, poverty; reformation from evil habits and customs; sobriety, generosity, good neighbourhood, peace. There must be a general reformation where the reformations of individuals are so numerous. The good minister declines all attempts at general enumeration, and so well may I. Even to the wife of his bosom he says: 'Too soon, my dear, to talk of numbers; time will count them, time may make sad reckoning of some of them yet.' Whatever be the issue, the number is large now; I made acquaintance with fifty, in part of two days. Every house I entered had its rejoicing inmates. To both sexes the happy change has come, and over all ages of human life the Holy Spirit has claimed his power. Youth is no doubt his favoured time, but hoary age of threescore-years-and-ten has not been forgotten. I visited an aged widow; she had been married to a Romanist, and, though he did not force her to mass, she attended no church, and was going down to the grave without God and without hope, when the words of a stranger, who had found Christ, laid hold upon her heart. Anxious days and sleepless nights she passed, but she submitted to God, took him at his word, and found peace. As she stood before me in her seventy-second year, cold must be the heart, I thought, which could continue sceptical with such a proof of God's work in view. There was no excitement, no fanaticism, not at all; what completely overcame me, as I gazed on her aged features, was the evident struggle to restrain feeling, to prevent the flood of feeling from rushing forth at her eyes, while she talked of God's infinite kindness. Emotion she did show, but it was not for herself, but for her son, her only child. 'Oh', said she, 'how happy would I live, and how blessed would I die, if God would show to my poor boy his wondrous loving-kindness, as he has to me!'

CHAPTER 5

The early history and first-fruits at Ahoghill—a spiritual 'hurricane'—family awakenings—the scoffer arrested—precursors and results—multiplied testimony.

THE Rev. David Adams, in his *Revival at Ahoghill, its Narrative and Nature,* plainly indicating that in his opinion the Revival originated in his own locality, writes as follows:—

> If by a *revival of true religion,* we mean, as is generally understood, that outpouring of the Holy Spirit of God *by which many souls are brought to Christ for their salvation, nearly at the same time and place,* in such a *sudden* and *wonderful* manner as to deeply and religiously impress the world and the church with a sense of their need, and the value of a living Christianity, then, I think, I may truly state that the present extraordinary religious movement in the North of Ireland, began in the south-west part of the parish of Ahoghill, County Antrim, about the commencement of this present year, 1859. Two or three years before this time, there were at Ahoghill, as elsewhere, several large drops of Heaven's grace seen in the conversion of both old and young, indicative of the coming spiritual flood; but these were, like angels' visits, 'few and far between'. For a considerable period previously, there was here, as at other places, a slow, silent work of salvation progressing satisfactorily. Some would call this a Revival, and so it was in a sense; but the torrent-flood of God's mercy did not come till the early part of this year, and then it was first manifested at Ahoghill. While I admit the existence of some prayer-meetings and conversions elsewhere, I deny that they were the beginning of the Revival, properly speaking. To say that the Revival, in the sense I have defined, began in September, 1857, at Castlegore School-house, near Connor, would be as true as to affirm

that it was commenced at Ballymena, in the summer of 1856, by Mrs C., or Lieutenant A.; and this latter statement would be as true as to say that it began with the visit of Mr Guinness, to Ballymena, in the spring of 1858, or Mr Spurgeon's visit to Belfast in the summer of that year. None of these statements are correct, not more correct than to declare that the late short and sharp summer campaign in Italy, originated with the Prince of Wales, because he had been at Rome in the previous spring. The very same Revival phenomena which have been everywhere in this country so characteristically similar, and which appeared first at Ahoghill, in January last, were manifested at Connor and Ballymena in May last, but not till then. In making this statement I have no wish to depreciate or honour any human being. I claim no merit. I merely mention what I consider an historical fact, and I record it simply as such, when I state that the present Revival, properly so called, began first near the village of Ahoghill, about the beginning of this year. It was there and then I first heard 'the sound of abundance of rain'. While bowing my knees, like the prophet on the top of Carmel, a herald of mercy told me of 'a little cloud that ariseth out of the sea', which, though then not bigger than a man's hand, soon covered the heaven, 'and there was a great rain', the refreshing shower falling fast, and the 'streams in the desert' *here overflowing* copiously.

But he adds,

I think the only proper account we can give of the rise of the present great Revival in America, Britain, and North of Ireland, is what d'Aubigné does when beautifully describing the origin and progress of the glorious Reformation, nearly at the same time in different countries—'As in spring-time the breath of life is felt from the sea-shore to the mountain-top, so the Spirit of God was now melting the ice of a long winter in every part of Christendom, and clothing with verdure and flowers the most secluded valleys and the most steep and barren rocks.'

As to *preparative and pioneering work*, Mr Adams says that the Revival 'did not come so suddenly and unexpectedly as some imagine'. From his ordination in 1841, he cherished an intense desire 'for such a time of refreshing', and had repeatedly preached to his people, and also on public occasions, with special reference to the quickening of dead souls, and the outpouring of the Spirit. He had also followed up the teachings of the pulpit by great diligence in pastoral visitation from house to house, thus dealing closely and continuously with the consciences of his people. Two discourses on 'Pentecost', and on 'the Conversion of the Apostle Paul', had been attended with special blessing. 'One said to me', says Mr A., 'at your request I prayed to God that I might be able to say, like Paul, It pleased God to reveal his Son *in* me; and *he heard me.*'

The institution of Sabbath schools, as well as the extensive circulation of the Scriptures and frequent catechetical instructions, were also the means of an extensive diffusion of religious knowledge. After ineffectual efforts for many years on the part of the pastor to form district prayer-meetings, in 1855 three were voluntarily established without his direct interference. To one which was held in the place of worship in winter evenings, crowds began to repair of persons both old and young; in many cases they came without shoes or bonnets, and in their working clothes.

In 1856 there was an unusually large number of persons who sought fellowship with Christ at his table. The congregation, also, became so large, that the erection of a new and larger church was found necessary, and it was opened in 1858. 'I regard it', says the pastor,

> as a singular token of God's good providence, that it was just ready for the great Revival harvest. If it had not been so, hundreds of devout inquirers after the truth could not have obtained accommodation. Some of our people thought it folly to attempt building such a large, handsome place of worship, but the Lord, notwithstanding, graciously led us in the right way, as all now thankfully admit.'

The first great Awakening at Ahoghill manifested itself on Monday the 14th March, at the Monday service which, both in Scotland and Ulster, follows the celebration of the Lord's Supper.[8] The attendance at this meeting amounted to 3,000 persons, and at its close the people still lingered. Roman Catholics, Episcopalians, and Presby-

---

[8] It was on similar occasions that great Revivals began at the Kirk of Shotts in 1630, under the preaching of Livingston, and at Kilsyth, near Glasgow, in 1839, under the preaching of the Rev. W. Burns, son of the parish minister, and now a missionary in China.

terians were present. A young convert addressed them, and under the mighty influence of his appeals many fell down on their knees in the muddy streets and amid chilling rain, and poured forth earnest cries and prayers. 'I know', says Mr Adams, 'that many date their conversion from that memorable night—a night which will never be forgotten by those who witnessed that amazing scene.'

From that period the Revival wave swept onward over the district,

meetings for praise, prayer, reading of the Scriptures, and exhortation, being held every night, and frequently at mid-day in the busiest season, in kitchens, barns, school-houses, churches, fields, wayside and hedge-side, while secret and family prayer became very general. The spiritually impressed were multiplied daily—eight or nine of my hearers being changed in a day. On a Saturday I find this entry in my journal:—'Went at eleven o'clock, A.M., to —. Many converted last night—*an all night of prayer and weeping.* Many careless men left work (corn-sowing and potato-planting), and crowded the house. Deep impression on old and young; and several under the power of the Spirit while I was speaking.'

In the end of April and the beginning of May the wind of the Spirit calmed, but about the middle of May it blew a heavenly hurricane, and the mighty wave of mercy swelled gloriously mountain-high, *sweeping across the dead sea of our rural population, and washing the rocky hearts of formal worshippers.*

It is worthy of notice, that this Awakening at Ahoghill had been preceded, as elsewhere, by earnest prayer by individuals in almost every one of the seven hundred families of which Mr Adams's congregation is composed. 'In almost everyone of these families', he says, 'there are *some who during the last eight months have been waiting and praying for the Holy Spirit.*'

As to spiritual results, the numbers awakened and converted, and the modes of the Spirit's operation, Mr Adams writes:—

Hundreds have been visibly and remarkably awakened, and many truly converted. It is utterly impossible at present to obtain accurate statistics of all, and *the day* will alone declare the *real* number as compared with the nominal. But from my own observation, and accurate lists which I have received from some of my elders, and other trustworthy persons, I am able to affirm that not less than *seven hundred* of our people [this refers to Mr Adams's own congregation *only*] have been graciously awakened by the Spirit of God since the Revival began, all, with a few 'stony-ground' exceptions, hopeful, and many of them decided Christians.

They have been brought under the Divine influence at different times and ways, and in different places. Some at night, others in the day; some in gloomy winter, others in warm summer; some in bed, others at work; some in the open air, either alone or at the prayer-meeting, in the field or on the wayside; and others at the crowded assembly, in the dwelling-house, or in the church.

From the lists before me I find there are as many as eight in one family, and so on, down to one. Within a small townland to the northern section of my district, the return shows forty-four impressed, varying in age from seventy-five to eleven; while thirty-eight are above the age of fifteen, and eleven of them are men. A townland in the east gives thirty-nine in all, thirteen of whom are men, highest age sixty-one, lowest six, and thirty-three above the age of fifteen. And a townland in the centre gives thirty-three in all, of whom eleven are men, highest age sixty-one, lowest age ten; and thirty-nine above the age of fifteen. On one day I was called to visit a grandmother of eighty years of age, and a boy of eight, both under deep conviction, and both very child-like in learning Christ. There have been a few so young as two years of age.

Mr Adams, in his own graphic way, gives the particular details of a number of cases, which, if our space permitted, would form in themselves a whole chapter of 'Revival Incidents'. In concluding, however, our notice of his account of the origin and early history of the Awakening, we cannot refrain from laying before the reader the following remarkable illustration of the *grace* of our Lord Jesus Christ towards one who was a 'blasphemer and injurious', and who yet obtained mercy. Cases kindred to this have been by no means infrequent over Ulster.

Behold this mocker, how he is 'smitten'. He is aged eighteen, a waif on society, a wild Arab. He never seriously attended a divine service. He was a mocker and a blasphemer, and delighted to mimic the awakened. On that never-to-be-forgotten Sabbath, the 22nd of May last, when God's Spirit was so copiously being poured out on us—(the sermon on the remarkable passage, Hosea 6:4)—he stationed himself near the entrance of the church, and there, in the language of grossest obscenity, he reviled, abused, and cursed the passing people. After some time he shouted 'Ha, ha! the devil will get hold of you today!' To others he said 'Run fast, or you'll not get the touch.'

Shortly after, I was called to visit an 'impressed one'. He saw the throes of the new birth; he heard my prayer and exhortation to all present, denouncing him who sat in the chair of the scorner. Scarcely had he left the house, and long before the separation of some of the assembled worshippers, that wicked lad was struck to the ground, as with lightning. He was prostrated in the very scene of his iniquity.

Some supposed he was dead, but the visitation was in mercy, not in judgment. With restored health, came the soul-piercing stings of an awakened conscience; words and gestures manifested his terror and despair. His agony reminded us of the torments of hell, which doubtless were present to his mind. Then slowly came awakening hope—'Lord save *me*—I Perish!' praying for himself most urgently and earnestly. We felt that a brand had been plucked out of the burning.

He warned sinners never to mock God's cause, or profane the Lord's day; and this soul-smitten sinner now limped to every prayer-meeting in the neighbourhood, spelling a little every day in the New Testament, which he kept often under his pillow, and is now regularly attending in Sabbath school and church.

With regard to the Originating Cause, and The Author of this movement, Mr Adams says:

Assuming that the Holy Spirit operates directly and immediately on the soul in the sudden and simultaneous conversion of many sinners, all the appearances, *bodily, mental, and spiritual,* connected with this Revival can be philosophically accounted for—that is to say, 'a sufficient reason' for their existence can be given, but in no other way can they be satisfactorily explained. Sympathy, contagions, hysteria, hot atmosphere, crowded meetings, the devil's agency, will not satisfy Baconian philosophers—whatever literary divines, sceptics, and *mere* churchmen may pretend: for, all these existed before without producing present religious results, such as prove that a vial, big, not with judgment, but mercy, has been poured out.

We can only account for what has occurred among us BY THE WORK OF GOD'S SPIRIT, 'whereby, *convincing* us of our sin and misery, *enlightening* our minds in the knowledge of Christ, and *renewing our wills,* he doth persuade and enable us to *embrace Jesus Christ for salvation,* as he is freely offered in the gospel.'[9]

There was no attempt to 'get up' a Revival, no human machinery or machination, no underhand plot: all was pure and simple, undoubtedly and manifestly the work of the Spirit, blessing in a most extraordinary manner the ordinary means of grace, such as praise, prayer, the word read and preached, the Lord's Supper, and the circumstances therewith connected. I may also add, that a large number of useful religious tracts were generally circulated, and were productive of much good.

The Rev. Frederick Buick, a zealous and godly Presbyterian minister, who had watched the movement from its origin, furnished me, early last summer, with the following summary of his impressions:—

It has no appearance of a work of Satan to mar a work of God. I never saw such holy, heavenly scenes of prayer and praise in all my life before. Characters often the most godless, and even maliciously opposing the work, have been stricken down under terrible distress, crying out for mercy from the Lord Jesus.

Even poor ignorant children, brought up in the midst of wickedness, are offering up prayers before the throne (such as perhaps the most learned divines never offered), in language the most exalted, and with amazing earnestness and power.

Delight in the word of God is most remarkable; never was it so sweet to the taste.

The Psalms of David are sung now as they never were before.

Whole nights are often now spent in reading the word, and in singing and prayer—especially where there are any parties in the house under conviction.

Frivolity is given up for seriousness of the whole deportment. Christ is all in all. Such love for him, such desires for him, such fresh and lofty thoughts of him, I never witnessed before. Oh! it would do you good to hear them. But to be thoroughly convinced, you must see the

---

[9] Westminster Assembly's *Shorter Catechism.* Answer to Question 31—*What is Effectual Calling?*

work for yourself. IT IS OF GOD. *Never in this country has Satan got such a stroke.*

From a carefully prepared report, drawn up by the writer of the foregoing, and presented to the Synod of Ballymena and Coleraine, it appeared that 'in all directions prayer-meetings had sprung up, and that without number', and that 'the Spirit had descended in power'. Referring to the physical excitement, Mr Buick says,

Through the instrumentality of the word and prayer, convictions, often the most powerful, even to the *convulsing of the whole frame, the trembling of every joint, intense burning of heart, and complete prostration of strength,* have been produced. The arrow of conviction pierces the conscience, the heart swells nigh to bursting, a heavy and intolerable burden presses down the spirit, and the burdened, burning heart, unable to contain any longer, bursts forth in the piercing cry of distress, 'Lord Jesus, have mercy on my sinful soul!' Under such convictions, the heart finds relief in pouring out its cries and tears before the Lord.

Under the awakening of the dormant mind, the stirring up of the slumbering conscience, and the powerful movement of the nervous system, the imagination is often called into lively activity in picturing out solemn scenes of the future, and in hearing words of warning and counsel. Such sights are easily accounted for, while they are often sanctified, in producing saving impressions.

Two great truths take full impression of the mind, namely, man is a sinner, under judgment unto condemnation; Jesus is the Almighty Saviour to deliver, and faith in him is the way of obtaining deliverance. Many—even hundreds—are giving the most pleasing evidences of being in Christ. Of drunkards, blasphemers, card-players, Sabbath-breakers, and neglecters of ordinances, and the wicked in general, it may be truly said, 'They are now, new creatures in Christ.'

Sin-besetting sin—is crucified. One man, proverbial for cursing and blasphemy, now declares that he never feels the slightest temptation to return to his former sin. Another, notorious for his love of strong drink, now says he shudders at the sign-board of a public-house. The love of a third for card-playing is now transferred to his Bible. Obscene songs have given place to the songs of Zion, scenes of revelry are exchanged for scenes of prayer and praise, and the reading of the word.

The tone of public morals is enlightened, sanctified, and elevated. Even upon that portion of the public who make no claim to be religious, a deep solemnizing influence has been exercised. It is like pentecostal times, when 'fear came upon every soul.'

From another paper—a Report presented to the Presbytery of Ballymena—it appeared that the facts of the great American Awakening of 1858, as detailed to their congregations by the Ulster ministers, were powerfully instrumental in stirring up the people of God to pray for kindred showers of blessing. During the winter Sabbath evenings, also, solemn impressions were produced, and some were converted and turned to the Lord, by means of brief, earnest, and pointed addresses. Afterwards came 'floods upon the dry ground', and a writer in an Ulster journal, dating his letter April 23rd, 1859, gives the following testimony:—

> I stood in the centre of a thickly-populated locality, recently a careless, irreligious, and riotous neighbourhood, and from my own intimate knowledge of the inhabitants I am prepared to assert that every house in view, within a mile from the spot where I now stood, is now a sanctuary for the worship of God at the family altar; public prayer-meetings are attended by crowds so large that no house of worship can accommodate the entire number.

The population in County Antrim being chiefly Presbyterian, the great majority of the converts were Presbyterians, but Episcopalians and other denominations received the blessing also. More than this, Roman Catholics attended the meetings, both public and private, read the Bible, ceased to go to Mass, and positively refused to send for their former so-called spiritual guides.

'Many Papists', we were told, 'are included in the movement; and in no case that I have heard of, will they let that enemy of God, the priest, near them, but they call for the Bible, whereby they are comforted.'

Episcopal clergymen in the neighbourhood took an early and active share in this blessed work. One of them was the Rev. D. Mooney, who 'held prayer-meetings every evening in town or country, turning many from darkness to light, and affording solace to all who attended.'

Great zeal and tender compassion were manifested by the new converts. No sooner did they receive comfort themselves, than they began to pour the oil of consolation into the wounded souls of others, and to be missionaries to the careless around.

Two eminent Belfast ministers early expressed opinions on the subject of physical manifestations. One of them, the Rev. D. Hamilton, who formerly was a beloved pastor at Connor (near Ballymena), where the Revival began, spoke as follows:—

> The movement in Connor has, during great part of its progress, been calm, steady, and onward, without any very violent physical manifestations. While we should not prescribe any mode in which the Spirit should manifest himself, neither limit the Holy One, I consider that the calm, deep feeling is the most healthful. I do not think that the feelings could in all cases be restrained, but I do think that in many cases they can. And while there are diversities of operations by the same Spirit, I think that the violent physical manifestations are not the most healthful or promising.

The Rev. Dr Cooke, after describing the facts of this Awakening in the county of Antrim,—the swearer declaring he could no longer swear, and the drunkard and dissolute becoming sober and industrious, while the churches in different towns became crowded, and in the streets of these towns, congregations of people assembled to sing the praises of the living God,[10]—proceeded to remark:—

> There, in the midst of this, when prayers were addressed to their Lord, strong men became weak, and strong youths fell upon the ground; loud cries were uttered, and many tears were shed, and some of those who came to mock, cried out for mercy, and remained to pray. 'What did he think of those outcries?' He believed that those who disapproved

---

[10] A person writing from Ballymena, on the 2nd of June, says:—'The 23rd, 40th, and 116th Psalms seem psalms of power in the hands of the Spirit in imparting indescribable joy. They are heard at the midnight hour, sung by bands of persons, old and young, returning from their prayer-meetings. Old 'Martyrdom', thus accompanied, and thus heard at twelve o'clock on the midnight breeze, has a wonderfully solemnizing influence.'

of this part of the manifestations had no solid foundation on which to found their disapproval. He would, however, pronounce no absolute judgment. But this he knew, that while he was assured by parties present there were cases of outcries where there was no evidence of any grace of God; yet, in other cases, there was every evidence that an honest man could ask for, that although these cryings might or might not be the grace of God, there could be no question but that the grace of God was there; penitence, humiliation, reformation, and love to the Scriptures were there. Let them not be dogmatic, but exercise their senses between good and evil. *He would warn all scorners to beware.'*

In the same spirit the Rev. John McNaughten, who had visited Ballymena early in the summer, remarked, 'This is not a movement to be made the subject of jest, ridicule, and scoff. Men had need to take care lest they run their heads against the testimony of God's truth.'

CHAPTER 6

The town of Ballymena—outburst of spiritual life—the atmosphere of prayer—Romish converts bearing the cross—Sabbath keeping, and its Popish contrast—a scene at Ballyrashane—Coleraine Town Hall a spiritual hospital—two officers, and their tour in Ulster—a labourer's letter, and a great social change—united prayer-meeting at Belfast—an Irish clergyman's testimony—letter from the Rev. H. Hanna.

AT Ballymena the Awakening appeared suddenly, and in great power. The whole town might be said to be filled with spiritual anxiety, and every minister of Christ was called, like Whitefield at Edinburgh, to hold daily, nay, hourly, a levee for wounded souls. A feeling of solemn awe came over the wicked, and for one night or more, sleep was withheld from the eyes of hundreds of the people. Strong crying tears and prayers were heard in the streets, and in almost every house, there was the manifestation of a Divine agent working mightily. Among the many striking results of the general Awakening in this town, it was found that those once the most careless, and wicked, and worldly, now crowded the different places of worship. Besides this, out-door assemblies, on a vast scale, were held on the Sabbath evenings, when addresses were delivered, and prayers were offered by ministers and laymen.

On the evening of the 19th of June, four or five of the new converts addressed the multitudes with great power. Their language was characterized by the unpolished but effective eloquence of nature, for they were thoroughly *in earnest*.

The ministers at Ballymena are well known to me, not only as men of great ability and piety, but also as persons of sound and enlightened judgment. The Revs. Messrs Dill and Moore, who took a most active part in these services, did not hesitate to recognize most fully 'the manifestations of God's power, and the work of the Holy Spirit', as exemplified in the conversions of many souls in the favoured community around them.

Prayer was the great characteristic of these gatherings. In the same neighbourhood there was a *mid-day* field assemblage of the people for *united prayer*. A large number of persons gave up their usual work, in order to be present. Mid-day meetings for united prayer were also held in the Town Hall of Ballymena, on every Tuesday and Friday. Episcopalians, Wesleyans, and Presbyterians, led the devotions on these solemn occasions.

Meetings of the market-people were also held on the afternoon of every Saturday in the open square of the Linen Hall; and thus 'the mercantile benches, designed for the use of linen buyers, were now alternately occupied by the heralds of a gospel "without money and without price"'.

The Roman Catholic converts in the same neighbourhood continued steady in their adherence to the reformed faith, and it was a significant fact, that one of them took a leading part in the business of a public prayer-meeting near Broughshane.

'The whole movement', wrote a visitor to Ballymena at the beginning of the Awakening,

> if you will admit the word, is characterized by this feature—that the Lord Jesus is the *only* object, aim, end, and desire, of those who have found peace in him; and there is yet another curious and blessed thing—I did not hear of any attributing of means to any person or persons, that is

to say, it was not under Mr So-and-so, but the praise is all to God. 'The Lord shall work, and ye shall hold your peace.' I had a brother with me, and we were both asked to speak or address a meeting to be held on the morrow (Lord's-day). He half consented, our hearts were so full, so I expected to be able, out of a full heart, to tell of Jesus; but, my dear brother, when I drew near to the meeting place (a large quarry), and saw about 5,000 people, my heart sank within me, and I felt as if God said this to me—'Stand back! don't imagine you have anything to do with this people, so just stand aside and let Me act, for the work is all mine.' I thank his name I was enabled to say, 'Go on, Lord God, and do thine own work, and to thee, not unto us, be all the praise and the glory.' And he did work; I think about fourteen or fifteen souls in that meeting of three-and-a-half hours were laid prostrate on the earth, crying aloud for mercy.

When I got forward to look, a young man, a new convert, was addressing the crowd in a clear voice, and most earnest deportment; he was an unlearned and ignorant man, truly, but I 'took knowledge of him, that he had been with Jesus.' He was about eighteen years of age, I suppose; he could not speak five words together grammatically, and had those five words been put together according to the rules of grammar for him, he, even then, could not pronounce them in plain or intelligible English, the accent and language of that part being so peculiar. But oh, brother, the gospel of Christ proceeded from his mouth and his heart, and power and unction accompanied him. In describing this man I also describe four or five speakers who followed, all burning to tell sinners of him who forgave and blotted out all *their* sins by his own blood. They may have varied their illustrations, but all tended to the one object—to exalt Jesus not the cold technicalities of Providence, the Good Being, the Deity, the Most High—all true in their way, but these are not the warm expressions of loving hearts. Nothing short of Jesus, the blessed Jesus, God the Father and his Holy Child Jesus, will satisfy these wondrous men. Near the end of the preaching, one old man stood up to address the multitude: he was a remarkable-looking man; I was beside him before he rose; a dealer in rags would not have given more than sixpence for all the clothes he had on his person; he bore the marks and tokens of a 'hard liver,' a confirmed drunkard. He spoke something to the following effect, as nearly as I can remember:—'Gentlemen', and he trembled as he spoke, 'Gentlemen, I appear before you this day as a vile sinner, many of you know me, you have but to look at me and recognize the profligate of Broughshane, you know I was an old man hardened in sin; you know I was a servant of the devil, and he led me by that instrument of his, the spirit of the barley. I brought my wife and family to beggary more than fifty years ago; in short, I defy the townland of Broughshane to produce my equal in profligacy, or any sin whatever; but ah, gentlemen, I have seen Jesus, I was born again on last night week, I am therefore a week old today, or about; my heavy and enormous sin is all gone, the Lord Jesus took it away, and I stand before you this day, not only a pattern of profligacy, but a monument of the perfect grace of God! I stand here to tell you that God's work on Calvary is perfect—yes, I have proved it—his work is perfect. He is not like an architect who makes a drawing of a building, and then he looks at it, and he takes out this line and that, or makes some other alteration, and frequently alters all his plan, and even when the building is going on he makes some other change,—but God drew out the plan of salvation, and it was complete, and he carried it out with his blessed Son Jesus; and it is all perfect, for had it not been so, it would have been incapable of reaching the depth of iniquity of —, the profligate nailer of Broughshane.' While listening to this speaker, various cases of smiting down to the earth occurred. I looked around in the direction of a small crowd surrounding a woman, and was attracted by seeing a little boy of about twelve or fourteen years, standing at the head of this woman: he was in earnest prayer for her, and truly his shoes were off his feet, he was barefooted, and he said, 'Lord Jesus, you know I do not know how to pray to you—you know I do not know how to say one word pleasing to you; but you have forgiven my sins, and oh, I ask you to show this woman your loving heart, and that you are willing to forgive her her sins also.'

I could tell a deal more that I saw, and I afterwards visited a great many who were converted, and I can just say that my soul was sweetly fed in being allowed to be a partaker of their joy. I asked one poor girl, bareheaded and without shoes, 'What in the world makes you appear so happy?' 'Oh, sir', said she, 'haven't I got Christ, and if he does not make a body happy, I do not know who can.'

42

Many seriously disposed members of the Roman Catholic Church began at this period to attend at the Revival meetings in the neighbourhood, and did so *in defiance of stern injunctions to the contrary.* 'We know', said the *Ballymena Observer,*

> of one poor boy who was inhumanly beaten by his parents for his disregard of an injunction of this nature; and when thus compelled to obedience, he, though unable to read, purchased a copy of the New Testament Scriptures, and presented it to a pious old neighbour, still poorer than himself, on whom he attends to hear it read on every available opportunity.

Sabbath observance, as contrasted with previous Sabbath desecration, was one of the results of this Awakening. By way of contrast, and as an illustration of what popery, and popish priests are in Ireland, we are assured, on unquestionable authority, that on the last Lord's day of May, 'a day marked by a mysterious and heart-searching power in Ballymena, as well as the lightning flashes of an elemental disruption', a large party was engaged in *playing cards,* and prominent amongst them was a Roman Catholic clergyman.

The Rev. J. S. Moore thus indicates the earliest cases of Awakening in Ballymena:—

> In Ballymena, the work began early in April; the first person brought under conviction of sin—I think I may truly say convert who is a resident in town, is a lad some sixteen years of age. His was a purely mental process; he was not smitten, like many, prostrate and helpless to the ground, in agonizing horror; he had deep anxiety, great fear, for some weeks; he found Jesus to be his own Saviour. He rejoiced in peace, yet with trembling, for among his companions he could find no kindred spirit, perhaps, for nearly a month. Others had been previously struck at Ballymena, in the streets and in the public-houses, on the market-days, but they were from the country. The second and third persons belonging to the town, and also the second and third persons whom I had seen under agonizing convictions of sin, were two females of mature years, pretty well instructed in gospel doctrine, and of good moral character; they continue faithful to Jesus, and I am persuaded will do so: the one sighed heavily and wept bitterly, the other seemed absorbed in thought, or overwhelmed in sorrow; I engaged in very earnest prayer, but I soon

had to cease, and remain there for perhaps ten minutes in silent admiration of the sweetest, most intensely anxious, powerful, and appropriate prayer I had ever listened to. The next visit I was called to make was to an Arian family, and soon afterwards to a Roman Catholic family: in none of these cases, except in the last-named household, did the now common hysteric phenomena make their appearance. On my return, after two days' absence at a meeting of Synod, I found the town in a state of great excitement; many families had not gone to bed for the two or three previous nights. From dozens of houses, night and day, you would hear when passing along, loud cries for mercy from persons under conviction, or the voice of prayer by kind visitors, or the sweet soothing tones of sacred song; business seemed at a stand-still. In some streets, four or five crowds of people, in houses, and before the open doors and open windows, engaged in prayer or in praise, all at the same time . . .

A goodly number of young men, in business establishments in town, and not a few young workmen, shoemakers, carpenters, sawyers, and labourers, who were depending for their daily bread on their daily wages, gave up almost their entire time, day and night, during the first week, to minister to the religious instruction, and physical and spiritual comfort of the poor stricken sufferers. I put this on record to the honour of these young members of the church. But for them, in this crisis, I do not see what would have been done, for, in their first alarm, the people of both town and country would demand that a minister, an elder, should be in a dozen places at once. Prayer-meetings, in town and country, became very numerous: in private houses they were held all hours of the day and night; at first they were held in the principal Presbyterian churches every evening; latterly they are held alternately in these churches: at each meeting addresses are delivered and prayers offered by converts, the minister presiding. In the parochial School-house, in town, a weekly meeting has latterly been held, for lecture and prayer; also in the Methodist chapel there are frequent meetings during the week. For four or five weeks past a union prayer-meeting is held in the Town Hall, on Tuesday and Friday, at noon, attended by ministers and members of the Presbyterian, Episcopalian, and Methodist churches. Persons from England, and Scotland, and many parts of Ireland, were to be seen perambulating the streets and lanes of Ballymena during the past month; ministers, missionaries, Sabbath-school agents, and cool, inquisitive business men, anxious to witness with their own eyes and ears this strange thing, of which they had heard in their distant homes- a half-dead soul revived by God's Spirit! a poor lost sinner, with God's arrows sticking fast in him—his crimes over him like a thick cloud—his iniquities a burden too heavy for him to bear—his heart sore pained within him, 'the terrors of death having fallen on him'—fearfulness, and trembling, and horror overwhelming him; now crying, again shouting, screaming for mercy—again unintelligible to auditors, a modern Heze- kiah, 'chattering like a crane or a swallow'. One in twenty of these in- quirers, perhaps, returned home apparently dry, cold, sceptical, puzzled; many returned having caught a spark of the celestial fire, to be fanned into a flame.

At Portstewart and Ballyrashane, especially the latter, and both in the neighbourhood of the Giant's Causeway, the Spirit of God was now working mightily. The minister at Ballyrashane, the Rev. J. Alex- ander, a college friend of the writer, stated that in that parish nearly every family had been visited. In some cases only one member, and in other instances the whole family had been brought under conviction. On Sabbath the 19th of June, at the morning service, 'there was a crowd of anxious and deeply impressed hearers. A few persons came under the influence of conviction, which occasioned a little confusion, but the effect was most extraordinary.' In the evening of the same day, there was an open-air meeting of 1,500 persons, addressed by some of the 'Awakened'. Upwards of fifty persons were brought under alarm- ing convictions, and were 'struck down'.

Prayer-meetings are held every evening in the week in the district, and *'the moral effect'*, says Mr Alexander, 'is beyond description. The cases are numerous and important. All around are, equally with my- self, well acquainted with this extraordinary but merciful dispensa- tion. *It is a great and good work of the Spirit of God,* and I firmly believe that great and good also will be the results.'

At Coleraine, the New Town Hall, the mode of the celebration of the completion of which, had been a subject of discussion among the citizens, was thrown open, not as some proposed, to the votaries of the giddy dance, but to a crowd of sin-sick inquirers. 'Its walls gave back', says the *Coleraine Chronicle*, 'the almost despairing groan of the stricken sinner, the heart-felt prayer of the believing penitent, and resounded with the adoring thanks of the redeemed saint.'

On the morning of Tuesday, the 27th of June, two Christian officers sat as guests and visitors at the breakfast-table of the Religious Tract Society, Paternoster Row. Both these gentlemen had just come from visiting the principal scenes of the Revival, and both were very deeply impressed with the conviction of its reality, extent, and power.

Captain Hawes went round the Antrim coast by Carrickfergus, and onwards towards the Causeway, having first spent the Lord's day at Belfast, where he found an unusual and deep interest prevailing on the subject of personal salvation. He also was present at a remarkable meeting at Whitehouse, near Belfast, where the presence of God was wonderfully displayed among the young people who worked in the spinning-mill. It was delightful to hear from him an account of the recent conversion of the proprietor of the mill, and also of his wife, and how both were now zealous evangelists in their own sphere. Here and elsewhere, he and Captain Orr his companion, had great liberty and boldness given them to speak to the people the words of eternal life.

Captain Orr found an episcopal clergyman rejoicing with exceeding joy over numbers in his parish, who had long remained in the sleep of spiritual death, but who gave the clearest evidence of having passed from death unto life. The clergyman was very sceptical to the movement, until it reached his own borders, and there it showed itself, to his amazement and delight, to be indeed divine. At Kilrea, Captains Orr and Hawes addressed a crowd of people, and favourable impressions were produced.

Other places in the county of Londonderry we pass over, to mention that in the city of Derry itself, meetings for prayer and praise now began to be held every evening in the week, in the Victoria Market: very full expositions of scriptural truth were given, and pungent appeals were addressed to the impenitent. A commercial traveller, at one of the hotels in Derry, who for a time suffered much mental agony, was visited and prayed with by the Rev. Dr Denham, and by another minister; and having obtained peace of mind through faith in the Saviour, he went on his way rejoicing.

Deputations of converts from Londonderry about this time visited Omagh, and other towns along the line of railway to Enniskillen.

A humble man, writing to a Wesleyan minister from the town of M—, said,

> I know young men of the worst characters, drunkards, cockfighters, and in short, the most wicked and sinful, explain the Scriptures, and make prayers far superior to any minister. It is not altogether confined to Presbyterians, but there are members of our church (Episcopalian), and even Roman Catholics. From the advice given by those seized with it, to shun drinking, there was not one glass of whisky sold in this market yesterday (June 7th), for every fifty before . . . It is the best thing ever came to our country, for it is the means of turning many, many wicked sinners to God.

The sin of intemperance in Ulster had long been a subject of mourning to ministers and others. Now, through the wondrous power of the gospel, drinking habits began to be rapidly abandoned. At Ballymena, the public-houses, if not shut up, were deserted; and (as Captain Hawes assured the writer) in the town of Coleraine, on a recent market-day, it was ascertained that up till three o'clock in the afternoon, not a single glass of whisky had been purchased in the town.[11]

Crowded meetings for united prayer here, now commenced in the town of Belfast. At the first of these meetings at least *sixty* ministers of various denominations were present. At the second, Dr Knox, the Bishop of Down and Connor, presided. The deepest solemnity always prevailed at these meetings.

A friend, who was present at the first meeting, informed us that there were several Unitarian ministers present, as 'lookers on'.

The Rev. E. F. F. Trench, an eminent minister of the Irish Established Church, and cousin to Dr Trench, Dean of Westminster, published about this time an account of his personal observation and inquiries. He had found a number of cases of 'violent affections' among

---

[11] One publican, comparing notes with another, each declared that he had not '*wet a measure*' that day.

persons in the *higher walks of life*. He related the case of a wealthy linen merchant, who was thus converted; he also detailed the results produced on notorious sinners, and concludes with the following very weighty remarks:—

> It has been my happiness not to meet with any ministers engaged in this work, who have not appeared to me to be sensible men, and sound in the faith. None of them attach any importance to the outward bodily affections. Some of them fear that great confusion and many extravagances may follow; but up to the present the fruit has been good, and almost without any root of bitterness in the places where I have been. I fear this has not been the case elsewhere, nor can it be expected where the work falls into the hands of teachers who attach an undue importance to the feelings in religion.
>
> But the fruits are the things which will be looked for, both by God and man. And what are they? In addition to those enumerated in my last narrative, I may specify a few things which I heard, and believe to be true.
>
> A solicitor in B— informed me that litigation had decreased; a publican, that no man could live by the trade; and policemen, that now they had less to do than usual. Beyond all doubt, the most abandoned of women have forsaken the streets, and cried to Jesus for mercy. I have heard interesting anecdotes of quarrels made up. I have seen it stated that deposits in savings' banks have greatly increased, and I can certify that political demonstrations, 'gendering strife', seem to be in abeyance. It is true, that the editor of a public newspaper has been entirely incapacitated from collecting his thoughts on any other subject. It is true, that compositors in a printing-office have been unable, through strong feelings of sin and bodily weakness, to go on with their ordinary work. It is true, that the business in factories has been stopped through the same cause; but I believe it has been already in some degree made up to their masters by the return on Monday mornings of 'hands' which used to be disabled by intemperance on the Sabbath. The more I see of this work, the more mysterious it appears to me; but with such fruit, what can we believe but that God is using these violent affections of the body for the good of souls? Why are we to doubt it? The fact of the body being affected by the mind is of constant occurrence; it occurs every time

we laugh or cry. We read in Scripture that under religious impressions Daniel 'fainted', David 'roared', Habakkuk 'trembled and quivered', John 'fell as dead', Saul 'fell to the earth', thousands were 'pricked to the heart'. Similar affections occurred in America, and led to President Edwards's book on the *Religious Affections*.

At this time I received a very full and interesting letter from the Rev. Hugh Hanna, of Belfast, narrating the results of his own observations, and very large experience, in connection with the Revival at Belfast. This gentleman is intimately known to me, and his letter is so full, clear, and satisfactory, that I give it almost entire:—

Belfast, June 25, 1859.

DEAR SIR,—The movement of the Spirit of God is widening and deepening. We have had no such day as Thursday last, since the origin of this work of grace. The cases of conviction in Sandy Row during the day were very numerous. There is not the same excitement at public meetings as there was during the first week of the Revival. But the meetings are still as largely attended in Berry Street Church—every evening crowded to the doors. The arrows of conviction are shot by the Divine hand, and, lodging in the conscience, the sinner surrenders—the next day, perhaps, He struggles against the power of God, but at last he falls to the earth in the agony of his soul, and cries aloud to Jesus for mercy.

Some soon find peace; others are kept for days under a cloud, and are sorely exercised. I have visited nearly 400 cases, and *nothing short of the blindest infidelity could fail to see that a mighty work of grace is on foot*. The five-sixths of all the cases are calculated to gladden the church. Many of them are quite surprising. When God enters the heart, he opens the lips, and fervent exhortations by the converts are addressed to all around—father and mother, brothers and sisters, being specially urged to flee to Christ for mercy.

Such touching scenes as one now daily witnesses, it would be impossible adequately to describe. Every street, in some districts of the town, you may discover a house full of the surrounding inhabitants. The voice of prayer and praise resounds. Some stricken soul seems to feel the very pains of hell, or with angelic rapture is pouring forth the most beautiful tributes of gratitude and praise to the Lord Jesus. 'Ah! I wish', said one, 'that I could tell you of Jesus' love; I would take all sinners in my arms if I could, and lay them at his feet.' One young woman acknowledged that she had often assisted in the street rows, and carried stones for stronger arms, wherewith to pelt the enemy. But she had no enemies now, for she would be a friend to all sinners. She would tell Romanists of the love of Jesus, and she could love them now even when they wronged her.

I entered a very poor dwelling the other day; but it was like a corner of Heaven. Three sisters, on one bed, were rejoicing in Christ. They were in a state of heavenly rapture. An aged mother, with tearful eyes, looked on her rejoicing children, and gave glory to God. Many most remarkable cases of wild, profligate, and brutal characters, created anew, in this gracious movement, might be adduced. They would fill a volume. The good done is incalculable. The lower and middle classes are pervaded by a spirit of seriousness and inquiry. Churches are crowded at all services. Open-air services are attended by thousands. The people seem never to have enough—they so hunger for the bread of life. It is impossible to get them to retire from the churches. Roman Catholics are overtaken in the mercy of God; and God's grace proves itself stronger than controversy in the pulling down of strongholds. I write with an interesting young woman, of vigorous mind and considerable intelligence, beside me. God has overtaken her. She had a great struggle with the priest; she dreads the displeasure of friends—not for her own sake, but for theirs. She has written to her father, who is at a distance, to tell him what God hath done for her. Her letter breathes a beautiful spirit; and concludes by saying, that though he should cast her out, she will ever pray for him. *Our hearts are full of joy. The Lord hath done great things for us, whereof we are glad.*—I am, yours in Christ,

HUGH HANNA.

When I read this letter I could not but feel that Christians, by continued fervent and believing prayer, should seek for such an outpouring of the Holy Spirit, that the whole United Kingdom may participate in the unspeakable blessedness of a revived Christianity; specially, that they should supplicate that Ireland—so early a land of light—may once more become a torch-bearer to Western Europe. For that country I do anticipate a glorious future, even as she had once—ere Rome enslaved her—a great past. And in believing anticipation of the dawning of that bright day, in a higher and holier sense than was meant by Erin's bard, the Christian Irishman may even now address his country and say—

> Though nations are fallen, yet still thou art young,
>   And thy sun is but rising when others have set;
> And though slavery's chain long around thee has hung,
>   The full noon of freedom shall beam round thee yet!

CHAPTER 7

Early history of the Awakening in Belfast—the first meeting and its issues—Christian professors quickened—a quiet yet mighty work—overwrought labourers—great prayer-meeting in the Botanic Gardens—Unitarians, Romanists, and Orangemen—The car-driver's logic.

THE town of Belfast, the commercial capital of Ireland, was stirred to its centre by the tidings of the work of grace going forward at Connor, Ballymena, and in the neighbouring towns and district of the county of Antrim. In the month of June a public meeting was convened in Linen Hall Street Presbyterian Church, for the purpose of hearing addresses from two converts from Connor. These men, with extraordinary earnestness, gravity, sincerity, and power, addressed the multitudinous assemblage. There was nothing exciting in their manner, but their words were as arrows, and ere the meeting closed, an awful sense of the Divine presence filled every heart. Some were stricken down, and cried out in agony and alarm of soul. Thus a movement was inaugurated which rapidly spread over the whole town, and which has led, it is believed, to the conversion therein of at least 10,000 souls. At Berry Street, Great George's Street, and other Presbyterian churches, vast crowds assembled nightly, and the Spirit of God displayed his power in the conviction and conversion of hoary-headed and hardened sinners, of open profligates, as well as young men, maidens, and little children. The labours of Episcopalian, Presbyterian, Wesleyan, Independent, and Baptist ministers were incessant. Arians and Roman Catholics were led in considerable numbers to renounce their errors.

One early feature of the Awakening in Belfast was the truly marvellous increase of spiritual earnestness and piety among the members of Christian churches. In a Presbyterian church well known to the author, and presided over by one of the most excellent of pastors, it was found necessary to provide large additional accommodation at the Lord's table, so numerous were those who desired to partake of the holy feast; and this large additional membership was not the result of conversions since the Revival movement began. Although these had been numerous, and there was an ardent desire on the part of many to commemorate Christ's death, the pastor, who is as cautious as he is earnest, desired to prove and test by a little delay these persons, and dealt with them as catechumens, to be instructed in the way of God more perfectly. The increase in the membership, therefore, arose from a thorough Revival among the body of professors themselves, or, to speak more accurately, and to give the exact truth as it was conveyed to us, the addition had arisen solely from the conversion of mere formal professors, and the increased spirituality of the true children of God. This last, we hold, is the primary result of a Revival in the proper sense of the term. The church prays, 'Wilt thou not revive us again?'—that is, 'Wilt thou not awaken into fresh vitality the faith, the penitence, the love, the holy consecration of heart, and time, and talents, which thou didst bestow at the beginning of our Christian career, when all things were made new?'

The application of such a truth is obvious. In vain do we look for the quickening of the spiritually dead in Great Britain, until Christians themselves are revived—until formalism in the church gives place to reality, and hypocrisy to truthful and loyal allegiance; and prayer, not from feigned lips, but gushing forth from hearts filled with the Holy Ghost, shall bring the blessing down; and so the dead shall hear the voice of the Son of God, and hearing, they shall believe and live.

Although the movement was now attracting universal attention, and in its very vastness was accompanied with much of outward manifestation, yet—and this we state on the very best authority—there was a mighty and quiet movement going on, which those alone who were mingling among the people, and who have their confidence, could know.

Great was the anxiety on the part of ministers and others that this blessed work should not be marred. In the *Banner of Ulster* appeared a letter, signed by four ministers of eminence, calling special attention to the probability, that Satan would endeavour to bring this Awakening into contempt, or to diminish its power by counterfeit manifestations, such as should give cause to the enemies of evangelical religion to blaspheme. Kindred anxiety was expressed also by an episcopal clergyman, who, in writing to me, spoke of certain parties more ardent than judicious, who had been guilty of 'excesses'. I found it, too, in the communication of an eminent Presbyterian minister, who feared lest by unbelief or self-seeking, or the exaltation of man, the work should be hindered. All these anxieties were tokens of good. 'Forewarned, forearmed'; these sober and unselfish Ulster ministers will, I said, be honoured of God to guide the movement, with Christian discretion, to a blessed issue.

The closing week of June seems to have been the most remarkable in the early history of the movement in Ulster; so said a Belfast journal of June 30th:—

> Several weeks have elapsed since the wonderful work of the Spirit, now effecting such momentous moral changes among our community, first commenced its work in Belfast and the neighbourhood. But the present week must be regarded as the great and special season of refreshing and revival the 'accepted time' to numbers who before dwelt in the shadow of death. This will be sufficiently evident from the deeply interesting details relative to the progress of gospel enlightenment throughout our immediate bounds, and the spiritual renewing which is going on silently, but with power, not only in localities where the Revival element had previously manifested itself, but also in districts widely asunder—some of them even remote from centres whence the Awakening influence

could have reached them by means of any mere human agency or sympathy.

Of the 'details' above alluded to, we now proceed to give a summary from various sources of information. A Belfast Presbyterian elder, while modestly declaring his incompetence to furnish me with a full summary of the work in that town, gave, as a second reason, *want of time*. He, with others like-minded, had been overwhelmed with toil arising from the blessed necessities of the crisis. Night and day had pious laymen been engaged, speaking with the awakened, and visiting them at their own houses. 'Everyone', wrote my friend,

> that has a heart for work is done up, the calls are so many. As the movement here has been much among the poor, our Town Mission arrangements greatly increase. The Lord is doing great things in our midst. In Fisherwick Place Sabbath schools about forty have found the Saviour within the last few weeks.

The Awakening among young persons was also marked and extensive. An instance of simultaneous conviction, at this period, among almost the whole children of a Sunday school at Belfast, excited much attention. Can there be, I ask, an object more worthy of intense desire on the part of British Christians than that the mighty rushing wind of the Spirit should pervade and fill our Sunday schools? The pupils are numbered by millions; the teachers are a quarter of a million at least, mostly all zealous and faithful; and yet the number of conversions, how few! From the elder scholars but a small number, comparatively, enter the church of Christ. It is an alarming and an acknowledged fact, that the gulf between the school and the communion table is unbridged. Is there not need, then, for instant, incessant, fervent, compassionate entreaty for a great Revival in our Sabbath schools?

A great union meeting for special prayer had been *the* event of this period. It had been considered highly desirable by the zealous friends of the movement, that an effort should be made to bring together, on one day, many persons from all the districts within a reasonable distance of the metropolis of Ulster, in order that information might be given, and, in connection with solemn addresses, prayer offered for the abundant outpouring of the Holy Spirit. From the counties of Armagh, Tyrone, Antrim, and Down, these came, by railway trains, which were crowded to excess, to different Belfast termini, and thence repaired, with all the solemnity and order of Christian Sabbath-day worshippers, to the Royal Botanic Gardens. Here, also, were gathered crowds from the town and immediate neighbourhood.

It was in the beautiful grounds of the Botanic Gardens that the Rev. C. H. Spurgeon, in the month of August, 1858, addressed the largest audience which ever assembled to hear a minister of the gospel in Ulster. But it is calculated that a multitude four or five times as great was now collected, numbering in all from 35,000 to 40,000 souls.

When this vast assembly was gathered together in front of the platform, and occupying every available spot of the entire ground be-tween the pavilion and the conservatory, the scene was certainly one of the most striking, as well as impressive, ever witnessed in the prov-ince. Crowds, however, continued to pour in through the gates for more than an hour subsequently, till at last the whole space in view from the platform was closely packed.

> Even the branches of the trees were taken advantage of by the junior members of the audience, as the most suitable situations for either see-ing or hearing; and there, while the sounds of praise were rising from the multitudes below, these young worshippers were heard joining in the song of thanksgiving. Nothing of holiday levity, nothing of the thoughtless mirth of youth was manifest among them; their attention to the proceedings was as marked, and their attention as well ordered, as that of any person in the vast assemblage.

The Rev. John Johnston, D.D., the Moderator of the General Assembly,—whose name was identified with Christian missions, Bible circulation, Sunday-school instruction, when these were little prized in Ulster, and who still more recently was the leader of that great open-air preaching movement which has acted as a pioneer to the present work of God,—was the chairman and president on this remarkable occasion. He opened with a deeply impressive prayer for the outpouring of the Holy Spirit upon those before him. After read-ing a portion of Scripture, he then gave out the 100th Psalm, and never before, in Belfast, did so many voices unite in such hearty accord in singing this favourite song in Zion.

The chairman then addressed the throng. The following is a portion of his observations:—

> When the destroyer of men's lives was vanquished at the battle of Waterloo, the crowned heads of Europe fell down on bended knees, and with uncovered heads acknowledged themselves grateful to that God who had put an end to the shedding of human blood; and when the God of peace is now treading underfoot the destroyer of men's souls, and is rescuing from his fatal grasp so many immortals for whom Christ died, shall we be ashamed to acknowledge his goodness, and the might of his Eternal Spirit, as we are this day met to do, and with one heart to pray 'Thy kingdom come?'
>
> > O Jesus, ride on till all are subdued,
> > And the universe filled with the knowledge of God;
> > Let the whole earth be filled with thy glory. Amen and amen.
>
> But, my friends, we are in a world that lieth in wickedness. There are scoffers who say, 'Where is the promise of his coming? for since the fathers fell asleep, all things continue as they were from the beginning.' Let us not give occasion to the enemies of God to blaspheme, by any levity, trifling, or impropriety, unbecoming this occasion. Let us set the Lord God before us, and so realize his awful presence in this place, that good may be done, and God may be glorified. We are especially met to do homage to the Holy Ghost, whose convincing and converting power has been so strikingly manifested amongst us for these several months; and let us not resist the Holy Spirit, nor grieve him, but ask unanimously, earnestly, and expectingly, that he will descend upon us on this day as he did on the day of Pentecost, in answer to the many prayers offered up, and to be offered, and that many sons and daughters may this day be born to the Lord Almighty.

While the addresses were being delivered, and the prayers offered, there were very many, who found it impossible to catch the sounds by reason of distance. Hence it came to pass that other congregations were rapidly formed and collected in other parts of the gardens, numbering from 500 to 1,000 each. In these smaller meetings many were 'struck down' under deep conviction of sin; some weeping bitterly, but silently: some crying out piteously for mercy, and others unable to utter a word. Some proceedings in one of these circles—where a coloured gentleman, agent to the Temperance League, and three others, were offering up prayer in a manner; the vehemence of which gave occasion to considerable remarks—'were', said the *Banner of Ulster,* 'not at all to our taste.'

Prayer-meetings among the young formed another feature of this remarkable gathering. In many parts of the gardens groups of boys and girls, some of them ragged, who had evidently belonged to the outcast classes, and were recently converted, prayed in language most affecting and impressive.

On the same day on which the united prayer-meeting was held at the Botanic Gardens, the regular weekly prayer-meeting was held at the Music Hall, and was largely attended. Week-evening services also continued to be held in the various places of worship; and these, as well as services in the open air, were crowned with results truly astonishing.

From Comber, Dundonald, Killinchy, and Killyleagh, in the County Down, from Glenarm, and other places in Antrim county, from various quarters in Londonderry, and from the city of Armagh, most cheering accounts were now received.

Unitarians and Romanists also continued to be brought under the power of the movement. At Carryduff, in Downshire, a woman, who was a Unitarian, who never attended one of the prayer-meetings— who did not believe that these revivals were of God, but mocked and scoffed at them, and who had never spoken to one of the ' convinced', was herself brought under deep distress of mind, and was led to cry to the Saviour for mercy. She refused to see the Unitarian minister, and was brought the same evening to the evangelical prayer-meeting, to be instructed and prayed for. This was done, and she went home full of peace and gladness.

Of the Roman Catholic converts at Belfast we were told, that 'their firmness in holding fast by the liberty wherewith Christ had made them free, was greater than that of the converts of any other persuasion.'

Marvellous indeed were the scenes now going forward night and day. This was the season of the year which recalled to the recollection of the writer many an anniversary of the battle of the Boyne, in connection with much that was painful as to spurious party zeal among the Protestant yeomanry of Ulster, and frequently collisions with Romanists. But now, in July, 1859, party spirit seemed dead. Instead of the favourite songs and airs of 'Croppies, lie down!' and 'The Boyne Water', and drum and fife,—in the summer evenings, were heard the high praises of God from groups met in holy concert, or returning to their respective homes as 'a band whose hearts God has touched'.

The reality of this Awakening was now so unquestionable, that scoffers were well-nigh silenced. A driver of a car at Belfast, who had seen many in a country district 'struck down', and had heard them crying for mercy, was asked what he thought it was? He replied,

> Why, sure it must be the work of the Almighty. The Catholics say it is the work of the devil, but I always say to them, , Would the devil teach people to pray? Sure, if it was the devil or glamourie,[12] it's drinking and swearing they would be, and not praying and doing good.'

We find also, as one of the fruits of this work, 'restitution' being made, as in the days of the great Revival of Scotland, a century ago. The social change in the community which was effected in two months was amazing.

The Rev. William Arthur, of London, who was now amid the scenes of this Revival, deliberately declared that it was a season of Pentecostal power and blessing.

---

[12] glamourie: (archaic) witchcraft, *Ed.*

CHAPTER 8

Extending interest in the Awakening—pilgrims from afar—their testimony—
Belfast toilers—general progress—abatement of party Spirit—bigotry and its
contrasts—the loving Bishop and united prayer—a clergyman's visit to Belfast—his good report—special cases—special prayer in America for Ulster—
case of 'trance' at Ballymena.

INTENSE interest soon began to be felt in this marvellous Awakening, not only throughout the United Kingdom, but also in Canada
and the United States, as well as over the continent of Europe.

Summer tourists repaired to Ireland, and among them, many earnest Christians not only embraced in their journey the glorious scenery
of Killarney and the west of Ireland, but also repaired to the north, to
see something still more glorious than even the Giant's Causeway and
the magnificent headlands of the Antrim coast—even the results of
the mighty creative energy of God the Holy Ghost.

Ulster in 1859 was in truth the scene of special pilgrimage, and,
having closely examined the facts, and become personally acquainted
with the sober-minded and judicious men who directed or co-operated in this great movement, men returned to their homes, saying, 'It
was a true report we heard—the half was not told us.' 'The Lord hath
done great things, whereof we are glad.'

Among the early visitors to Belfast, was M. Napoleon Roussel,
an eminent minister of the French Protestant Church, well known
as the author of *Religion D'Argent*, and other controversial treatises,
which have dealt heavy blows and sore discouragement to the Church
of Rome.

A well-known minister at Belfast wrote to me at this period, of the
overwhelming fatigue which he and his brethren underwent, in visiting, conversing, and praying with awakened persons. Several of them
were thus engaged till two or three o'clock in the morning; and he
himself, although just recovering from severe illness, was thus occupied till twelve o'clock at night. It was only late on a Saturday evening

that he could snatch a little time for pulpit preparation for the services of the Lord's-day. Such labour, however, was one of love, and we doubt not that many faithful men throughout the kingdom now almost envied the hallowed 'weariness' of their Belfast brothers, and would have been more than glad, to be called to 'endure hardness' kindred to that of these good soldiers of Jesus Christ, in fighting his battles, and in winning souls to him.

Another correspondent at Belfast, writing to me, said,

> You will see by the papers that the Revival work is still going on and increasing all over Ulster. While we cannot approve of all we see and hear, yet we must not condemn; and there is no doubt of the great change wrought in the community as to sobriety, decrease of party and sectarian spirit, and also as to religious feeling.

In reference to the usual Orange demonstrations on the 12th July, in commemoration of the battle of the Boyne, our correspondent adds, 'I do not think we shall have any party processions or displays here next week, which in itself is a great matter, and a token for good.'

It was stated in a Belfast journal at this period that a clergyman of the High Church school found a Presbyterian layman administering consolation to a young woman who had been grievously oppressed both in body and soul, that he ordered him out of the apartment with words of extreme sectarianism, and intimated at the same time to the father of the girl, that the landlord would be much displeased with him in not sending for his own clergyman. We rejoice to say that this exclusive spirit had found no countenance from this gentleman's own brethren.

While some stood apart from co-operation with other Protestants, yet anti-Tractarian,[13] anti-Romish, Evangelical, is the prevailing characteristic of many clergymen.

Thus it was that the Bishop of Down, Connor, and Dromore, presided at the first meeting for united prayer in the Music Hall, Belfast. He opened it with an address so full of brotherly love, as to remind

---

[13] *'We have too much of the real thing (i. e. popery) in Ireland'*, was the expressive reason given by the Bishop of Cashel, why Tractarianism found sympathy from few or none of the Irish clergy.

us of that amiable predecessor of his in the seventeenth century, who, when a Presbyterian ordination was being held in his diocese, asked leave to be present, not as a prelate, but as 'a simple presbyter'; and who put his hand on the head of the candidate, in common with, and in loving recognition of, the Scottish ministers as his fellow labourers, and the servants of a common Lord. We have already given the testimony of the Rev. F. F. Trench, an Episcopal clergyman, as to what he saw and heard on a recent visit to Ulster. Kindred testimony had been borne by two of his brethren—the Rev. W. Marable, of Dublin, and the Rev. J. P. Garret, rector of Kellstown, County Carlow. The latter gentleman told his own parishioners that he was about to visit Belfast, and that, on returning, he would communicate the results of his observations. He now 'fully corroborated what others had written', and desired that the facts published by him might 'redound to the glory of God, from whom all these great things proceed'. His first visit was paid to a daily meeting for prayer, held at the factory dinner hour (two o'clock) by a number of young women in the school-room of Linen-Hall Street Presbyterian Church. The local ministers were so pressed with urgent duties that he was asked to preside. We give what followed in his own words:—

> Having given out a suitable hymn and prayer, I then read the first fourteen verses of John 16, especially dwelling on the 7th and 13th verses. I felt my heart drawn towards these people, and after using expressions to stir up convictions, I assured all true subjects of conversion that when the Heavenly Physician commenced his work, he would perfect it, and carry on his stricken one to the rest in glory.
>
> Then occurred a scene I shall never forget: a strong girl sat near me, named Agnes J., twenty years of age, who, throwing up her hands, fell back with a suppressed moan. Three girls next her, held her from falling; her body quivered, tears fell, perspiration broke out over her face, her lips moved, the names of Jesus, Saviour, and Holy Spirit, were audible.
>
> We joined in the 40th Psalm, and after it was sung, two of the converted girls, at my request, prayed in turn, and never did I hear a more earnest prayer—so simple, so scriptural; beautifully they expressed themselves whilst wrestling with God in behalf of her they now called sister.

Not one in the whole meeting but now held down their heads, and all seemed to pray as with one heart and one soul. Just before the conclusion of the meeting, the Rev. Mr Knox, the Presbyterian minister, entered, and feelingly he prayed in behalf of the oppressed and stricken one. She was then carried to his house, which was at hand. I followed. We then praised God together, and again prayed for her, and I left her with the intention of seeing her next day when taken to her home.

Another girl, aged eighteen, called Rachel O., was stricken at the same moment, but she was able to suppress outward expression of what was passing within her. The next day, Wednesday, quite unexpectedly I called with a Scripture-reader of Christ Church, whom I had known for above twenty years, and we found Agnes in bed, very weak but very happy. She knew me at once, and her bright eyes bid me a joyous welcome. She told me, in answer to many questions, that she had for nearly three weeks been under conviction of sin; but that assurance that 'God never commences his own work in a soul but he perfects it', went like a dart to her heart. She was overpowered, and fell. She said her heart felt as if it would burst; but now the load was gone, and sin was pardoned. She was full of gratitude—humbled in the dust for past sin and neglect of God, but, blessed be his name and his Holy Spirit, all was now changed. 'Never, oh! never', she exclaimed, 'will I doubt; he will never let me go.' The girl who was also stricken at that meeting came in while we were there, and actually rushed to the bed, and threw herself into the arms of Agnes. They felt they were new creatures—one in Christ, and sisters for eternity.

Mr Garret adds, with regard to those who have found peace and joy in Christ:—

The striking brilliancy of their eyes was extraordinary, but this is observable in nearly all who are brought under this gracious work of conviction and salvation. Some Roman Catholics have become impressed, and I had a most interesting conversation with one. The feelings of everyone I visited are forcibly expressed in the following lines:—

'Other refuge I have none—
Hangs my helpless soul on Thee;

Jesus, Thou my Saviour be
Sweet it is to trust in Thee!'

All false trusts on human aid, all false teachers, are rejected. God's Spirit has enlightened the soul, and I believe men or devils shall not gain a final ascendancy over these stricken but now rescued ones again, for nothing but Bible truths and Bible teaching will satisfy them. All sectarian and unkind feelings pass away, and their love for Christ and for each other is wonderful.

This excellent clergyman called for prayer on behalf of the stricken ones. 'Pray for them', he said, 'and for the noble ministers labouring with all their strength, and some above their strength', and he gave as a reason for special prayer—'These stricken ones will be tried; Satan and his confederates will set up hypocrites to cast discredit on this work, and if possible keep the masses in ignorance of truth and under the shadow of spiritual death.'

Prayer for the north of Ireland was expressly asked for last year by a Christian lady at the daily prayer-meeting in Philadelphia, at the time when the American Awakening was in the fullness of its vitality and power.

I received at this time a copy of the *Sunday School Times,* from the excellent and well-known George H. Stuart, Esq., of Philadelphia, who is the President of the Sunday School Union there; and in its columns I found the fact—for the first time it may be—was distinctly announced in connection with that Awakening in Ulster, the tidings of which had reached America.

Surely there were many such answers to prayers thus offered for America itself. But here was prayer for a locality beyond the great Atlantic, and believing suppliants, could recognize and record the answer in the flood-tide of blessings pouring over 'the north of Ireland'—the scene so earnestly pleaded for. What a twofold encouragement was here, first, for *specific* prayer; and, secondly, for humble, patient, yet confident waiting for a gracious answer to the united prayers of God's children!

While the physical agitations were not by any means universal, yet cases were constantly occurring. Thus, of one Episcopal church, on the first Lord's day of the month of July, the *Belfast News Letter* said, that 'about nine of the congregation were brought under a similar influence to that felt in other congregations and throughout the province.' At Berry Street and Great George's Street Presbyterian churches, numerous cases occurred.

> Parties of men could be seen passing in almost every street, conveying their fellow men in a state of utter physical prostration to their residences. Individuals, who were not so much weakened, were taken a short distance from the church, and on the footpath in the adjacent streets prayer was engaged in with and for them, and many of them returned to their homes rejoicing.

At this period all the places of worship at Ballymena were crowded to excess, and in the parish church four or five cases of spiritual arrest and physical agitation occurred, one of which is so strange and peculiar, that we give the account as it is furnished by an eyewitness. The case was that of a child, eight years old.

> She had earnestly besought her father's permission to accompany him to church; and, while there, had paid marked attention to the devotional exercises which preceded the usual sermon of the day. Some expressions of the Rev. Mr Mooney, in his discourse from the pulpit, must have arrested the child's attention, for, on two or three occasions, she pressed her father's hand, and, looking upward, whispered in solemn and impressive tones, 'God bless him!' Soon afterwards she suddenly bowed her head upon her father's knees, and instantaneously fell, speechless and motionless, into a trance—and in that state she remained for a period of about four hours. With respect to the extraordinary sensations experienced by this child, while in a somewhat similar condition on the preceding Tuesday, a correspondent has referred us to the event recorded in Acts 10:10—'But while they made ready, he fell into a trance, and saw heaven opened.' We do not presume to offer any opinion upon the subject—our statements on every matter having reference to the present Revival being limited to a simple narrative of facts. After the congregation had dispersed, the girl was carried to an open passage of the church, and placed in the arms of her father, who had there seated himself upon the floor. In that position we had every opportunity of observing her

for half-an-hour. Her physical condition was neither epileptic, nor in the slightest degree resembling that induced by an ordinary fainting fit. The colour of her face was natural—neither pale nor flushed. When previously affected, her eyes had remained open during the entire time of visitation, but they were now firmly closed; and with the exception of an occasional gentle movement of the lips, and a tremulous motion of the eyes, clearly perceptible beneath the eyelids, her features were in profound repose. Her pulse was full, and beat with strength and perfect regularity, but considerably slower than it is usually found in children. The heat of her body was natural; and, in general, she breathed calmly; but there were several momentary intervals wherein her respiration became extremely hurried—a fluttering motion being then perceptible about the neck and chest, accompanied by a slight nervous movement of the arms and hands. She was restored to consciousness in about three hours; but for more than an hour afterwards she was unable to move her lips, or articulate a single syllable. Her eyes, when first opened, did not appear to be cognizant of any object within view, but they subsequently assumed an expression of tranquil happiness; and, when she regained the power of speech, she did not, as on the former occasion, make reference to any scenes which had been presented to her imagination during the interval of visitation. The loss of speech is a new and very mysterious feature in some of the recent cases where mental impression is accompanied by external influence upon the body.

On this trance-like sleep, and on physical agitations generally, I shall afterwards remark in a separate chapter. Meantime let me quote the remarks of the *News Letter,* writing at this time. It denied, with regard to the great majority of *'stricken'* persons, that they had committed 'extravagances'. 'They have merely confessed their consciousness of sin, implored mercy from God, and sought the prayers of those around them. As for the cases of those rendered helpless for a time, they had, after restoration, "become new creatures"' It was added :-

That some profess to have seen visions we do not deny; nor are we disposed to regard the sort of second sight they have assumed as anything but a result of mental excitement leading to self-delusion. But these cases are the few amongst thousands; and again we say it is utterly wrong to measure the movement by any such. That a genuine revival of religion, in the best sense of the phrase, is afoot, all who have calmly examined for themselves admit. It has resulted in an enormously increased attendance at religious services, both on Sundays and week-days; in a decrease of drunkenness and depravity of every kind; in a more serious feeling pervading the general community; in many special conversions of noted evil-doers; in the conversion, also, of numerous Roman Catholics; and, if these results are to be approved, on what prin-ciple can the movement be condemned? We have ourselves seen troops of mill girls walking along the roads in the suburbs singing hymns and psalms in the most serious manner, persons who used to make it a con-stant habit in the summer evenings to go in companies singing light songs, and making light jokes with every passer-by. A clergyman of a neighbouring town tells us that the last fair-day there was 'like a prayer-meeting', and that not one quart of whisky was sold, according to the report of the publicans. That the good will abide and increase is to be hoped. We shall know it better by its lasting fruits; but for the present its fruits, now continued for several weeks, proclaim a work in which the Spirit of God has been sensibly amongst us.

CHAPTER 9

Irish General Assembly—report on the state of religion—solemn recognition—recommendations—Mr Moore's testimony—Dr Cooke on false peace—converts and their addresses—strength in prayer—opposition overruled for good—'an overwhelming array of witnesses'—lay preaching, and Brownlow North.

IT is a great advantage to be able to test any movement by authentic information.

This is obtained from the testimony of personal observers or actors, and when to this are added the conclusions of deliberative bodies, who have sifted evidence, and have carefully eliminated facts, public opinion is alike enlightened and satisfied.

We are thus enabled to add to preceding statements, furnished from the private and personal observation of trustworthy persons, the solemn and deliberate estimate formed of the Awakening in Ulster by the General Assembly of the Presbyterian Church in Ireland.

This, the Supreme Court, is composed of the ministers and elders of more than five hundred congregations, and is the representative body of nearly one half of the Protestants of Ireland. Its creed is emphatically scriptural and evangelical. Its ministers preach with fullness and earnestness the depravity and guilt of man, the necessity of regeneration and sanctification through the truth and by the Holy Spirit, as well as of justification by faith in the obedience and sacrifice of our Lord Jesus Christ, and, by evangelical motives, they urge the people to live holy and peaceable lives in all godliness and honesty.

At its annual meeting, held in Dublin, in the beginning of July, 1859, the Assembly had brought before it a 'Report on the State of Religion', by the Rev. Dr Kirkpatrick. This document embraced a review of the condition and progress of religious life throughout the congregations of the church during the preceding twelve months. In other years, the Committee on the State of Religion had much that was encouraging and hopeful to report, as to Sabbath-school instruction, a self-denying and laborious ministry, as well as increased liberality on the part of the people to the cause of Christ; and especially as to a great open-air preaching movement, which had brought the gospel to at least 50,000 persons of the ignorant and outcast part of the population. Still there was much to deplore, and there were few evidences of anything like an extensive quickening of the dead and formal. But the Report this year opened in jubilant and thankful strains as follows:—

> We are enabled on this occasion, for the first time since this commit-tee was formed, to report, to the praise of God's sovereign and infinite grace, an awakening of many hearts to the claims of vital religion. This great blessing has been long the subject of earnest desires and prayers, yet it has taken us by surprise on its actual arrival. We had been so long accustomed to the previous state of things, that we were filled with won-der when it pleased God to hearken to the voice of our supplication, and to pour out his Spirit from on high. Yet it is true—it is assuredly true—the Lord hath done great things for us, whereof we are glad; and it be-comes us, with thankfulness and joy, to acknowledge his mighty hand, and humbly and faithfully to hear the lessons which he condescends to teach.

With regard to the pioneering and preparatory work, it appeared that pastoral visitation from house to house, plain and pointed appeals from the pulpit to the conscience, the increase of meetings for united prayer and an expectation of a coming blessing, together with an increas-ing respect to the Sabbath and its ordinances, a growing sobriety among the masses, and the decrease of open ungodliness, had been observ-able. 'But', adds the Report, as to the reality and fullness of blessing vouchsafed,

> the grand distinguishing feature of our spiritual history during the past year has been the outpouring of the Holy Spirit over an extensive dis-trict of our church. This remarkable movement, commencing in Connor, Ahoghill, and Ballymena, has spread over a large portion of the county of Antrim, and of the counties adjacent. Those who are the most intimately acquainted with its origin and progress, shrink from assigning any human effort as even instrumentally operative in bringing about this blessed result. There can be no doubt, however, that, under the guidance

of the God of all grace, some previous preparation had been made in addition to the ordinary faithful preaching of the word, and prayer. The reports of the American Revival had tended greatly to quicken the minds both of ministers and people. Many sermons were preached on the work of the Spirit, and many supplications offered up for the special visitation of his grace. Prayer-meetings were multiplied over the district. At length there was a sudden and public manifestation of the power that had been long secretly leavening the minds and hearts of the people. The work of conviction and conversion having thus begun, was carried forward from heart to heart, and from district to district, with unprecedented rapidity.

The following summary of the leading features of the Awakening is presented in the Report:—

1. Persons of both sexes, of all ages, of different grades of society, of various denominations of professing Christians, including Unitarians and Roman Catholics, have been at once convinced of sin, and apparently converted to God.

2. These spiritual emotions have been accompanied, in a very large number of cases, by physical impressions producing bodily infirmity, and continuing, in some cases, for hours, and in others for days, and usually terminating in peace of conscience, and sometimes in joy unspeakable and full of glory.

3. The two great truths on which the converts prominently, and almost exclusively, dwell, are the sinfulness and utter spiritual helplessness of men, and the all-sufficiency of Christ as a living personal Redeemer.

4. No heresy has been started in this new and unusual state of religious excitement. The whole movement, in its various aspects, tends to give striking and vivid illustration of the great doctrines of the gospel, as they are set forth in our catechisms and confession of faith.

5. The effect produced by this Awakening on the life and character of those who have experienced it, is decidedly evangelical—a deep sense of sin, especially of the sin of having neglected the great salvation, fervent love of Christ, intense brotherly kindness, earnest desire for the conversion of sinners, habitual communion with God, and delight in his word, worship, and service—these attributes of character are assuredly the fruit

of the Spirit, and those are the characteristics of multitudes who have lately declared themselves the servants of Christ. The drunkard has been made sober, the libertine chaste, the blasphemer and Sabbath-breaker devout, the worldling constrained to think deeply and penitently of his sins, and to flee from the wrath to come. These are surely trophies of Divine grace, and many such trophies as those have been raised to the honour of God since the commencement of the present Revival.

6. The work has been carried forward in many districts by the agency of the converts themselves. As many as have been brought to know Christ have taken delight in telling to all around them what a precious Saviour they have found.

The fear of man is completely taken away; and uneducated persons of humble station are heard to offer up prayer to God with fluency, propriety, and fervour, in the presence of multitudes, and, without embarrassment or trepidation, to call on their assembled fellow-sinners to repent and believe in the gospel.

As indicating how little there was of the merely impulsive in the minds of ministers throughout Ulster, and how earnestly they desired not only to extend but also to give healthy vigour and permanence to true godliness among the people committed to their charge, the following 'suggestions' are worthy of being recorded:—

That increased attention be given to the observance of family worship, to the catechising of the young, and to the formation of Bible classes for the benefit of those who have passed the ordinary age of Sabbath-school attendance.

That the private members of the Church be encouraged to exercise their various gifts for its edification and enlargement.

That Sessions be enjoined to meet more frequently for prayer, conference, and mutual encouragement of their members in the work of God.

That ministers hold meetings for the special purpose of personal edification, and of increased ministerial usefulness.

That religious intelligence be more widely circulated throughout our congregations. That our people be instructed to make themselves well acquainted with the Westminster Confession of Faith.

That circulating-libraries of standard theological works be established for the benefit of ministers, many of whom, from various causes, find it difficult to gain access to books necessary to enable them to meet the demands of this intelligent and inquiring age.

It was further recommended—

> That, in this season of spiritual awakenings, notes of cases of conviction and conversion should be taken, with the view of more accurately marking the operation of the Holy Spirit, and of furnishing materials for the narrative hereafter to be drawn up of this wonderful work of God.
>
> That wherever it is practicable and expedient, classes be formed of those who have been recently converted, with the view of establishing them in the faith, love, and hope of the gospel.

As to the deliberate judgment of the Assembly on the spiritual character of the movement, and the mingled cautions and encouragements held out to its ministers in connection with its further progress, important resolutions were adopted.

In moving the adoption of the foregoing resolutions, the Rev. Samuel J. Moore, of Ballymena, who had been called to take so active a part in that district, as well as to co-operate with brethren elsewhere, made some valuable statements. He dwelt on the necessity of distinguishing between mere bodily agitation and conviction of sin, and the conversion to Christ—

> It is a fearful mistake that any person should be under any impression for a few hours, or under bodily suffering or mental anguish, and yet imagine that he is brought to Christ.

In the same spirit the Rev. Dr Cooke spoke of a case of great distress followed by 'peace'. But Dr Cooke said to the woman, 'Now, can you tell me of any word of Scripture, which you take as God's warrant for your peace?' No, she could not. It was only a feeling. 'I took the Scriptures, and endeavoured to found her feeling upon faith, and not faith upon feeling. We should be most careful of these parties.' Mr Moore mentioned that some of the true converts held 'that it was impossible to be a true child of God and not to know it'; and explained that this arose from the extraordinary change which had passed in themselves.

A man who had led a wild and wretched life—a man who has requested his fellow workmen to gather around him for ten minutes, to hear how he could blaspheme the name of God—a man such as this, the next week but one, cast down by agonizing and burning convictions of sin, and feeling himself dragged down into perdition by the power of the great enemy, will, on being brought to realize the grace of God, realize also the deep consciousness of the change that has passed over him. The very countenances of some of the converts have a luminous joy, and look like the faces of angels.

Mr Moore explained that those young, uneducated men who had spoken with such power over the province, found their strength and courage only in prayer. Thus were they able to tell boldly what they had been, and what grace had made them.

I find a great difficulty in getting one of these young men, at our united meeting, to engage in any exercise, without first praying—prayer is, indeed, the very atmosphere they breathe. The impression seems to be that they could not live without prayer. I tried, a number of evenings, to urge some of them to deliver an address, and I found that, beginning with prayer, they became steady and energetic.

'Family prayer, presented by converts', was also a marked feature of this Revival. 'They engage in it', says Mr Moore, 'until by sheer persecution, or by physical violence, they are driven away from it.' He related the case of a family, where every member but one—and this the husband and father—had gone through the usual ordeal of bodily and mental struggle, 'and found peace, according to their own opinion, and some of them, I believe, have true peace in Christ.' He added:—

On a market day, the landlady of an establishment was sitting behind her counter preparing to dispose of her spirits; but the Heavenly Spirit descended on her, and she was—not smitten to the ground—but some darkness came over her mind, and some trembling, and weakness came over her body. She struggled upstairs, and there, in her bedroom, on her knees, she continued for the remainder of the day. I was sent for to see her, and when I went in, she was praying most earnestly—praying for mercy. She did not seem to feel that she had found the mercy of Christ. I sat down, and allowed her to go on with her supplications; for, as I have stated before, these supplicants can pray better for themselves than I or you could do. By-and-by, I observed a change in her tone and countenance, and by-and-by, the wild cry of despondency passed away, and like a little child, I thought I saw her, as a worm, crawling up to the cross of Christ, and in humility of heart, asking and finding mercy. Her language was—'Wilt thou not have mercy, Lord?' 'I know thou wilt, for thou hast said it.' Now, in all such establishments as these, wherever there are converts, youthful or aged, there is domestic prayer.

With regard to the opposition and ridicule which had been presented to the Awakening, by Unitarian ministers, Romish priests, and their organs of the press, the following statement, from the 'Report on the State of Religion' already quoted from, is important and weighty:—

A visitation of Divine grace, so sudden and so unusual, has naturally provoked the contemptuous ridicule of some, and the fierce hostility of others; but their opposition has been overruled for good. It has led many persons of matured Christian wisdom and experience, from various sections of the Protestant church, to examine and to judge for themselves; and we have now an overwhelming array of witnesses to testify with one accord, that the work is undoubtedly of God. It is true that the ordinary operation of the Holy Spirit is slowly progressive, and almost escapes observation. Yet who shall venture to say that it may not also be immediate, public, powerful, and extensive as his sovereign will? Why should we deem it strange if the Holy Spirit—especially in times like these, when men are so much occupied and engrossed with material objects and pursuits, when the boundary between the church and the world is so dim and so little discernible, when such exaggerated importance is attached to mere office, and order, and outward ceremonial—why should we deem it strange if the Spirit of God come forth in power, and send such a peal of awakening through the hearts of careless, worldly, self-complacent professors of religion, as shall effectually rouse them from their slumbers, and enable them at once to discriminate between truth and error, between right and wrong, between shadow and substance, between the form of godliness and the power thereof? Further we find that, in point of fact, the history of the church of Christ, both before and since the Christian era, has been marked by signal and extensive manifestations of Divine grace; and that in the community of the people of God, as well as in the individual believer, the life of religion has been forwarded by impulses rather than by continuing progress.

In reference to lay preaching also, the Irish Assembly cordially united in its recognition, as has already been done by the Free Church of Scotland. An eminent Episcopalian gentleman, Brownlow North, Esq., of Aberdeen, once wild and reckless, now full of Christian zeal and compassion, had been preaching in the Presbyterian pulpits of Belfast, and a vote of thanks to him was passed by the Assembly in Dublin. On this Dr Cooke made some remarks of a very judicious character:—

I know myself full well, sir, that Mr North neither wishes nor needs our thanks, and, rather than moving the thanks of the house to him—although that is the form in which it is—I return my thanks to Almighty God that he has raised up such a man to go forth as an evangelist. I have always been one of those who saw no objection to allow laymen to preach. I would not put a layman to rule the church; but I think, if a man has any knowledge of the things of God, the more he proclaims it the better. I know that the kings of Israel and the nobles of that land, in some of the reformations they enjoyed, became the harbingers of the gospel, as it was then understood, in the types and prophecies of the Old Testament, and were lay preachers in their days. I have often been delighted to hear Lord Roden preach a sermon. I have heard other noblemen and laymen-gentlemen like Mr North—preaching sermons, and I have been delighted with them.

The resolution adopted on the occasion was as follows:—

That this Assembly has heard with much satisfaction the address just delivered to them by Brownlow North, Esq. That we acknowledge the singular grace of God, in raising up such an eminent evangelist. That we recommend all our ministers to avail themselves of his ministerial services, so far as he may be enabled to visit, and that we pray he may be long spared to labour in the advancement of the kingdom of Christ.

The address of the Moderator to Mr Brownlow North was also marked by a loving and enlightened spirit:—

> We esteem it a happy circumstance in our ecclesiastical constitution, that it is so broadly Catholic that we can not only hail you as a brother in the midst of us, but bid you, from the heart, 'God speed' in your evangelistic mission. We would see in you a living illustration of the great truth, obscured though it may have been by the conventional-isms of men, that a God-made ministry is the only ministry, and that the spiritual church is, strictly speaking, the only church of Christ—the church for the sake of which all prophecies, promises, types, services, and ministrations have been given and ordained. Let me, in the name of this Assembly, return our grateful acknowledgments for your faithful admonitions and fraternal counsels. Let me also invite you to the culti-vation of a still more intimate relationship, even to the occupancy of our pulpits and the hospitalities of our homes. You have come among us at a season of blessed in-gathering, and happy shall we be if you thrust in the sickle, and mingle with us in the reaping-time, with its songs; but whether you abide in Ireland or return to other fields now whitening to the harvest, be assured that we shall not readily forget the hallowed interest which your presence has diffused; and that among the incidents of this Assembly, this shall not be the least memorable—that we have seen your face and grasped your hand, and been encouraged by your sympathies, your exhortations, and your prayers.

The Assembly devoted a whole day to mutual and devout confer-ence on the Awakening, and the Rev. Dr Begg, in referring to this after-wards in an address to his own congregation at Edinburgh, declared that it was one of the most solemn meetings ever attended by him.

The Rev. Mr Guinness was now preaching at Belfast to great mul-titudes.

The general progress of the movement in Ulster was also very cheer-ing. The *Banner of Ulster* wrote thus:—

> Our reports with regard to the work of the Spirit in our borders con-tinue as favourable and gratifying as at any former date. Outward and visible excitement may be somewhat less intense; but the silent and penetrating influence of the revival element becomes more powerful as

the other passes away. The labours of the ministers, lay assistants, and recent converts, in carrying forward the work in every locality and in whatever manner these services can be rendered, are truly indefatigable. Numbers of Scottish ministers and laymen have during the past week arrived in Belfast, in order to ascertain for themselves the nature, progress, and results of this great movement. We have heard (says the *Banner*) more than one of them state that the reports they had heard of the work, fell far short of the reality when witnessed by them.

CHAPTER 10

Rapid progress—the ministers absent, the master present in his power—the reclaimed infidel—prayer and blessing—a children's gathering—decay of party spirit—the Romish priests—the Irish Wesleyan Conference—spiritual marvels at Newtownards—Episcopal sermons and labours—Mr Chichester on 'epidemic'—Unitarian Synod and the Awakening.

SOLEMNITY and spiritual earnestness now prevailed in Ulster. The outward manifestations were not so numerous as at the commencement of the Awakening; but the conviction and conversion of sinners, by the 'still small voice' of Divine mercy, had made amazing progress. 'In proof of this', said the *Banner of Ulster,*

> we point to the unceasing anxiety of multitudes to become acquainted with the plan of salvation, who have hitherto been living without God and without hope in the world; to the number of persons who are to be met, who are weary and heavy laden with sin; and to that increasing throng, whose countenances, radiant with joy, proclaim that they have washed their robes, and made them white in the blood of the Lamb.

In the absence of nearly all the Presbyterian ministers from Belfast, during the meeting of the Irish General Assembly in Dublin, the usual meetings were held on week-days and evenings, in churches and in the open air, and the attendance was not in the least diminished. The open-air meetings were chiefly conducted by converts.

Not the least interesting of these meetings was that held at Queen's Island, Belfast, during the dinner hour, by the men engaged at the iron-works. A hasty meal was taken, a large number of the employees assembled on the central lawn, a psalm was sung, a portion of the word of God read, and some practical observations were made, after which the meeting was closed with praise and prayer.

The discourses of the Rev. H. G. Guinness at this period were characterized by a clear, simple, and earnest enforcement of the truth. Frequent allusions were made during their delivery, to the great work going on in Belfast and other places, laudatory of the work, so far as it was God's, and condemnatory of it, so far as it was man's.

In Great George's Street—where the Rev. Thomas Toye has, for years past, ministered the word of truth with unusually quickening power, and whose knowledge and beautifully appropriate use of Holy Scripture in preaching, have seldom been equalled—the Awakening had displayed itself in marvellous extent and energy. Not only was the house of worship crowded nightly to excess, but outside a multitude was always collected, and a garden in the rear was filled.

Among those who had recently addressed the throng, was a young man, who publicly acknowledged that he had been an infidel; but now felt the sacred influence of Bible truth upon his heart. Another, a foundry-man, who was converted by means of a little girl inviting him to come to Jesus, said that he had been a cockfighter, a gambler, a drunkard, a swearer, and a Sabbath-breaker; that he had renounced his former course of life; that his body was strong; and that he had resolved to devote that strength to the service of his Saviour.

In a neighbourhood well known to us (Lepper Street, Belfast) prayer-meetings had been held almost every evening for some weeks, apparently without results. About the middle of July, at an evening meeting for united prayer, 'the first drops of the genial shower were observed to fall upon the people, upwards of twenty persons being brought to feel the hardness and sinfulness of their hearts by nature'. 'These cases', it was added by a local journal, 'have, we are informed, resulted in genuine conversion.'

Next morning (the Lord's day)

at an early hour, another meeting took place, which was largely attended, and greatly blessed of God. At half-past nine, when the Sabbath school assembled, it was evident to the teachers that there was a solemnizing influence in their midst. It was pleasing to observe the expressions of love interchanged among scholars who had found peace in Jesus.

Also at this period a mid-day children's meeting was held in Berry Street Church, Belfast. About 300 were present, and probably one-third of them had been awakened to a sense of sin, and had found peace in Christ. President Edwards records how little children were brought to Christ in numbers, in the days of the New England Revivals; and Robert M'Cheyne gives cases of similar early conversions in connection with the Awakening at Dundee, in 1839. Children need conversion, and when the Spirit comes in power, as it did now in Ulster, we see that they too share in the blessing. At the above meeting, 'two of the boys in very poor attire, one of them bare-footed, prayed. They were both but barely able to read their Bibles; they poured out their souls before God, with a fervency that the Spirit of God can alone kindle in the heart.'

The decay of party spirit, as indicated on the anniversary of the battle of the Boyne, has already been noticed. But the following is a further pleasing illustration of one of the happy fruits of the Revival.

A young man, driving a bread cart down Durham Street, the scene of last year's unhappy party excitement, was, a couple of days ago, silly enough to exhibit an orange lily on the horse's head. This very foolish act would formerly, of course, have created a tumult in the neighbourhood. A very different result followed on this occasion. A number of young lads (Protestant converts) standing at a corner, seeing the driver pass, consulted as to the proper means of putting a stop to the party exhibition. Two of their number were deputed to follow him to the first shop at which he might stop; they kindly remonstrated with him as to the imprudence of displaying the obnoxious emblem, asking him to have the goodness to remove it, with which request he at once complied.

The Romish priests were greatly alarmed and enraged at the numbers of their flocks, who had been arrested and converted, and who steadfastly resisted all solicitations addressed to them to return to their old faith. In one case, a young Presbyterian girl, under conviction of sin, had knelt down in a field to pray. She was observed by three Romish priests, and the following was the issue,—disgraceful to the priests, and strongly illustrative of what Romanism is:—

> While on her knees, she was observed by three persons in clerical costume, who turned out to be Roman Catholic priests, and who entered into conversation with her. She was asked if she would cross herself, but declined, stating that she did not believe in the efficacy of crossing. Another inquired whether she believed in the efficacy of good works to save her. She answered, 'No'; that her conviction was, that works, when really good, were evidence of the work of God in the believer's heart. The colloquist told her that if she would do as he desired her, he would enable her to do good works. Her reply was, that none but Jesus Christ possessed such power. A proposal was next made, and insisted upon, that a car should be got to remove her, for which the priest would pay. To this she firmly refused to consent. One of them then said that he had a mixture in a bottle, suitable to her case, and a portion of which would revive her. Being very weak in body, she was persuaded to swallow a small quantity of the liquid, and the consequence was, that she became partially stupefied. While the three persons were endeavouring to induce her to allow them to remove her, two young men approached and overheard some of the conversation, and the girl praying, 'Lord Jesus, forgive them, they know not what they do.' The young men then drew near, and warned the priests not to attempt to remove her—that if they did so, they (the young men) would resist force by force. Their reverences then left the spot; and a Christian woman, who chanced to be passing a few minutes afterwards, took compassion on the sufferer, and, with assistance, conveyed her to her house, where she has remained and been kindly treated since, and, we are informed, has found peace in believing.

An interesting young Roman Catholic convert had been visited by two priests. One of them engaged the owner of the house in conversation, while his coadjutor endeavoured to re-convert the girl. He even proposed to forgive her sins, but without effect. She remains steadfast in her resolution, and was present in Townsend Street Church on the next Lord's day.

The Wesleyan body have taken a very active part in advancing the cause of Christ in Ulster, and in Ireland generally, for many years. In the revival season of earnest labour for Christ and the souls of men, they were among the most active, and their work of faith and love was largely blessed. A blessing also attended the visits of ministers and others to 'stricken' ones in their houses, in the awakening of friends and relatives who are present. Scoffers were thus arrested; and spectators mention the astonishing and sudden change that passed on their countenances, 'indicating an equally rapid change of opinion with regard to the Revival movement; and this change reaches its height, when they hear the persons affected bitterly condemn themselves for having mocked some of their neighbours when in the same state.'

Here is a sketch of what was going on at Newtownards, in the county of Down, and is a fair sample of the then wide-spread Ulster Revival:—

A minister was lately called to visit a person under conviction. He was directing his attention solely to the party in distress, pointing out the desert of sin and the way of escape, when a person standing behind him dropped suddenly on her knees, and with her clasped hands lifted up above her head, and the tears literally streaming down her cheeks, she cried out in agony, 'May the Lord have mercy on me for my sins!' Prayer was immediately offered on her behalf; and, when the benediction was being pronounced, another individual leaning against the door instantly assumed the same attitude, and began to utter a similar cry. They have both since found peace in Christ. In one case the person affected was asked to remember that, though our sins were red as crimson, Jesus could make them white as snow. The words fell like a thunderbolt on the ears of a poor sinner, who was standing in the middle of the room, and, falling instantly into an attitude of prayer, she cried aloud for mercy. Interesting cases sometimes occur of several members of the same family coming under the power of saving grace, and in some of these there is a fine illustration of the different ways in which the Spirit works on different persons. In one instance three members of the family had been long exercised with the most acute convictions before they found peace, while the Spirit fell on another member of the same family like dew, descending noiselessly and gently on the tender herb. A number of Roman Catholics have been privileged to find the true cross. It is scarcely necessary to add that the Presbyterian, Episcopalian, and Methodist ministers, the elders and other office-bearers of the several churches, with the Town Missionary, are so constantly occupied as to need much the fulfilment of the singularly appropriate prayer of one of the stricken, 'that they might run and not be weary, and walk and not faint'.

While some Episcopal clergymen expressed doubts on the reality of this movement, it was all the more gratifying to find a number of evangelical clergymen thoroughly agreed with their Presbyterian and Wesleyan brethren, in the conviction that the work was Divine. Their own labours were very abundantly blessed. The Bishop of Down and Connor preached in the month of July two sermons in Ballymena, and made repeated references to the Awakening as a genuine work of the Holy Spirit. The Rev. Mr Mooney, Rector at Ballymena, with other clergymen, continued to labour with much success. The Rev. G. V. Chichester, curate, of Portrush, County Antrim, writing to a friend in Scotland, dwelt with delight on the movement, saying, 'Every day's experience only tends more and more to confirm my belief in the reality of what I see.' With regard to the aspersions cast upon the Awakening, he added,

> It is easy to sit at a distance and theorize; but I am unable to conceive how any rational person could be in the presence of those converted, without acknowledging them to be epistles of Christ. All the fruits of faith are there: such a sense of sin, such self-abasement, such rejoicing faith in Christ, such peace with God, such glowing love to him and to his saints, I have almost never witnessed before, and this is not only in grown people, but in children. These are things so plain and undeniable, that no one could presume to argue the point, unless he belonged to that class of persons who would deny that Christ was risen from the dead even while looking into the empty sepulchre.

Then as to this being 'only an epidemic', Mr Chichester says:—

I do not remember any epidemic producing deep and agonizing conviction of sin. I do not read of any epidemic developing itself in a new power of utterance, and in the most intense and fervent prayers. I do not remember that the symptoms (or at least the results) of an epidemic have hitherto been those of faith in Christ, peace with God, joy in the Holy Ghost, love to the great Head, love to every member of his body, earnest desire and the most self-denying exertions to bring others into the same membership—to save them, as many of them most justly and truly express it, from the burning lake. Do epidemics produce thirst for the Scriptures, and an eager application to all the means of grace? Do they make drunken men sober? blasphemers men of prayer? thieves honest? deceivers truthful? sensual men spiritual? vindictive men patient and forgiving? Do they cause the maid to forget her ornaments and the bride her attire, and to put on the adorning of a 'meek and quiet spirit'? Is it, in short, the usual result of epidemics to bring men, women, and children from darkness to light, and from the power of Satan unto God? If so, let us henceforth rejoice in the prevalence of epidemics. Yea, let special prayers be introduced into our public services, that we may long experience this happy atmospheric pestilence.

And yet, after all this, we find the Remonstrant Synod, and the Unitarian Association, at their annual meetings at Belfast, ridiculing the work, denying that the fruits of the Spirit were in any measure its results, and saying that it was an unmixed evil and an abomination. Unitarianism decreases in Ulster; the Revival has robbed it of a considerable body of adherents. The system is one which has never flourished in the atmosphere of a spiritual and apostolic Christianity.

CHAPTER 11

Coleraine and its press—the convert's address—growth in grace—drunkenness disappearing—crowded sanctuaries—united prayer—Rev. John Graham—the clergyman's 'Caution'—address by Mr Guinness—a Revival scene—an Edinburgh minister's testimony—blessings carried to Scotland—an Antrim minister rejoicing—continuance in prayer—converts baptised—multiplied meetings—Brownlow North's sermons—a physician on the Awakening—a market-day 'like a Sabbath'—a scene of weeping—theory and fact as to 'excitable Celts'—summary of results by a clergyman.

AT Coleraine the Awakening continued to manifest itself with great power. Of the weekly narratives contained in *The Coleraine Chronicle*, a literary gentleman on the staff of the *Glasgow Guardian* said with great truth and justice—

> They have been largely instrumental in arresting the attention of the careless, and in stirring up, by way of remembrance, the pure hearts of God's people. If the influence of the press were uniformly put forth in the same direction, there would be an instrumentality for good in our land second only to the preaching of the word.

Here is an extract from the address of a young convert, delivered in an open-air meeting, as reported in the *Guardian;*—

> Dear friends, I was a great sinner, but Christ has been a great Saviour to me. Thanks be to God, he has brought me from darkness to light, and from the power of Satan unto God. If there be an unconverted soul before me, I would just ask you to seek Christ this night. Let it not pass without finding him. Oh, let it not pass without finding Christ to be precious to your souls, for oh! he is lovely, altogether lovely to them that find him. Ah, what is hindering you from finding him this night? What is hindering you? Is it not your unbelief? Will you not believe Christ's word? He says, 'Come to me, all ye that labour and are heavy laden, and I will give you rest. Take my yoke upon you, and learn of me, for I am meek and lowly, and ye shall find rest to your souls. For my yoke is easy, and my burden is light.' Ah, yes, the burden of Jesus Christ is easily borne; ah, yes, it is easily borne, dear friends, besides the burden of sin.

Ah, yes, some of us here felt the burden of sin, and we know the change now, God be thanked. I would just ask you this night to seek him who can take away that burden of sin, who can enlighten your minds, and bring you from Satan's bondage, and set you free. Is there anyone here this night who would refuse Christ's offer? Ah, I think not. Surely I do not look upon one who would say, I refuse Christ; Christ is all and in all to them that believe. I would ask you to come while it is day, for the night comes when none can work. Work now, come now. Do not wait till tomorrow; perhaps tomorrow will be too late. The devil's time is tomorrow; he told me tomorrow; and he is telling many here that you are too young to come to come to Christ, that you have time enough yet. But, ah, friends, heed not the devil. Seek Christ, seek Christ this night; seek him, for he is precious, he is precious. Oh, my friends, how long will you be slaves to sin? How long? Oh, think for a moment what it is to be under Satan's power. Will you not turn? 'Turn ye, turn ye', says the Lord, 'why will ye die?' Will you choose to die, and go down to destruction, rather than seek God, and go to happiness? There are two classes of people here, the believers and the unbelievers. Ah, think of this, think of this. There are one of two places we must go to, just the two places; there is no third place. And there are but two roads. Which of the two will you choose? Will you take the broad road that leadeth to destruction, or will you choose the narrow road which leads to everlasting life? Will you choose to go to destruction, or to heaven? Which, which? You have your choice this night; now which will you choose? Ah, think for a moment, dear friends, is there any of us would choose that road that leads to destruction, any of us that would take hell for our portion? Oh, think of that, my dear friends; be warned this night, and flee from the wrath to come. Oh, the wrath of God, the wrath of God abiding on you; what an awful thing! The wrath of God abiding on you, morning, noon, and night, in your lying down and in your rising up. Picture to yourselves, any of you that have a master; picture to yourselves that he should be angry with you, and his wrath abide upon you day and night. Would you find happiness? I am sure you would not. But, ah, what is the wrath of man to the wrath of God? Oh, think of this, my dear friends, and flee from the wrath to come. Oh, seek Christ, seek Christ now, for now is the accepted time, and now is the day of salvation.

The manner and spirit of the young speaker were in beautiful accord with his address, and are thus described:—

> We must just add that the reporter's art can give little idea of the power of an address which owed so much of its effect to the intense earnestness of the speaker. There could not have been a finer specimen of natural eloquence—the eloquence of the heart—than were afforded by this young disciple of Christ. There was no enthusiasm, no shrieking or vociferating, but melting appeals addressed with the tenderest affection to fellow-sinners. The speaker appeared as if he could not bear to part with his hearers until he had prevailed on them to come to the Saviour, who had done such great things for him. He saw so clearly, and felt so powerfully that there were peace, joy, and salvation in none but Christ, that he seemed as if he could not believe that his hearers would hesitate to take him for all their salvation, and all their desire, when he was freely offered to them.

Growth in grace and in knowledge was now evident among the converts. In addition to this, drunkenness had almost disappeared at Coleraine. One who was much among the lower classes, and who was looked upon by them as a 'friend', to whom they could successfully apply on a Monday morning for as much money as would relieve their thirst, declared that 'since the Awakening began, no professing Protestant has presented himself in that condition which formerly so frequently followed a Sabbath evening debauch.'

Episcopalian, Presbyterian, and Wesleyan ministers were extremely active and faithful in the advancement of the work. The places of worship were crowded on every Lord's day, and, 'indeed, few inducements, save the certainty of hearing the gospel preached in its purity, were now needed to induce as many to leave their homes as to fill all the open churches with devout worshippers.'

At the ordinary morning service in the New Row Presbyterian Church, on Sunday, the 24th of July, a case of special conviction occurred. 'The individual affected was a very intelligent man, and quite the reverse of excitable. He was not prostrated, but in an agony of mind remained fervent in prayer for a long time.'

At the Union Prayer-meeting, on the 25th July, presided over by the Rector of Coleraine, the Rev. John Graham, of Craven Chapel,

London, delivered an impressive address, and concluded by expressing the gladness of heart which he had experienced when he first
heard what God was doing in Ulster, and said that he had seen more
of God's work in Coleraine since he came than he had expected.

A collection had been made at Mr Canning's church the previous
day, for the purchase of a Bible, to be kept 'as a memorial of the work
of the Lord in Coleraine'. Mr Graham offered some money to aid in
this, which was respectfully declined; but it was ultimately handed
over to Mr White, to assist in the distribution of Bibles and Testa-
ments in the town.

The Rev. F. F. Trench, an Episcopal clergyman, from whose statements of what he had himself witnessed we have made extracts in
a former chapter, was present on Wednesday, July 27th, at a great
meeting in Coleraine, and gave 'a beautiful and persuasive address'.
He cautioned the people not to cry 'Peace, peace', when there was 'no
peace'. On the evening of the same day an immense assembly, num-
bering 7,000 persons, was brought together to hear an address from
the Rev. H. H. Guinness. 'During the progress of his sermon several
people were convicted, and carried away.'

'In the afternoon of the same day', says the *Coleraine Chronicle,*

we were privileged to witness a Revival scene of intense interest. In a
small house in a neglected portion of the outskirts of the town, a child,
some eight years of age, was made the instrument in God's hand of
awakening three others—all members of different families; and one of
them, a young man, who the evening previous had 'sat in the scorner's
seat', and who was loud in his scoffs at any whom he heard ascribing to
God's Spirit the work of Awakening which he derided. Now the hand
of God in mercy broke in pieces the hard heart, and laid the young man
prostrate at the feet of Jesus. He belonged to the 59th Regiment, but is
now discharged, and in all the *abandon* of earnest seeking after spiritual
things, the uniform of his earthly sovereign was soiled unheeded, while
he sought on his knees the garment of righteousness, provided for all
who in sincerity own allegiance to the heavenly King. By him sat a
young woman who an hour or so previously had found peace and joy in
believing; and in the same house two other young women experienced
saving knowledge of Jesus.

As an illustration of the numbers on pilgrimage at this time to the North of Ireland, it may be mentioned that at one meeting in Coleraine there were present ministers from India, Malta, Edinburgh, Glasgow, London, and from many other places. 'Hosts of laymen are also among us, all deeply interested in the work of Revival. The ministers and others visit in the houses of many of those who have been converted, and take away interesting accounts of their interviews.'

The Rev. Moody Stuart, of Edinburgh, after a short visit in Ulster, gave a statement at a public meeting, of what he had witnessed. He said that the 40th Psalm was a favourite psalm amongst the converts and others, and that it had been sung by publicans, harlots, and blasphemers. He then described the effect which had been produced upon Roman Catholics who had attended some of the meetings, and said that he had seen a young man belonging to this persuasion completely borne down with grief on account of his sins. He was much struck with this when in Ireland,—that there was a constant appeal to the mighty power of Jesus to save them, and at the same time a constant waiting for the Holy Spirit with the whole heart, so intense were the feelings. At a meeting at which he was present, attended by 300 or 400 persons, in Coleraine, there arose a bitter cry of 'Lord Jesus, have mercy on me!' from one of the most abandoned women in the whole town. This was a cry often heard; and it would be followed by 'He will come', so great was their confidence that he would graciously reveal himself. He then described how, after being in intense anguish of spirit, joy would be seen beaming upon the countenance—perhaps it was after a week, sometimes sooner, and sometimes longer—and they would declare that Jesus had taken away all their sins, and that they had found peace. Another thing that struck him was, that when they found peace themselves, they began to interest themselves about others. Referring to the Orange anniversary on the 12th July, Mr Stuart said, it was a very saddening thing, to find a minister in Scotland ascribing this Revival work to the cause which he did';[14] and when he spoke about it stirring fierce fanaticism, he was guilty of great

---

[14] The Rev. G. Gifillan, of Dundee, had ascribed the movement to satanic influence, but has since withdrawn the statement.

ignorance, for in the Orange districts of Belfast, and in other parts of Ireland, all had passed over quietly, and instead of the usual scenes of fighting and drunkenness, the sounds of praise and prayer had been heard. Surely nothing was more striking than to find that all had been peaceful in Ireland, while bloodshed, and even the loss of life, had occurred in Scotland in connection with the 12th of July. Instead of leading to fierce fanaticism, this Revival created a love to the Roman Catholics; and those who were its subjects were solicitous about their eternal welfare, and were to be seen going about comforting their neighbours. Love for the Lord Jesus and for one another, were the characteristics of the blessed work now in operation in Ireland. Mr Stuart then mentioned one or two cases where a wonderful reformation had been produced in individuals who were formerly notorious drunkards and profane swearers; and concluded by saying that they in Scotland ought to be much in prayer, that they might be sharers in the blessed work of Revival.

It is here worthy of notice that some Scottish visitors to Coleraine, after their return to Glasgow, had become the instruments of commencing an extensive Awakening in that city.

Returning, however, to Ulster, a minister in County Antrim, who ministers the word of God with great usefulness to crowds of people, wrote thus to a religious journal:—

> I have been quite delighted to see among the audience many who scarcely ever entered the house of God before, and being so deeply affected with the offers of a free gospel, that tears stream down the bronzed cheeks of men unaccustomed to weep. In the experience of the oldest minister, there never was a time when people engaged in praise with the same heart, and I trust with the same understanding. You cannot go out to walk in the stilly eve, without the voice of psalmody falling upon your ear, like the sound of many waters, echoing from hill to valley. The whole country district is vocal with the song of redemption. No gathering now to laugh, and jest, and sneer, and sing profane songs; no mocking at holy things, as was too frequently the case formerly.

The weekly Union prayer-meeting was still held in the Music Hall, Belfast. The Earl of Roden was among those who were present. The attendance was very numerous. 'There was a solemn stillness over the whole house during the three minutes set apart for secret prayer (as is the custom), towards the close of the meeting.' A number of youthful converts were at this time baptized by the Baptist minister at Belfast. It was a very solemn and impressive service. While at Belfast physical prostrations still occurred, 'yet', says the *Banner of Ulster,*

> the work of conviction and conversion is now principally mak-ing way without any exterior signs of the change, which is being wrought silently in the heart; other than an increased gravity and solemnity of manner, an avoidance of light and frivolous conversa-tion and amusement, and of thoughtless companions, and an anxi-ety to mingle and commune with those who have experienced the Spirit's influence in refreshing their souls.

At Comber, Portaferry, Dundonald, Rathfriland, and other places, in the county of Down, meetings were being constantly held, and with marked results. At Ballymena, Brownlow North, Esq., delivered four impressive discourses to densely crowded congregations in the Pres-byterian churches, and also addressed an open-air assemblage, num-bering 11,000 persons. In the parish church extra services were held, and some of the Presbyterian churches were open every evening. Here as well as elsewhere physical prostrations occurred, in some cases ac-companied by a continuous, trance-like unconsciousness. Dr Wallace, Scottish medical missionary at Parsonstown, King's County,[15] having written a series of articles on the subject of the manifestations, while attempting to account for them, on the principles of mental emotion reacting on the nervous system, wound up as follows:—'Of the deep, glorious, ever-spreading, ever-swelling river of God's manifested grace, on the surface of which these manifestations are but froth, I have said nothing, because I feel that the fittest attitude in refer-ence to it is to stand by and adore.' We are persuaded that this is the 'attitude' towards this wondrous movement which should have been assumed, from the first, by all earnest lovers of Christ and of perishing men.

[15] Now known as County Offaly, in the Republic of Ireland, *Ed.*

A person now writing from Cookstown, County Tyrone, said,

A solemn impression seemed at this time to rest on almost everyone. The great bulk of the people left the weekly market long before the customary hour; and, as a sensible man observed, 'it was more like a Sabbath than a market-day.' *This is, indeed, God's work, and marvellous in our eyes.*

The movement was now spreading into the county of Down, the Yorkshire of Ireland. On the 30th May, an immense assemblage was addressed at Comber, by converts from the neighbourhood of Ballymena, and a deep impression was made. On Thursday, 9th June, strong agitation showed itself, while the pastor, Mr Killen, addressed a crowded prayer-meeting. On Sabbath, 12th June,

at the morning service, the church was a very Bochim; the people seemed so bowed down as to be able only to give vent to their feelings in sobs and tears; some cried out, and others had to be removed. Mr. K. was employed constantly, when not preaching, in visiting the converts, or those under conviction of sin.

It is not to be forgotten that this Awakening appeared mainly among a Presbyterian population, the calmness of whose temperament, even in matters of religion, presents a striking contrast to the old Celtic race among whom they dwell, but with whom they have never inter-mingled. And when I found such spiritual budding, and blossoming as the rose, in places where a cold orthodoxy had long reigned, I could not but recognize adoringly the Spirit's presence and power, given in answer to the continued prayers of a faithful remnant of God's people in Ulster. It seemed but *the beginning* of a glorious extension of Christ's kingdom. The heart's aspiration was, 'Oh, that the living and life-giving wave may spread over the whole of a land which once was full of scriptural light above all the countries of Western Europe, and that, as in the days of Columba and Columbkill, Ireland may be called, and may become, "the Island of Saints" again!'

The following conclusions as to *reality and results,* as arrived at by the Rev. C. Seaver, an Episcopal clergyman at Belfast, who had watched the movement from the beginning, are worthy of attention.

1. There has plainly been an outpouring of the Holy Ghost in answer to prayer. 2. This has not been in the usual way of human agency, but is the direct work of the Spirit himself. 3. Physical manifestations have accompanied, but have not necessarily been connected with it. The number of those seriously impressed has been far more than of those physically affected. 4. Its tendency is to unite in closer bonds the members of Evangelical churches. 5. It has pervaded all classes of society. 6. The abiding fruits of the Spirit have been manifested in the altered lives and conduct of those under gracious influence, the careless and ungodly becoming anxious, the drunkard sober, the profligate abandoning his vices and becoming pure.

Map of Ulster, showing most places mentioned in Weir's narrative

Atlantic Ocean

DONEGAL

Giant's Causeway
Dunluce Castle
Carrick-a-Rede
Bushmills
Portrush
Portstewart
Coleraine
Ballyrashane
Lough
Foyle

The North Channel

Londonderry
Newtownlimavady
Aghadowey
Ballymoney
Loughguile
Kilraughts
Garvagh
ANTRIM
Kilrea
Clough
Rasharkin
Glenarm

Raphoe
Donagheady
LONDONDERRY
Galgorm
Broughshane
Portglenone
Ballymena
Larne
Strabane
Ahoghill
Connor
Kells
Ballycarry

Bellaghy
Drummaul
Ballyclare
Carrickfergus
Castlederg
TYRONE
Magherafelt
Antrim
Muckamore
Bangor
Gortin
Cookstown
Oldstone
Whitehouse
Holywood
Donagha
Omagh
Crumlin
Dundonald
Newtownards
Belfast
Comber
Dungannon
Carryduff
Boardmills
Lisburn
Saintfield
Killinchy
FERMANAGH
Hillsborough
Dromore
Killyleagh
Portaferry
Portadown
Lurgan
Waringstown
Dromara
Richhill
Gilford
Donacloney
Clogher
Armagh
Tullylish
Enniskillen
Cremore
Banbridge
DOWN
Monaghan
Markethill
ARMAGH
Mount Norris
MONAGHAN
Keady
Bessbrook
Rathfriland
Clontibret
Clones
Newry
Warrenpoint
Irish Sea
Rostrevor
Cavan
CAVAN
Carlingford Lough
Dundalk

PART TWO
PERSONAL OBSERVATIONS
AND INQUIRIES

CHAPTER 12

Personal visit to Ulster—one day's observations and inquiries—visit to the minister's study—the countryman's account—a Roman Catholic Judge on the fruits of the Revival—the mill girls' prayer-meeting—a mourner in Zion—the Town Missionaries—the worst saved—a week-evening congregation—the 'Evangelical Union' Chapel—the ministers' counsel to the anxious—the first Sabbath in Belfast—two memorable scenes—Mr Hanna's letter on the Belfast Awakening—a 'sleeping' case—a young convert—Great George's Street Church—testimony of converts—Rev. T. Toye—Hon. and Rev. H. Ward.

WHEN, after an absence of three years, my eyes rested upon the beautiful hills on either side of the Belfast Lough, bathed in the light of early morn, and when I trod once more the streets of the great town itself, I felt that kind of glad relief from metropolitan heat and long-continued toil, which many clerical brethren realize at the 'holiday' season of the year. But my thoughts were mainly fixed on one subject—the Ulster Awakening. The providential opportunity was now furnished me, for inspecting with my own eyes, some of those scenes throughout the province which had been made sacred by the recent footprints of the Divine Saviour himself.

One day's observations and inquiries, let me now furnish. My first visit was paid to the suburban dwelling of the excellent minister of the Presbyterian Church, York Street, Belfast. Independent of old friendship, I could not have visited anyone who was better qualified to satisfy my preliminary inquiries. For here was a man of ripe experience in the Christian ministry, calm, cautious, and discriminative. Here too was one who in his earlier days was a pastor at Connor, in the county of Antrim, the birthplace and home of the Awakening, and who had recently visited his old flock, and had been, with the present pastor, dispensing the Lord's Supper to a great company of disciples, many of them the genuine and living fruit of the movement. Moreover he himself, as a pastor, was in close contact with souls in the various stages of anxious inquiry, of trembling hope, of settled peace, of exulting gladness. He had also seen 'strange things', for which he did not profess his ability to account, but which he promised that I myself should see them, and form my own opinion.

All that I learned from my dear friend at two interviews on the same day, it would be impossible to detail. As to physical agitations, he has always deprecated and discouraged them. While by no means saying that they were always the result of injudicious stimulants applied by zealous spectators to those already under terrors of conscience, he always judged them by their fruits, not regarding the 'peace' that followed after hours or even days of prostration and weakness as worth anything, save when it was clearly produced by a believing and intelligent trust in him whose blood, applied to the conscience, can alone give 'the peace of God'.

My friend, after an extended observation over a period of more than two months, and over wide districts, gave it as his deliberate and solemn conviction, that in its main features the work was Divine; and that it was marked by a depth, extent, and power, to which the history of religion in Ireland could furnish no parallel. In another church he had been an eye-witness of what might be regarded as the first case of awakening, marked by such mental distress, as to prompt the loud outcries of a soul almost despairing of mercy, nothing being uttered by the preacher at the moment. The time was evening; the place was the Berry Street Presbyterian Church, and a large congregation was assembled. Suddenly a strong, powerful man raised in the midst a loud and bitter cry, and fell down. He was carried speedily out of doors. There were no appearances of epilepsy, nor of any contortions of the face, or loss of consciousness. Indeed, as he lay helpless on the ground, extended on his back, and the people gathered around, some one remarked that 'he was quite conscious'. 'Yes', he said, with a look of unutterable horror of soul, 'yes, *awfully conscious!*'

This case was a remarkable one. It was not that of one who had been of profligate habits. He had been for some years a recognized member of a Christian church, and a teacher in the Sabbath school. But he had been led to the deep and awful conviction that he had been a formalist and a self-deceiver. My friend visited him during the period when by bodily weakness he was confined to his house. He had no doubt whatever of the reality of the change, and on his relating the whole circumstances to a body of ministers soon after, one of them a Professor of Theology, they unanimously declared that this was nothing else than the special work of the Holy Spirit of God.

In my friend's own congregation, a case of deep anxiety of soul, on the part of the professor, had recently led to a request in writing by the party thus distressed, that meetings should be held (in addition to the evening prayer-meetings in the church) for conversation with any who might desire it. The announcement was made accordingly. Two such meetings were held during the following week, attended by unexpected numbers,—not the poor only, but the better classes also,— not scarcely at all the profligate and outcast classes, but those who observed the decencies of life, regularly attended on divine ordinances, and professed Christ before men. In some cases my friend regarded it as a *deepening* of the work of grace in the hearts of those who were already God's children, but in others that it had been the Spirit acting as a detector of unsuspected formalism, which, if undisturbed, must have ended in death eternal. This secret agitation and softening of men's souls was now general in Belfast and over Ulster. Backsliders were arrested in large numbers, and after passing through a 'horror of thick darkness', received the seal and the earnest, the white stone, the new name, the baptism of the Holy Ghost afresh. It was *re*-vival; new, fresh life for those already alive, but who were 'ready to die'. This must surely be regarded as the work of God. It affected ministers themselves. It filled them with deep self-searchings; it led repeatedly to the cry, 'Deliver me from blood-guiltiness.' One minister of reputation, I was informed, had publicly related how, when a student, he once saved a companion from a dreadful death by seizing his garments, and dragging him back just as he sprang lightly over what appeared to be a fence dividing from another field, but which really skirted, while it concealed, an awful precipice on the coast of the County of Down. This minister, publicly referring to this, said with tears, that he feared that he had not been as earnest in seeking to save souls from death eternal, 'pulling them out of the fire', as he had been on that memorable day, when with a loud cry and eager haste he seized his companion, and saved him from death temporal. Has this confession no voice of suggestive warning for ministers everywhere?

After making an appointment with my friend, to the fulfilment of which I shall refer afterwards, I proceeded towards the town. As I walked along the road, I overtook a plain countryman, and we speedily fell into conversation, which almost at once glided into the subject of the present Awakening in Ulster. He was himself a resident at Stoneybridge, not far from Crumlin, but he had relatives and connexions in the neighbourhood of Connor, which he had recently visited. He was very rapid and voluble in his utterances, had a wonderful knowledge of Scripture, and somewhat hesitatingly inquired of me what I thought of these things now going forward. He evidently had formed his own convictions from what he had seen, and he had told me much to confirm the testimony of other witnesses. Encouraged by my answers, he went on to tell of publicans who had given up their business altogether, and how they, with other converts, would have no fellowship with persons whom they regarded as ungodly, not even speaking to their old neighbours. After some conversation, we agreed on two points—that we were not to judge rashly as to physical agitations; and further, that while Christians were not to have social fellowship with the ungodly for the sake of sinful enjoyment, they mistook the prohibitions of their Master, and did not follow his example, if they left the ungodly around them to perish without warning or entreaty, or if they declined to associate and eat and drink with them with the object of doing good to their souls. The social changes which this man had seen were precisely such as have already been indicated as witnessed elsewhere as the fruit of the Revival. And I may here add that Chief Baron Pigot, in his charge to the grand jury of the County Down, had, a few days previously, expressed his delight and satisfaction at these results of the movement, including the decline of party spirit, and the diminution of crime, and expressed his hope that it would penetrate the very depths of society. This recognition was an emphatic rebuke to the Unitarian mockers and to angry Roman Catholics, and was all the more remarkable as it has come from the lips of a judge who is himself a member of the Romish Church.

At two o'clock, P.M., I attended the daily united prayer-meeting of young women employed in the adjoining factories. It is always held in the school-room attached to Linen-Hall Street Presbyterian Church. I found, at the foot of the staircase, the pastor, the Rev. R. Knox, who, from excessive labours in the holy cause, both in Belfast and throughout Ulster, was almost voiceless, and well-nigh broken down. He was, however, handing to each young person as she passed to the room, a handbill tract. The service was conducted by A. D., Esq., a Presbyterian elder, with great solemnity. There were no outcries, but there was deep feeling, and tears flowed. At the close of the half hour, the young people went to their accustomed toil. One young woman remained, in deep distress, and Mr Knox, and an American minister, conversed with her. Her face was indeed the picture of woe. She had, as she supposed, found pardon, but now she deplored her want of assurance, and feared that she was not among the saved. What could be done but speak forth the free gospel to such a 'bruised' one? I could not believe that she would be permitted to continue 'comfortless'.

In the afternoon I met two town missionaries, and also the elder who spoke at the prayer-meeting at Linen-Hall Street; and from all these parties received most valuable information. The missionaries are educated young men, licentiates of the General Assembly, and devoted to the work of their Master. While opposed to all excitement, and condemning the movement of a number of ministers (from different parts of Ireland, meeting here at an annual gathering), who had almost dragged the people to 'anxious seats' in the open streets, these young men clearly recognized God's hand in the movement, and testified very fully to its power over the worst of the population. It appeared also to them as if the 'striking down' of the very wicked was permitted, in order to arrest those companions in sin, who, under all other means, had been unmoved, but who were thus filled with terror, and, in many cases, brought to true repentance.

Next day, I proceeded with the Rev. D. Hamilton to visit a 'sleeping' case, attended by circumstances and 'visions' so very peculiar, that I shall specially notice it again in this chapter. Afterwards I went to the evening meeting held at Berry Street Church, which, I found, was a special preparatory service in connection with, and in prospect of, the celebration of the Lord's Supper on the Lord's-day. The minister, the Rev. H. Hanna, sat in the pulpit, while (when I entered the gallery) a discourse on Isaiah 40:31, was being brought to a close by the Rev. Mr Denham, of Holywood. The language was weighty and well chosen, and the sentiments were striking and impressive. Earnest appeals were made to the unconverted. Warnings were also addressed to those who had recently found peace in Christ, against self-confidence, reminding them that the Christian life was a conflict, and that their only safety was 'waiting on the Lord'. A congregation of about 1,000 persons was present, chiefly, if not entirely, working people. Deep seriousness prevailed, and the closing song of praise struck me as peculiarly jubilant and animated. This church had been the spiritual birth-place of hundreds recently, and was 'holy ground'.

It was now growing late, and as I wended towards my domicile for the night in the southern suburb, I saw a lighted building, and heard the sound of a human voice. I entered, and found a minister in the desk addressing about sixty persons, mostly men, and encouraging those who were anxious about salvation not to be timid, as too many were, in making known their case to the ministers of Christ. He himself had once been thus backward, but he had found the servants of God willing, frank, and affectionate counsellors, and so would they. This, I was told, was an Independent Chapel; more properly it is connected with 'the Evangelical Union', or Morrisonian denomination. As I left, two tracts were put into my hands, one of them improving, in a series of stanzas, the subject of the 'Life Boat', to urge Christians to zeal and compassion in the great work of rescuing sinners from destruction.

I shall append to this chapter a letter, received since my return, from the Rev. Hugh Hanna, of Belfast, giving a clear and accurate account of the origin and early history of the Awakening in that great town:—

> Dear Sir,—When we heard, during the last year, that the Lord had visited and refreshed his heritage in America, the church here was moved to more earnest prayer for a time of refreshing; but especially when we heard of the Lord's doings in Connor, Ballymena, and Ahoghill,—how that he was prosecuting his glorious march from district to district of the county of Antrim, our expectation was increased, and our hope and faith acquired fresh energy. On the first Sabbath in June, a meeting was held in Linen-Hall Street Church, and was addressed by two lay converts from Connor. The meeting was very large. The converts were intelligently acquainted with the Bible, and had felt the power of grace in their hearts: they possessed little learning beyond their knowledge of Divine truth, and but for their great earnestness would not for five minutes have been listened to by any assembly in Belfast. But God hath chosen the foolish things of this world to confound the wise, and the weak things and things that are despised hath God chosen to overthrow the mighty. And God owned them. He signally put his approbation on their testimony. One woman fell down in a pew as if she had suddenly been smitten by an invisible but resistless energy. She cried out for mercy. The meeting was impressed indeed; but the impression was not very deep. Incredulity, despite our expectations, was very great. The woman may have been excitable. She may not have been a person of very strong mind, and other imaginations started up to account for her prostration, independently of the Spirit of God. And so the meeting dissolved.
>
> On the following Tuesday evening a Revival meeting was held in the Berry Street Church. It was addressed by the Rev. Mr Knox, of Bel-

fast, and the two converts before alluded to. Another soul was brought down at Jesus' feet, and constrained to cry for mercy. After the meeting was formally dissolved, the people were reluctant to depart. The meeting was reconstituted, prayers were offered, and two others were brought to a deep conviction of sin, and expressed their feelings in such a way as made a profound impression on the audience. The hand of God was visibly at work, and acknowledged in our midst.

The next evening was that of the congregational prayer-meeting, conducted by the elders and other praying people in the congregation. There was no minister present; there was no exciting address; but God made bare his arm in a most marvellous way. Many were convinced and converted. The meeting was large, and great fear fell upon all the people. It was resolved to continue every evening the meetings that God had thus signally owned.

There had been, for many months, in Great George's Street Church (the Rev. Mr Toye's) a faithful band who, on every evening of the week, besieged the throne of grace. They waited, like the believers of old, for the 'Consolation of Israel'. With the exception of these, the meetings in the Berry Street Church were the first assemblies identified with the Revival movement in Belfast. And so they continued for six weeks on every evening of the week. The church was literally crammed; every available spot within and around it was occupied. Many thousands of souls must have been brought within the influence of the truth under the most solemn circumstances during those six weeks. Not only from the population of the town were their audiences drawn, but many earnest souls came from great distances in the country. It was now no uncommon thing for persons to travel forty miles for the sole purpose of seeking God where he was pleased so marvellously to manifest himself, and an incalculable good was done. During that period nearly eight hundred souls were visited at their own houses by the minister and office-bearers of the church—all brought under conviction of sin at the Revival meetings. Many more, and by far a larger multitude, there is reason to believe, were overtaken by the grace of God, and brought to Christ by the silent inspiration of the Spirit. We are receiving proofs of this every day.

The whole population was aroused. The Lord's people rejoiced greatly. The churches were opened to accommodate the thousands that thronged with deepest earnestness to hear the word of God. And so the wondrous movement continued until flesh and blood could stand it no longer. The great excitement that worked the first stage of the Revival subsided, and the gracious work continued, but under a quieter aspect. The world that walks by sight thought it external, and said it was so. The irreligious press gloried in preaching the fiction to be a fact, as it had done all it could to disparage and misrepresent it during its more active manifestations. But the work continues very auspiciously still. In the churches of Townsend Street, Eglinton Street, Great George's Street, Berry Street, among the Presbyterians, in Christ Church, Trinity, St Paul's, and St John's, among the Episcopalians, where faithful ministers labour; Donegal Place, Wesley Place, and Salem, among the Methodists, the Spirit of God has been mightily manifested. Many trophies have been rescued from the hands of Satan. In Belfast alone some tens of thousands have been brought under serious impressions. There is probably no evangelical church in the town where the attendance is not greatly increased at all the services. It was somewhat difficult once to get the ear of the people for the gospel. But it is open now, and hearts are open also. Wherever a minister chooses he may have a congregation in a short time, the great majority of whom will listen to him with the most reverent attention. It is undeniable that a mighty change has been effected in the character of society; that a mighty good has been accomplished. Multitudes, I believe, have been savingly converted to God, and the gracious work is progressing still. Every day we are accosted by some in tones and terms of heavenly rapture, as they tell of the same struggles of soul they had heard of in others, and of the precious Saviour they have found. Sincerely yours,

HUGH HANNA.

With Belfast, as the scene of continued observation and inquiry, I shall now refer to two scenes which makes memorable to me the 7th of August, 1859. It was the evening of the Lord's day—I had addressed a crowded congregation, in the church of my friend and brother D.H. the word of life and reconciliation. The last psalm had been sung, and the parting benediction had been pronounced. Amid the soft shadows of the 'gloaming', I accompanied my friend up a narrow street, and stopped with him at the door of No. 29. He lifted the latch—the apartment was nearly full of people. We entered—the pastor asked a question which scarcely required the answer, 'She is asleep again.'

In this apartment we had stood together two days before. There, in a low bed, with a wooden framework around, sat up, a young girl of twenty-one years of age. Her face was radiant with joy, her language was of heaven and the Saviour, of the angels, and their song before the throne. She had been 'away', and while absent, she had seen and heard, as she believed, the glories of the upper sanctuary, and Jesus as the central attraction there. My friend the minister had been with her conversing the night before, and she told him and all around that she would 'go away' at ten o'clock the same night. He waited till the hour came; and she fell at once into a profound trance-like sleep, and had 'come back' (woke up) at the precise hour which she herself named the night before. More than this, while 'away', she had seen, she said, J. N., a girl in an adjoining street; and when she awoke, she said that the latter had 'come back' before her. On inquiry, it was found that this was true; and also that J. N. had had a corresponding vision, and knew the time when her friend was to 'come back'.

Calling again, as I have said, on the Sabbath evening, we found her, as her father stated it, 'asleep the seventh time'. She had 'gone away' precisely at the hour previously mentioned by her. During the waking intervals she took some light food. There was no sickness or faintness, nor the least appearance of derangement of the mental faculties.

I expected that the sight of the trance-stricken one would have been something painful. On the contrary, it was peculiarly pleasing. Never did I see an infant's slumber more soft or undisturbed. There she lay on her side, the parting light of day coming through the casement and falling on her head—that head almost pillowed on the open hand. The face was tranquillity itself: no shudder nor smile passed over it. I felt the pulse—it was slow, healthy, and regular; the skin was cool and unfevered. I twice placed my ear to the mouth and lips—there was no respiration to be detected; and but that I knew from the pulse and saw from the cheeks' warm hue that the heart was in action, I might have supposed her dead.

I asked, 'Is there nothing which could awake her?' 'No, sir.' 'What, if she was lifted up and shaken violently—or if loud cries were raised in her presence?' 'No.'

Here was a solemnized circle, and in its midst the father of the maiden, once under my own pastoral care, and a true child of God. There sat, in the background, a young girl, his step-daughter. A peculiar gladness, mingled with humility, rested on her face, as the minister took her hand and said, 'I was hearing of you today, and was glad.' The explanation of this will give some insight into the quiet, yet powerful and penetrating work of the Spirit, now going forward all over Ulster, amid exceptional scenes of strangeness or agitations. The last time but one that the minister had been here to see the afflicted girl, he had offered prayer, and before going away, he asked her sister, in a subdued tone, 'Have you found Christ?' An answer indistinct, but apparently assuring, was given, and he left. That question was the Spirit's arrow, and all the more as the young girl accused herself of having deceived the minister as to her real spiritual condition. Her soul was now tempest-tossed. She went to the sanctuary on the Lord's day, and during the morning service she was so wretched that she was compelled to leave ere the close. She went home, and entering the closet, threw herself on her knees, cried to the Saviour for mercy, and she found it. And now she sits here before me on this Sabbath evening, as one of the saved. Oh! how happy her aspect, and, oh, how meek and lowly too!

Returning to the case especially described, I have to state that whatever this 'sleep' was, it was not an attempt at imposture. The vision which the girl related in my presence—of having been in heaven, seen the Saviour, and mingled with angels—I explain *by the joyful frame of soul into which she had passed after a season of terror*. She was thus led to believe that she was in heaven. She had previously scriptural knowledge, and therefore heaven, as set forth in harps, crowns, and songs, naturally presented itself to her imagination. To hold that in this, or in any similar case, the Spirit of God was fixing the truth on the mind by symbols, seems to me altogether inconsistent with the sufficiency of the Bible as a Divine revelation.

The Sunday evening service was over in Great George's Street, but the building was still lighted up, and when I entered, I found a large congregation standing and singing a verse of the 69th Psalm (Rouse's translation). These lines had been read out by the pastor, the Rev. Thomas Toye, and sung by his people as the short but emphatic utterance of a redeemed and grateful soul. On the morning of this day, the Lord's supper had been celebrated, and the number of communicants was *threefold* larger than on any former occasion. Such was one of the evidences of the mighty operation of the Holy Ghost in this place, and it had parallels elsewhere.

Mr Toye, standing in the pulpit, read from one of the Gospels the account of the ten lepers healed by the Saviour, and their subsequent conduct. He then addressed himself to the members of his church thus:—

> Communicants, there is one of two courses open to you this night. You may either imitate the ingratitude of the nine lepers, who received a bodily cure at the hand of Christ, and yet did not return to thank him; or you may imitate the one leper, who received both a bodily cure and a soul cure, and who with a loud voice glorified God. I am not about tonight to call on anyone by name but whosoever of you feel the love of Christ in your hearts, be not ashamed of Christ, but rise up and declare what he hath done for your souls.

After a short pause, a young man stood up in a pew in the centre of the church, and a second and a third followed. Each of them, in fervid language (marked, indeed, by occasional provincialisms and grammatical blunders) briefly addressed the people. One spoke in solemn warning, instancing the case of a young, cheerful, and godless woman whom he had known, but who had been cut off suddenly. Another, standing at the foot of the pulpit stairs, said, 'I am not ashamed of Christ or his cause; this (holding up a pocket Bible), this word of Truth is his cause. I am not afraid to own what Jesus has done for me; I am always sorry when I have only a few to tell it to—I would like to have millions.' He went on to tell of the exceeding great joy of heart which had been his at the Lord's table on that day, and urged others to come to Christ for salvation without delay.

This prayer-meeting had been opened by a venerable minister from Wick, in the north of Scotland. A middle-aged man rose up after two or three younger men had spoken, and, alluding to the minister's prayer, referred gratefully, as a seaman, to deliverances wrought for him from danger and sudden death, in other days, off the northern Scottish coast.

After remaining about half an hour, I retired. I observed another young man waiting for an opportunity to speak, and I learnt afterwards that two women, who had been Roman Catholics, ere the service closed (it lasted two hours), bore testimony for Christ, and against the errors of Popery. I may add, that sometimes the meetings in this church have been protracted till early next morning. On the week previous, after the benediction had been twice pronounced, and the people still lingered, it was found necessary to close the doors upon them. There is no doubt whatever but that this place has been the birthplace of many souls. Still it was the impression of some of the most judicious and earnest, that, at times, there had been a little too much excitement. Nevertheless, there is special adaptation in Thomas Toye to a particular class. He is a 'free lance' among the Presbyterians; he is not like them of the calm Scottish temperament; and if any English tourist in Ireland wishes to hear the real rich brogue of the southern Irish in its perfection, and to listen to a discourse, marvellous in its scriptural fullness, and direct appeals to the conscience, let him repair, on the Sabbath morning or evening, to Great George's Street Presbyterian Church, Belfast.

I shall reserve for another chapter an account of an intensely interesting visit paid to a district in the county of Down, where the word of God grew mightily and prevailed. Meantime, let the reader peruse the following letter from a Presbyterian minister to his brother in London, as furnishing a fair illustration of the glorious scenes then realized in Ulster:—

> God has been pouring out his Holy Spirit upon us here very abundantly. We have an Awakening in my congregation, I think I may say a Revival, that is most cheering. I have a meeting for prayer and exposition nearly every night in the week. Hundreds have been awakened; in

some instances, strong bodily manifestations. The individual falls down, or gradually sinks, clasps the hands, or lifts the eyes, or both, and cries, 'Oh, my sins! Lord, have mercy on me! None but Christ,' &c. A gradual desire for prayer, and an increased anxiety about spiritual things, have been visible for more than eighteen months here; but we had no bodily manifestations till about one month since. For the last three Sabbaths the meeting-house has been crowded to suffocation, and on each of these many had to be helped out who were either stricken down, or likely to be so, under a sense of sin. Our week-day evening services are sometimes even better attended. Last night we held our meeting, by appointment, in the open air. I had a number of clergymen to assist; among the rest, the Hon. and Rev. H. Ward, rector of Killinchy, who has taken a lively interest in the movement all along.

Dear brother, I am not nearly grateful enough to God. I believe it is all of God, and must redound to his glory. What hath God wrought! Dear brother, I will supplicate a throne of grace for such an outpouring on your church and congregation. I am satisfied we have nothing to do but ask and have. Prayer-meetings are starting up in all districts. Four female prayer-meetings in one evening. You would be delighted to hear the prayers of those who, a few weeks since, were only blasphemers and mockers.

In reference to what the Presbyterian minister in Downshire says in the foregoing letter, of the co-operation of the Hon. and Rev. H. Ward, rector of Killinchy, the following testimony borne by that excellent gentleman, which appeared at this time in a Dublin journal, will be read with interest:—

I am the incumbent of a large parish, and having laboured among the people for five-and-thirty years, I know them well. The great majority of them are Presbyterians, living scattered over a district exclusively agri-cultural, and not congregated, as in towns. They are intelligent, industri-ous, well and scripturally taught, calm and reserved in their disposition, and, as regards the reception of Divine truth, would be considered by strangers, perhaps cold. The spirit of Revival visited us not very long after it made its appearance in the county of Antrim. In reference to the results of these Revival meetings, which have been continued now for three weeks, it would be impossible to speak with any accuracy. The grand total of good already done must be left unreckoned until 'the day shall declare it'; but 150 persons of all ages and conditions are known as having been, in an extraordinary manner, brought under conviction of sin. I have met them in a class for special instruction, and have visited many of them in their houses.

I may add, that the spirit of these newly awakened persons is all gentleness, teachableness, and humility; while the fruits of the Spirit—love, joy, peace—rule in their hearts most manifestly. The spirit of our meetings throughout the week is all harmony and love—the Presbyterian not annoying the Episcopalian, the Episcopalian not vexing the Presbyterian. The labour being divided between the ministers of the two denominations, no distinction is made, and the hearts of all are knit together in one holy bond of Christian fellowship. There is no exaltation of man or means—no novelty, no unnatural excitement, no confusion; all order, solemnity and devotion. There can be no imposition practised here; such a thing, from the deep feeling of seriousness which pervades this part of the country at the present time, would not be tolerated by the people. Now that this work, so far as it has come under my observation, is the work of God, I have no more doubt than of the truth of the Philippian jailer's conversion.

I have to add that I found that the movement was rapidly spreading into new districts, and that, although it was more quiet in its manifestations, it was not arrested. The word of God—the good seed—took root, grew up rapidly, and fresh spiritual harvests were gathered daily.

CHAPTER 13
PERSONAL OBSERVATIONS
AND INQUIRIES

An unexpected change in the journey—a visit to a well-remembered scene—
Lurgan, Waringstown, and Donacloney—early days—the staid people deeply
moved—first sight of one stricken—publicans abandoning their trade—visit to
native parish—Banbridge, Glascar, and a great revival.

IN a beautiful rural district, familiar to the writer since childhood,
an ancient seat of the linen manufacture, irrigated by the Lagan
and the Bann, with Lurgan, Waringstown, and Banbridge, as its
principal towns,—there was a mighty work of real awakening now
in full progress. I had not expected to be able to visit this part of the
country, however desirous to do so. I was preparing to leave Belfast,
and to pass along what some one has called the 'trunk line' of the
Revival—by Ballymena and Connor, to Ballymoney, Coleraine, Portrush, and the Giant's Causeway, and from thence to Londonderry.
But a minister well known in days past, the pastor of the congregation where I had been brought up, meeting me in the street, so moved
me by a stirring tale of the 'great things' going on at Donacloney,
that I seemed to see a Divine hand beckoning me away to that well-
remembered region.

I am thankful that I went thither; the recollection of what I saw
and heard will always be sweet and grateful. Arriving by railway at
Lurgan, we drove across the country southward. At Waringstown we
were joined by a godly young Presbyterian minister, who told me of
the spiritual marvels that had been wrought in Lurgan, and in his own
district. Very many had been 'stricken down' in agony of body, and,
said he, 'The people around me—the weavers at their looms—are at
this moment almost unable to go on with their work, by reason of the
spiritual distress which they suffer.' 'I have', he added,

living opposite my own house, a man who was recently a notorious infidel—who, a short time since, told me that the Bible was a fable, and that he had books to prove it to be such. But now, he is awfully convinced of the reality of God's wrath, and of the truth of his word, and is earnestly asking what he must do to be saved? The same is the case with his brother-in-law, who was an infidel and a wicked, hardened man, like himself.

Passing rapidly to the old and venerable place of worship whither we were bound, the pastor ascended the pulpit, and commenced the devotional meeting, for which—as on every other night in the week, except Saturday—a large number of persons, of all ages and both sexes, many of them coming from great distances, had assembled. In this gathering I saw a fair specimen of what had been common, and I might almost say universal, in nearly every part of Ulster, during the last two or three months. Prayer was the characteristic of the movement, and were there no other proof of the divinity of its origin, this were alone sufficient.

Here, for example, was a place where, for nearly 100 years the old truths of the gospel—brought hither by the followers of Ralph and Ebenezer Erskine of Scotland, when Pelagianism and Arianism had come in like a flood—had been fully and faithfully preached by faithful men. But meetings for united prayer, as distinct from the devotions of the great congregation at the regular services of the Lord's day, were almost unknown.

Here also was a people peculiarly unimpressible, in the emotional sense of the term. They held fast the truth, with a comprehensive, intellectual grasp, and many of them were truly devout; but, true to their Scottish blood and origin, they were not wont to shed tears, or to be demonstrative in any sense, in their devotions. What a change presented itself to my eyes in that old familiar place! Here was a large body of people, who on a week evening had come together, not expecting an address from a stranger, knowing who would address them, and thinking mainly, if not entirely, of praise and prayer. And when the prayer of the pastor (the Rev. J. Moorhead)—full of solemnity and unction—was over, I could not help marking, with glad surprise, the eyes of strong men wet with tears. A psalm was sung, and I then entered the pulpit. It was to me a solemn moment, and a very solemn place, and all the more did I feel this, because I had come thither so unexpectedly to myself. I could not help giving expression to the deep and strong emotions which filled my breast, by some opening references to the former pastor, George Hay (once a student of John Brown, of Haddington), by whom I had been baptized, and to the family pew where I had sat by the side of father, mother, sisters, and brothers in boyhood's days, and from which I had stepped forth and sat down side by side by a mother (now in heaven), to commemorate for the first time a Saviour's dying love. By such references and allusions my feelings were relieved, and my mind was prepared for speaking to the people the word of life. What could one say amid such a people, but tell them of sin and its penalties, and of pardon, peace, life, and healing, through faith in a Saviour's name, and by the grace of his Holy Spirit? As words of this import were spoken, my ear was startled by a suppressed cry proceeding from a pew to the left of the pulpit. I looked and saw a young woman in great agitation, but there sat by her side one of the elders of the church, who took her hand in his, and calmed her. But a little time later, her emotions and physical sufferings were so great that it was found necessary to remove her.

The address was closed: prayer was offered by the young minister of Waringstown, the closing psalm was sung, and the benediction was pronounced. Proceeding to the adjoining session-house or vestry, I found a crowd of persons gathered before the door. Entering the house, I found the young woman in a state of great prostration and weakness on one of the benches, her head leaning on the breast of an elderly female. Words of instruction and consolation were spoken to her. I found that she was an orphan girl in humble circumstances. I asked her, had she felt anything of this kind before? She replied, 'Yes, once or twice'; but there had been no external manifestation till that evening. She gradually revived, and spoke of going homeward. She was taken into the open air, but she found herself so weak and oppressed, that a chair was placed for her, and the people gathered around her.

The Rev. Mr McMurray standing near, prayed very earnestly, and all the people bowed their heads, and worshipped with him. I then proposed a song of praise—the first verses of the 40th Psalm.[1]

The poor girl hailed the idea with delight, crying out, 'Oh yes, do sing!' and the soft sweet swell of that song of a redeemed soul, rose up on the evening air and died away. It seemed to act on the sufferer as did the harp of David on King Saul.

In this, the first case of 'conviction' which I had witnessed, there were precisely the two characteristics which I had heard of as being universal:

First, there was great distress of countenance and aspect, accompanied by a burning sense of pain in the chest, and by great difficulty of breathing. Secondly, along with this, and evidently the cause of this, was deep horror of soul, by reason of a sense of guilt and exposure to the wrath of the Almighty, which could only find relief in sighs, and supplications for mercy.

It was not for me, then and there, to pronounce on the genuineness of conversion in this case, because I was leaving the neighbourhood; but time has since attested its reality by fruits.

I was struck with the fact that the *sole* source of comfort (apparently found ere I departed) was *Christ trusted in*. An increased clearness of apprehension marked the last utterances which I heard from this young person, as contrasted with those *first* expressions as to the way of salvation (correct but obscure) which had reached my ear.

Many such cases had occurred in this district, but it was the first I had seen, and I could thus begin to understand why (if these physical agitations were indeed from a Divine influence) such manifestations were permitted. For, by this one case occurring on that evening,

[1] These verses are now called 'The Convert's Song', all over Ulster. They run thus in Rouse's metrical version of the Psalms:—

I waited for the Lord my God,
    And patiently did bear:
At length to me He did incline,
    My voice and cry to hear.

He took me from the fearful pit,
    And from the miry clay:

And on a rock He set my feet,
    Establishing my way.

He put a new song in my mouth,
    Our God to magnify:
Many shall see it, and shall fear,
    And on the Lord rely.

an emphasis and an application peculiarly solemn were given to the words of warning and invitation which had been spoken; and more than this, the sight of this girl thus 'stricken' brought again within the sound of gospel truth the careless and the undecided, and compelled them to think of eternal things.

It was thus that all over Ulster, God seemed to be using these agitations for the glory of his name, and for the awakening and conversion of very many, including the worst and vilest of society, as well as formalists and hypocritical professors.

I had afterwards satisfactory replies to inquiries made as to the progress of the work of grace going on in this district.

In the town of Lurgan the Episcopal, Wesleyan, and Presbyterian ministers went hand in hand, and were 'abundant in labours'. So numerous were the cases of persons 'stricken', that it was found necessary to summon by telegraph the Rev. Mr Barklie, the Presbyterian minister, to return home immediately from the meeting of the Irish Assembly in Dublin.

An intelligent, pious master of a national school, mentioned to me that he had been conversing with a man who kept two public-houses on the roads leading from Waringstown to Banbridge. The man said,

> If these times continue, our trade will be done up, and I shall never take out another licence; and, indeed', he added, 'at this I am not sorry, as I think it will be better for the country that the people give up whisky drinking.

Giving it up, they certainly were. All along the road-sides of County Antrim, publicans were about to take down their signboards,—some from conscientious feeling, and all agreeing that the business could not pay. That was an illustration of a great social change in Ulster, not affecting the Roman Catholic population. They still drank freely at markets and fairs. But their priests and their men of business could not but acknowledge that the Protestant population were becoming very sober. They 'hated the change' while recognising it, and were greatly enraged at other results of the Revival as trespassing on their domain. The priests were quite awake to their own interests, and when Romanists were 'stricken down', their spiritual advisers went to them with bottles containing a healing mixture. As these bottles were often renewed before the 'cure' was complete, and a sum of money was demanded and paid for each, the profits of the Roman Catholic Church, even under circumstances otherwise adverse, must have been very considerable.

Thank God, the many Romanists convicted and converted, were now able intelligently to give a reason for the new-born peace and hope which were theirs. They could also say to their former blind guides, who now would have 'healed' them by false teachings and consolations, 'Physicians are ye of no value—miserable comforters are ye all.'

At Tullylish Presbyterian Church, where the venerable John Johnson, D.D. (the father of the Irish open-air preaching movement, and late Moderator of the Irish General Assembly), has been pastor for nearly half a century, I addressed a very large assembly. This was to me an affecting scene, for outside the walls, in the family burying-ground, lay the dust of my parents and sisters, of whom I could say with truth, 'These all died in faith.' Since the period of my visit, the Awakening has made great progress in this district. The Rev. Mr Bewley, curate of the parish, writes,

> Hitherto ministers had considerable difficulty in persuading the people to attend public worship: now the difficulty is to find room for the multitude who press forward both on Sunday and week-days. The badness of the weather has absolutely no effect in diminishing their numbers. The communicants in the parish church have been doubled within the last few months.

At Banbridge—an important manufacturing town—and in the neighbourhood, the Awakening displayed itself suddenly with great power. It began at an open-air gathering, in a bleach-field, on Thursday the 21st July, and on the following evening, at another meeting addressed by three students of theology, sixty-four cases of prostration occurred. Many of those present on this occasion had come from a distance. Thus the influence of the Awakening was diffused far and wide, and fresh missionaries were raised up to call friends and neighbours to repentance, faith, and newness of life.

At this town I was taken to see two cases of the convicted. One had been an 'unfortunate'. A Christian gentleman found her at ten o'clock, P.M. (after the meeting already alluded to, but not one of those who had been present), lying on the ground near the bridge, and in awful distress both of body and mind. Her despairing and warning cry was, 'Let all sinners of my class beware!' It afterwards appeared that her conscience had been upbraiding her. I was taken to see her. She had been placed in the house of a pious family till she should recover. Her first anxiety, after finding relief, was to implore that efforts should be made to save her two younger sisters, still uncontaminated, from the perils that surrounded them. I felt deeply in looking on that thoroughly subdued, humble, penitent one.

The next case was that of a young woman of blameless life, but led to Christ after deep agitation. The radiant joy of her countenance, coupled with a beautiful meekness, was just what was to be seen in the converts everywhere. A young person here resident also, who had been a confirmed Unitarian, and who had not attended any public meeting, had been stricken down. She was in a respectable position in life, and very intelligent. Her former faith in the hour of distress was found worthless; she turned to an Almighty Redeemer, and cried out, 'My Lord, and my God!' This was the town in which ministers a Unitarian pastor, who had recently, at Belfast, poured ridicule and contempt on those manifestations which marked the Revival.

There were not wanting instruments in the hand of God in preparing the way of the Lord in Banbridge. Many of the young men of the town had been gathered into Bible classes, and several of them were truly converted to God. These converts became willing-hearted workers in the evangelization of the neglected and outcast population. They established cottage prayer-meetings, and also local Sabbath schools, and there was thus an extensive sowing of the good seed of the kingdom ere the Awakening appeared in its power. To crown all, prayer, united, continuous, and believing, had been *long* offered in faith and fervour by this band of young men, and by other associated Christian friends. In addition to this, evangelical truth had been long and faithfully preached in the town and neighbourhood. The public mind here', a friend wrote me soon after my return home, 'was never in such a prepared state for the reception of the good seed, and I feel that he who has thus prepared it by his Spirit, will satisfy the desire he has created.' The confident expectation thus expressed has been since largely realized.

I visited the house of the Rev. James Rogers (an old college friend) in this neighbourhood, and found him from home. His wife told me that he would not return till a late hour in the evening, from visiting cases of persons who were 'ill' from the agitations through which they had passed. This is the district of Glascar, County Down. A more sober-minded pastor, and a more staid people, are not to be found anywhere, and yet here also the Sovereign Spirit caused strong men to 'cry out for fear'. 'Anything like the earnestness', wrote Mr Rogers on the 17th September,

> manifested by the people generally on the subject of religion has never been witnessed in our day. Multitudes who never attended a place of worship in times past, now rush to every meeting, and can with difficulty be got to leave. In my own congregation we have men who had grown grey in the neglect of ordinances, who are now waiting regularly, and with all attention and seriousness, on the means of grace. The appearance of the congregation is entirely changed. *They come into the sanctuary as a people prepared for the Lord,* and the attention paid to the word, and the spirit of the worship, are as different as it is possible to conceive. *The singing is like the sound of many waters.*

CHAPTER 14
PERSONAL OBSERVATIONS
AND INQUIRIES

A student convert—his testimony as to a great Awakening—the town of Newry—Scots and Celts meeting, but not mingling—the Irish language—the 'Big Sunday' at Newry—Protestantism revived, and the Sabbath honoured—decrease of intemperance—a Romish Magistrate on the 'Revival'—a solemn meeting—the alarm and cry—an address to awakened ones—a Union meeting, and addresses—a Rector's testimony—the voice of Psalms—the Indian Colonel's plea.

A STUDENT of the General Assembly at this time gives an impressive account of the Awakening, as it had manifested itself in a district about seven miles north-west of Newry. His letter was put into my hands by Alexander Dickey, Esq., of Belfast, and is as follows:—

CREMORE AND TYRONE'S DITCHES.—The first prayer-meeting at this place was held on the 7th of July, and was conducted by the minister, no converts from other places, addressing any of the meetings in the neighbourhood. The writer, a student of the General Assembly, was one of those blessed by the Lord at the first meeting. There could not have been less than fifty cases of conviction on that night. The people did not leave the church, till four or five o'clock in the morning. Since then, the work has been advanced with astonishing rapidity. Meetings are held every evening in various places, and though the physical manifestations are not so numerous as at first, the meetings are still crowded. These have been conducted by the local ministers and some Presbyterian students, and no strangers have yet visited the place. There are some unbelievers in the movement, but they cannot deny the great change that has taken place in the country; they cannot deny that intemperance, Sabbath breaking, blasphemy, &c., are now almost unknown; they cannot deny that more than one public-house has been closed. This neighbourhood was notorious for its religious sectarianism, but God has broken this heartless bigotry into ten thousand pieces. You can now see Covenanter, Seceder, Assembly-man, Episcopalian, and Methodist, sitting side by side listening to the story of the cross, when formerly, they would scarcely have looked at one another. Many Roman Catholics have been converted, and the last person the writer spoke to, as he entered the train for Belfast, was a converted Unitarian.

At Rathfriland, seven miles to the east of Newry, in Downshire, the power of the Holy Spirit had been displayed continuously for many weeks together. Strong and stalwart men had been prostrated to the dust, and large numbers of true penitents had been brought to the Saviour's feet. In other districts of the County Down, as in the neighbourhoods of Hillsborough and of Saintfield, as well as at Dromara and Boardmills, the same triumphs of grace were now witnessed.

The Rev. G. H. Shanks, of Boardmills, a minister well known to the writer, has been permitted to gather an abundant harvest of precious souls. In August, a devotional meeting of 1,000 persons was held in his district at a place called, 'The Temple', which had been long infamous as the scene of cock-fighting and other abominations. A missionary from India, who had been present, described the gathering to me as intensely interesting. An entire revolution of habits and morals has passed over this district, and probably nowhere has the visible and moral reformation been more decidedly or more extensively the direct and immediate fruit of the operations of the Holy Ghost.

The town of Newry is the barrier town between the province of Ulster in the north, and the province of Leinster in the south-east of Ireland. Its site amid hills and mountains is picturesque, and the scenery of Rostrevor and Carlingford Bay, in its vicinity, is 'beautiful exceedingly'. Here, too, you may study the native Celtic population, and the descendants of the Scottish and English colonists of the seventeenth century; and mark and ponder a striking contrast in face and form, and even in language and religion.

In the market-place, mutual bargains are made in the Irish tongue by the peasantry of the county of Louth; and from the Romish chapel door, you could have watched with interest, a crowd of real native Irish people—men in their frieze coats, and women with their blue or red cloaks—issue forth, after a mass in honour of the 'Assumption' of the Virgin Mary.

Were there any tokens of the presence and power of the Awakening in such a town as this? We reply, Yes; but it had *not* reached the Roman Catholic population of the town or neighbourhood, nor has it told upon their social habits. This, however, it had done on the Protestant population of the town, and especially among the farmers and peasantry northward. In proof of this, I was told, when at Newry, that on the 'big Sunday', the 14th of August (an anniversary and holiday among Romanists), there had been 400 fewer pleasure excursionists to Warrenpoint this year, as compared with the corresponding day of 1858, and this a Roman Catholic magistrate of the town, in the hearing of a personal friend of my own, expressly attributed to the 'Revival'.

In like manner, the use of ardent spirits is much diminished in this neighbourhood among Protestants, and drunkenness is scarcely known. I had no means of ascertaining the decrease of excise revenue in this district, as I had afterwards with regard to that of Coleraine, where the collector reported a diminution of receipts for the quarter, of £400.

At Newry, I attended two meetings, marked by deep and peculiar interest to myself. The first was on a Monday evening, in a house of prayer which I had been the instrument of building for the worship of God and the preaching of his word. Here I stood up in the presence of a large assembly of various evangelical denominations, and surrounded by many to whom for years I had ministered the word of life, and introduced into the church of Christ. The pastor, the Rev. J. Dodd, opened by solemn prayer; and not without much emotion did I address the assembly.

While speaking, there was a noise in the gallery, and the sound of footsteps of parties hastily retiring. Immediately afterwards, I heard a loud cry outside, twice at least repeated. The sound was peculiar; a lady afterwards described it as a 'wail'. But to me it suggested the idea that some intoxicated person, or a Romanist, had got into the grounds surrounding the church, and had raised this cry in mockery.

After the service was over, the pastor came to me, and informed me of the true cause of this strange outcry. A young man sat in the gallery that evening, who had received a religious education, but who had wandered from God and his ways. A companion sat in the same pew, and about the middle of the service, his friend suddenly turned to him, and said, 'I am very ill. Come out with me.' They then hastened forth, and as soon as the area in front was gained, the young man, unable to control his feelings any longer, gave utterance by agonizing cries to the fear and agitation which oppressed him.

He was afterwards conducted to his father's house, and there I visited him. I am not able to say that this was a case of real conversion, but I give it as a specimen of the effects produced by an alarmed and an awakened conscience, and in illustration of those physical agitations which, in the great majority of cases, have been preceded by deep feeling. They are marked by an intensifying of the sense of guilt and misery to an anguish intolerable, and are generally followed by a true change of heart, in connection with repentance toward God, and faith toward our Lord Jesus Christ.

Immediately after this service, a meeting for awakened persons was held in the vestry, which was addressed by the Rev. R. Lindsay, minister of a large Presbyterian congregation at Drumbanagher, three miles to the north-west of Newry. There, as well as at Bessbrook, numbers had been brought under conviction, and—as Mr L. believed and declared—had been hopefully converted.

The second meeting at Newry was one for united prayer, presided over by Dr Bagot, Dean of Dromore, Here, five clergymen of the Church of England, three Presbyterian ministers, and an Independent pastor, were lovingly associated. Although the rain fell heavily, the large room of the 'savings'-bank was crowded to excess, and a most solemn and devout feeling reigned to the close. Among the speakers was the Hon. and Rev. H. Ward, rector of Killinchy, a clergyman remarkable for his piety and zeal in every good cause, as well as for his catholicity of spirit. His striking testimony as to the reality and power of the great Awakening, as witnessed in his own parish of Killinchy, in the county of Down, has been already quoted. From his own lips, however, I learned much more. He stated that there had been about 260 cases of persons 'stricken', the great majority of whom (and he is a man of exceeding caution, and of ripe years and experience) he now regarded as the genuine children of God. There had been no attempt at excitement; no 'converts' were brought from a distance; no young persons were encouraged to address the assembled people. The Presbyterian minister and himself had been present together at each meeting, and all things were conducted in perfect order. At the public meeting in Newry, Mr Ward dealt with objections and objectors to the movement, in a very powerful manner, and at the same time appealed to the hearts and consciences of his audience. I know not any man, in whose judgment and opinion I would place greater reliance, and his testimony, therefore, was all the more valuable. It was very solemnizing to hear his statement about a notorious infidel in the parish, whose soul had been shaken with terror to its centre. And touching was it, to hear his description of the breaking up of each evening meeting, the people marching in a body to the cross-roads, singing psalms and hymns all the way; and when compelled to part, each band departing by a separate road, and the still night and the starlit skies made vocal with their anthems of praise.

An excellent gentleman residing in the neighbourhood of Newry, and a retired Colonel of the Indian army, published at this period *A Few Plain Words to Objections* in reference to the Revivals in the North of Ireland.

He deals with the three classes of objectors—such as unreservedly vilify and repudiate; such as object to the physical accompaniments, and while they admit that there may be, to some extent, good in it, say they must wait for more permanent results; and those who declare its author to be Satan 'transforming himself into an angel of light'. As to the first class, he regards reasoning and argument with them to be futile, as they are mockers who disregard the operations of God's hand. To the second class, Colonel R., who is an Evangelical churchman, addresses himself in the following weighty words:—

> I would say, How long will you halt between two opinions? Does the friend of the convalescent postpone his joy, saying, I must wait to see if

your cure is permanent? Does he condemn him if, having passed from a state of depression and pain to the enjoyment of health and life, he gives expression to unwonted feelings of thankfulness and delight?

Are men to be cast down when an earthly calamity befalls them, and is there to be no manifestation of alarm, no mental or bodily depression, when the realities of the eternal world are brought suddenly before them in all their vivid signification, when the awakened soul feels itself hanging over an unfathomable abyss of horror?

May the emotions of the prodigal's heart be rapturous when his earthly parent's arms are outstretched to receive him, and is the spirit to be unmoved when it feels that it is reconciled to God, and that the terrors of hell are removed?

As regards waiting for further evidence, how long does the historian of the Acts of the Apostles declare the interval to have been between Peter's first sermon, and the conversions which followed it? 'The same day', he says, 'there were added unto them about three thousand souls.' The willingness and power of the Holy Spirit are the same now as then, and this is evidenced in the altered conduct and dispositions of those upon whom he now operates. Vicious habits are abandoned, a desire for services in which intercourse with God may be enjoyed, is exhibited to an extent unknown before, and which all previous human efforts had failed to excite.

Marvellous fluency in prayer is possessed by the most illiterate, and often by very young persons. A boldness in acknowledging what God had done for them is shown, and an ardent desire to make known to others the love of God in Christ. These things cannot be gainsaid, for whole districts proclaim their existence. How is it that you know them not? Is it because you are unwilling to know them, and will not take the trouble?

What if God should refuse you further evidence, leaving you to the performance of frigid rites and the possession of barren hearts?

To the third class he says—

Though Satan can transform himself into an angel of light, he cannot make men produce fruits of the character just mentioned, nor would he if he could, as he would then be working against himself.

In estimating this work to be evil in its origin and operation, take heed that you are not committing the unpardonable sin 'blasphemy against the Holy Ghost', and beware lest the words to you are applicable, 'Behold, ye despisers, and wonder and perish, for I work a work in your days, a work which ye shall in no wise believe, though a man declare it unto you.' Whether you believe or disbelieve, the work will go on, and souls will be gathered into the garner of Christ, with a rapidity proportioned to the shortness of the interval remaining for its completion. The joy of angels over one sinner that repents must spread until heaven's arch is filled with the reverberation. The kingdom of God has long been offered to those who heed it not; it is time, therefore, that the inhabitants of the highways and hedges of the earth should be gathered in to enjoy for eternity, the rich provision God has prepared for them.

CHAPTER 15
PERSONAL OBSERVATIONS
AND INQUIRIES

Visit to Ballymena—the minister and his guest—hospitality—the Ahoghill district—the rich man's conversion—the Bible class—the evening gathering—the young preacher—cases of deafness and dumbness—the converts' joy—Mr Moore, and the power of prayer.

THE town of Ballymena, in the county of Antrim, as we have already indicated, has peculiar interest clustering around it in connection with the history of the Revival. Within a few miles of it on the one side—to the north-east—is Connor, where the Awakening had its origin; and on the other side—to the west—is Ahoghill, where its development became truly marvellous in the early months of the present year. But in Ballymena itself—a prosperous market town, the seat and centre of the linen manufacture in Antrim—the Awakening has been so marked and manifest, that no Christian tourist could with propriety, or without a great deficiency in his records of ascertained facts in connection with the Revivals, pass it by.

It was on the afternoon of Thursday, the 18th of August, that I found myself able to realize my purpose of visiting Ballymena. It was the first place which, after an examination of the spiritual condition of Belfast, I had marked down on my programme. But Providence ordered it otherwise; and I shall always be thankful that, by strange and unexpected causes, I was led to visit other scenes dear to me from childhood's associations and family ties, as well as the town where I first ministered the word of life.

Parting at the Ballymena station with an Indian missionary, who was passing on to Coleraine, to supply, on the coming Lord's day, the pulpit of a minister whose health had broken down under excessive toil, I penetrated speedily into the town. I inquired my way to the manse of the Rev. S. M. Dill, by whom I was most hospitably received. Here I found myself at once in the atmosphere of Christian life and activity. First of all I found at Mr Dill's house the brother of the Rev. J. H. Guinness, the well-known evangelist. This younger brother, in his vacation recess (he is a student at New College, St John's Wood, London), was now on a visit to his native country, and was preaching almost daily. The evening before, he had addressed an immense audience at Carrickfergus, and this evening was about to preach in Mr Dill's church. Meanwhile, we three were driven out to dine with—Y., Esq., at a beautiful mansion, which had originally belonged to the noble family of Mountcashel. Our route lay along the highway which leads to Ahoghill, in which village I had, years before, preached for several Sabbaths. I tried to recall the features of the neighbourhood, but, in doing so, I was irresistibly led to ponder with thankfulness on the blessed change which, not without some hopeful antecedents and providential preparations, had passed over this district. In itself, it presents as fair a specimen of prosperity as Ulster can supply. The soil is rich, the population is numerous, and yet not squalid, but in comfortable circumstances, while the dwelling-houses, with their whitewashed walls and their superior size, tell how the linen trade has long been the source of wealth to this special locality. It was to the top of one of the round hills of this neighbourhood that, as related in a previous chapter, an inhabitant not long ago took a Christian visitor, and pointed out to him a particular district, studded with its farm-houses, into which the Spirit of God had come with such regenerating power during the present year, that almost every family had undergone a social revolution.

Returning into town for the evening service, there was pointed out to me a large suburban house, or rather mansion, occupied by a wealthy merchant. He had, up till a recent period, been living without God in the world, but very soon after the work of grace displayed its presence in Ballymena, was privately brought under conviction of sin,—whether accompanied by physical agitation or not was not known,—and his resolve, as soon as he was led to the Saviour's feet, was that of Joshua—'As for me and my house, we will serve the Lord.' This is not the only instance of persons in the higher walks of life having been converted during this awakening time. Many such there are in various districts of Ulster.

At eight o'clock, P.M., Mr Dill's church began to be rapidly filled by a congregation comprising almost every grade in society, and including working-men and youths, just as they had come from their toil. Previously Mr Dill had met a large Bible class of young women, nearly all of whom were recent converts, and many of whom had been physically affected. He laboured to build them up in the faith, and, as a good shepherd, to feed them with knowledge and understanding. This, in truth, is the special care of almost all the Ulster ministers with regard to the young disciples, and is as apostolic in its spirit, as it is full of promise for spiritual stability and permanent results.

With these young people, at Mr Dill's request, I engaged in prayer; and here, as well as elsewhere, found it very sweet and joyous to give thanks to God on their behalf, while yet asking special guidance and guardianship for them. And could you, dear reader, have looked on them as they rose from their knees, you would have seen the gladly tearful and glistening eyes of many of them, ere they moved away to take their places in the church at the evening service.

Mr Guinness, jun., was the preacher in the evening, but I was asked to take the introductory services. The view from the pulpit was indeed heart-stirring. At least 1,200 persons were present, and in song and prayer, in reading and briefly expounding, it was impossible to feel aught of the isolation of a stranger, in a pulpit surrounded by a people so thoroughly alive and earnest.

Mr Guinness preached from the text, 'Be ye reconciled to God.' His sermon was a series of scriptural pictures, ending with the Agony and Crucifixion, illustrated by anecdotes, and, based on these, was an appeal to sinners at the close. His appearance and manner were winning, and marked by gentleness and goodness. There was little direct teaching in this discourse. Its import and aim, however, were evangelical; and next evening a fuller message was delivered—from the words, 'Come unto me all ye that labour, &c'. —to an equally numerous audience. No doubt Mr G., after mature study and further experience, will prove, like his brother, an evangelist indeed. His spirit is very amiable, and it is impossible to know without loving him.

On Friday morning I paid several visits to young persons who had been physically affected, and some of them in a very remarkable manner. One girl with whom I conversed in her father's house had been twice, for days together, both deaf and dumb. Unlike others who had suffered from blindness (in the sense of having the eyes constantly closed, and of inability to open them), she saw perfectly during the whole period of these visitations, one of which, if I mistake not, continued a whole fortnight.

During all that time, she was able to go about the house, but could neither speak nor hear. She told me that she had suffered from a choking sensation in her throat, and in saying this, she grasped her throat midway with her hand. Her father, a shoemaker, seated at his work, confirmed her statement.

With a little band I had previously united in prayer in the house of a Christian widow, whose husband had been a pious elder in the congregation of Connor for years, and whose daughters, forming part of the circle, had all been brought into subjection to the Saviour's authority.

Passing to a third house, whither I was conducted by a little female guide, I was again permitted to see and share in the joy of young persons who had recently passed from death unto life, after severe conflict, both bodily and mental in its character. The warmheartedness, the simplicity, and godly sincerity of these converts were most evident, and, in truth, but the counterparts of what I had already seen and was yet to witness in others throughout Ulster.

Happiness beamed in every eye. Each had suffered agonizing convictions,

> As if an accusing angel held the candle of the Lord to the record of their deeds. The idea of little sins, excuses for sin, or hopes of self-redemption, could not live in that awful light. Guilty, guilty, guilty! Unclean, unclean, unclean! Lost, lost, lost! This was the feeling.'

But here at Ballymena, as at Coleraine and Portrush, as well as at Connor, 'clear, happy conversions had taken place'; as the Rev. William Arthur expresses it—

> conversions which made the person changed go on his way, walking and leaping, and praising God. No longer now the spirit of bondage, but that happy, holy cry, 'Abba, Father!' burst as naturally as a child's greeting for an unexpected, long absent parent, from the unwonted and wondering lips of recent disciples.

At one o'clock, P.M., I attended a daily prayer-meeting intended for the higher classes of society, which was presided over by a leading physician of the town. At this meeting, which lasted an hour, several tourists (strangers) were present, and two ministers from a distance took part in the exercises.

Leaving Ballymena on Friday afternoon, I had just time to shake hands at the railway station with the Rev. J. S. Moore, one of the ministers of the town, who has been remarkably blessed in his labours in connection with the Revival. He was returning from County Down, where he had addressed large public meetings. In the few words which he uttered, ere we parted, he dwelt earnestly on the power of believing prayer. He expects great things, and, 'according to his faith', so has he found the results to be. Oh, for a wide diffusion of this spirit!

CHAPTER 16
PERSONAL OBSERVATIONS
AND INQUIRIES

Coleraine—the labouring man and his converted son—Bellaghy and its minister—Coleraine and the first Awakening there—the Town Hall—the Irish Society's school—prayer-meetings—Dr Mitchell's address—a band of converts—daily morning prayer-meeting.

I ARRIVED by train at Coleraine, reluctantly passing by Ballymoney, in the evening, and proceeded at once to the house of the Rev. Joseph Macdonald, about one mile north-east of the town, on the road which leads to the Giant's Causeway. As I left the station, I saw before me on the road a labouring man, and with the familiarity of a brother Ulsterman I called out, 'Will you not wait for company?' The man stopped till I came up to him, and ere we had walked side by side three minutes we were conversing about the Revival. It was to him a delightful topic. He had been a Christian indeed before its blessed advent, but his soul, as a father, had been filled with gladness because of it. His dress was mean, and his aspect rugged, yet here was a 'brother beloved, partaker of the benefit', at once found and recognized. He spoke of the wonderful scenes that had occurred in the Town Hall of Coleraine, and throughout the place generally, at the outset. He was a labourer in a farmer's service, but with awe-struck tones and reverent air he said to me, 'I did not work for several days then; I didn't think it quite right to do so.' 'You felt that God was specially near?' 'Yes.' 'Were you at the Town Hall on that memorable night, when so many were struck down?' 'Yes; and I had one of my sons with me.' 'Did it make a great impression on him?' 'Yes; he said to me next day, "I feel as if I was to have it tonight!"' This implied that the youth had the beginnings of conviction of sin within him, and that he had a glimmering hope of mercy. He then described how the youth went to the prayer-meeting, and how next day he had borne testimony, before all the men in the farm-yard, to what God had done for his soul. He added, 'When my boy came home that evening he looked at me very solemnly, and said, 'Father, will you let (allow) me keep family worship?' I said to him '—(and here the father was deeply moved, as he spoke)— "Well, James, I am very glad to hear such a word as that from you." And so he took the book (the Bible) and read; and then he knelt down and prayed—such a prayer!'

Such was the substance of this wayside, casual converse with a poor working-man. Thank God, there are thousands like him in Ulster at this hour.

I had passed by the village of Bellaghy, on my journey this afternoon, but cast a glance of deepest interest upon it and the district around. For—as indicated by a letter from the Rev. A. Hunter, printed in Dr Massie's *Facts and Documents* with regard to the Revival—this is truly the 'transformed village', above most others in Ulster, by reason of the mighty outpouring of the Holy Spirit upon the people. It was in this neighbourhood that a Member of Parliament, and a nephew of a late statesman, attended with his wife an open-air meeting. He had made no profession of religion previously (more, perhaps, might be said than this implies), but so powerful was the impression made on his mind, by what he saw and heard, that he declared that now he believed that religion was a reality, and his household can now testify with gratitude, to the blessed results of the change.

It was from this village of Bellaghy, in the county of Derry, that the Rev. Mr Pennefather, incumbent of Barnet, invited Mr Hunter to pay him a visit with the express object of doing good in his parish. Mr Hunter was present at the Conference of Christians at Barnet, which extended over three mornings.

On one afternoon, Mr Hunter gave an address to 500 persons in the school-room, illustrated by incidents from the Irish Revival; and at an evening meeting he gave an account of the Awakening in his own neighbourhood, and 'the transformation of what had been one of the most wicked districts in the north of Ireland'. 'The interest attached to the report of one who had been on the spot from the beginning', writes BETA, in *Evangelical Christendom,* 'was enhanced by the fiery energy, and the air of truth and reality with which he spoke.'

I heard much that was interesting about Mr Hunter, while in Ireland, and of the glorious change wrought in a district where, by the desperate wickedness of the people, he had been almost driven to despair,

Coleraine was a town where, as I previously knew, great things had been done. The beginning of the Awakening is thus described by the Rev. W. Arthur:—

> The town of Coleraine is beautifully seated on the banks of the Bann, and, like Ballymena, was prosperous. Here the spiritual power of the Revival seems to have been manifested, in a degree, perhaps, surpassing any other place, at least up to that time. Much prayer had been offered, and when the work came so nigh as Ballymena, faith and hope grew stronger. At length united meetings were held, indoors and out of doors, of Churchmen, Presbyterians, Methodists, Independents, Baptists,—all classes who preach salvation by grace through faith,—working together, with one heart and one soul. A mighty power of the Spirit was shed down. If they had often wondered at the barrenness of their utmost efforts, now, looking on the blessed results of every meeting, they were as men that dream. When I asked a friend how matters were going on in the town, his reply was, 'For the last three weeks, it has been one continual Pentecost.' Conviction of sin had appeared to be granted to hundreds of the people at once, and that in the clearest and most awakening form. In cottage after cottage, groups were gathered to pray around penitents, or to read the Bible, and sing psalms and hymns. One day the newspaper had to delay its publication, for the convincing Spirit had touched the hearts of the compositors, and, instead of being at work, they were wrestling in agonies of prayer. A new Town Hall had been built, and was to be opened by a ball; but such a power of repenting grace came down upon the people, that place must be sought on all hands for mourning penitents to meet and seek mercy. The court-house, in another part of the town, was filled; and instead of the dancing throng, the new Town Hall was thrown open to a company of the weary and the heavy laden, who were resolved to wait at the feet of Jesus till

he bade them 'go in peace, and sin no more.' The *Coleraine Chronicle* says: 'Instead of the joyous dance and the stirring music of the ball-room, the walls of the hall gave back the almost despairing groans of the stricken sinner, the heartfelt prayer of a believing penitent, or resounded with the adoring thanks of a redeemed saint. So hour after hour of that memorable night passed away. One after another, ministers and good men, who had prayed with and comforted the mourners, retired worn out.' But the editor saw one whom no time or toil could weary:—'In the niche of a window', sat a mother, 'for six long hours', holding in her lap the head of a son, a wicked son, who now lay prostrated under the awful power of conviction. Would not God, who had borne with her boy in his years of waywardness, vouchsafe to him 'a sight of the cross'? Her patience was rewarded; before his dark soul a clear light dawned upon the great atonement, and he went home 'rejoicing that even such a sinner as he could be received by the Lamb of God.'

At one period it seemed as if it was *no longer a shower but a fall of awakening influence*. On all hands were men and women seeking God, pressed with an overwhelming sense of their sins, and resolved not to rest till, 'being justified by faith', they had 'peace with God through our Lord Jesus Christ'. A Methodist minister, coming down the town about midnight, worn out with his own share in the blessed labour of pointing penitents to the Cross, found upon the street a group, among whom a Presbyterian minister was earnestly discharging the same office.

Mr Arthur also describes the remarkable awakening which took place in a large school, belonging to the Corporation of London, or that body connected with it, known as the Irish Society, who are the landlords of Coleraine, and of much property around.

In it, a boy was observed under deep impressions. The master, seeing that the little fellow was not fit to work, called him to him, and advised him to go home, and call upon the Lord in private. With him he sent an older boy, who had found peace the day before. On their way they saw an empty house, and went in there to pray together. The two schoolfellows continued in prayer in the empty house till he who was weary and heavy laden felt his soul blessed with sacred peace. Rejoicing in this new and strange blessedness, the little fellow said, 'I must go back and tell Mr—.' The boy, who, a little while ago, had been too sorrowful to do his work, soon entered the school with a beaming face, and, going up to the master, said, in his simple way, 'O, Sir, I am so happy: I have the Lord Jesus in my heart.' Strange words, in cold times! Natural words, when upon the simple and the young the Spirit is poured out, and they feel what is meant by 'Christ in you the hope of glory', and utter it in the first terms that come! The attention of the whole school was attracted. Boy after boy silently slipped out of the room. After a while, the master stood upon something which enabled him to look over the wall of the playground. There he saw a number of his boys ranged round the wall on their knees in earnest prayer, everyone apart. The scene overcame him. Presently he turned to the pupil who had already been a comforter to one schoolfellow, and said, 'Do you think you can go and pray with those boys?' He went out, and, kneeling down among them, began to implore the Lord to forgive their sins, for the sake of him who had borne them all upon the cross. Their silent grief soon broke into a bitter cry. As this reached the ears of the boys in the room, it seemed to pierce their hearts: as by one consent, they cast themselves upon their knees, and began to cry for mercy. The girls' school was above, and the cry no sooner penetrated to their room, than, apparently well knowing what mourning it was, and hearing in it a call to themselves, they, too, fell upon their knees and wept. Strange disorder for schoolmaster and mistress to have to control! The united cry reached the adjoining streets, and soon every spot on the premises was filled with sinners seeking God.

I shall not dwell at any length on the memorable evening spent at Coleraine. First of all I accompanied my host, Mr Macdonald, to his own church, to a meeting for united prayer. The building is comparatively modern, and its erection was the result of the strenuous and self-denying zeal and devotedness of a former venerable pastor, the Rev. James Hunter. Of the company here assembled, the pious elders arrested my special attention. Nearly all were aged and experienced Christians, who, when spiritual religion was low in Coleraine, had been earnest and faithful.

I might dwell also on other prayer-meetings held that evening in different places of worship, at which addresses were delivered by various ministers from a distance. But sweeter still was the closing and special meeting with converts, in a large upper school-room connected with one of the Presbyterian churches. It was crowded to the doors. A pious citizen presided, and around and immediately before him were gathered ministers and lay gentlemen—pilgrims to Ulster, that they might see what God had wrought. As I had marked elsewhere, so at this meeting, the sweetness and jubilant exultation of the song and shout of praise was delightful, and proceeding as it did from a host of recently awakened and rescued ones, it was like the echo of the blessed symphony of adoring gratitude of the upper sanctuary, 'Salvation unto our God that sitteth on the throne, and unto the Lamb.'

Mingled with the prayers and singing was a very impressive and touching address from Dr Murray Mitchell, Free Church missionary at Bombay. He said that he had been about to leave, for his field of toil, but could not go away without first visiting the scenes of the Revival. He blessed God that he had come, and for what he had seen, adding, very naturally and beautifully, as well as with deep emotion, that he would go back to his labours greatly encouraged by the knowledge that many new supplicants would henceforth be pleading before God for the heathen world. In connection with this, he dwelt on the 67th Psalm, 'God be merciful to us'—the church seeking mercy, and quickening for herself;—why? 'That thy way may be known on earth, and thy saving health among all nations.' Never did I feel so strongly or perceive more clearly, that the revival of the church itself, and the awakening and conversion of the dead in sin, are the destined presages and pioneers of the salvation of the race.

I left Coleraine that night with deep emotion. As my friend and brother, Mr M'D., conducted me towards his house in the country, there suddenly fell on my ear the sound of singing at a distance. I thought, from old remembrances, that it must be a band returning from a drinking party, who were singing Bacchanalian and party songs. But my friend knew better, and as we ascended a rising-ground on our way, distant, clear, solemn, and beautiful, there was wafted us from the valley westward, the choral harmony of an air, familiar as it was sacred. The words could not be distinguished, and night threw her sable mantle over the singers. I longed to come in contact with them, and so traversing a country lane rapidly, and just as we reached the cross-yards, lo! we came upon the head of a column of about thirty young men, marching four or five deep, with steady, regular tramp, and filling the listening woods around, and the solemn starlit heavens above, with the high praises of Jehovah. This was a band of 'United Irishmen', indeed. In 1798 such a band might have been seen marching in military order, with firm tread, with gleaming pikes, in silence, under the stimulus of mistaken love of country. But now the Author of peace and Giver of concord had been welding all hearts together by the grace of his Holy Spirit, and inspiring these hymns of praise. These are some of the converts whom I saw two hours ago in the upper room at Coleraine. They are returning home, and, like thousands more over Ulster, they beguile the way with songs of rejoicing. And see! there is a coloured young man (who had been at the meeting, and who had since addressed them seperately), and two of them, with their arms entwined in his, bear him on to a night's hospitable reception and repose.

At our invitation, the young men stop their homeward march and joyous song, and they gather around us. They are then briefly addressed as to the importance of watchfulness, prayer, and holy self-denial, that so they may retain the fervour and freshness of 'first love'. They are reminded that while they may—in the present glow of ardent affection to the Redeemer—suppose that the decay of this love is impossible, yet that the church at Ephesus did lose it (*Rev.* 2:4), and that they need a constant supply of the Holy Spirit's grace, otherwise they may yet dishonour their profession, and deny their Lord. Very touching is it to meet the upturned, thoughtful eyes of the young converts, as words like these fall on their ears. We then sing a part of the 103rd Psalm, which is followed by prayer and the benediction. All of us linger on a spot which is to us as 'the house of God, and the gate of heaven'. At length we part, to meet, I trust in glory. That scene I can never forget—those voices still ring in my ears. Here was one of the many bands, who all through the summer and autumn, have nightly, and ofttimes till near the dawn, poured out their gratitude to God with a kindred fervour and continuance to those seraphs before the throne,

> Who all night long unwearied sing
> High praise to their eternal King.

Next morning, at half-past nine o'clock, was held the daily half-hour meeting for united prayer, in the New Town Hall of Coleraine. Here the Spirit of God had displayed his marvellous power at the opening of the movement, and here this morning was gathered an assembly, of all ranks and ages, including an ex-M.P., strangers from a distance, and many of the labouring classes and the very poor of the town, who had been brought to Christ. There knelt beside me an aged man, evidently poor, with patched clothing, and with worn and rugged face. Oh, with what fervour and importunity, yet in subdued undertones, did he back the petitions offered up by the successive suppliants! Here—as he rose up, and I grasped his hand—I felt was one of those 'secret ones', who in Ireland have long been waiting for and expecting the blessing which now gladdens their hearts, and who continue to wrestle for blessings greater still. Fain would I linger over my reminiscences and impressions in connection with this thrice-favoured town of Coleraine, where ministers, press, and people, have all been baptized with the Holy Ghost. But other scenes are yet before us, and other reminiscences, gladdening and delightful, are to be recorded. Portrush, Dunluce, Derry, and other places, have yet to unfold some of those wonders of life, light, and power which shall always make so memorable to me the month of August, 1859.

CHAPTER 17
PERSONAL OBSERVATIONS
AND INQUIRIES

Carrickfergus—Bushmills—the Giant's Causeway—Dunluce Castle—a
Sabbath at Portrush—remarkable conversion of an old Waterloo soldier—the
young maiden's prayer—the press and the Revival.

ALONG the coast of Antrim, so magnificent and bold, by the
shores of the Lough of Larne, at Glenarm, and the mountainous
region round about, and stretching onward by Carrick-a-Rede and
its famous suspension-bridge, spanning an awe-inspiring gulf on the
sea-shore, and also in the inland belt of Antrim County lying behind,
the Awakening has exercised a powerful influence. Nearer to Belfast,
however, at the old town of Carrickfergus, where the French landed,
about the middle of the last century, and where the military chaplains of Scottish regiments, in the service of King Charles I, in 1641,
formed the first presbytery of a church which now numbers nearly
600 ministers, and nearly half a million of people;—the power of the
Lord has been present to heal and save many souls.

Night after night meetings had been held at Carrickfergus, and
the people had come in crowds to the places of worship and elsewhere. The conversions had been very numerous, and the moral and
social change wrought on the community had been marvellous.

My respected friend, the Rev. J. White of Carrickfergus, has given
a striking account of the daily prayer-meetings held by the workers
in the salt-mines, many hundred feet underground. Here, it may
be interesting to mention that a brother of this gentleman, the Rev.
Verner M. White, LL.D., a minister in Liverpool, and a native of
Ulster, since his return home, has been holding meetings, almost every
evening, in his own church, and that there is good reason for believing that a real revival of religion is progressing in that great town. It is
thus we trust that other visitors and eye-witnesses of the Awakening

in Ulster, have been honoured of God to stir up the people of England and Scotland to pray believingly, penitently, perseveringly, until shall be heard from heaven 'the sound of abundance of rain'.

Immediately after the morning prayer-meeting in the Town Hall of Coleraine had broken up, I was joined by two friends from Tottenham, and proceeded with them on an excursion to the Giant's Causeway. The Irish jaunting-car, with its fast trotting horse, bore us speedily onward to our destination. The day was bright and beautiful; the sun poured its golden tide on fields white to the harvest, and on those farm-houses and white-washed cottages, which met the eye on every side.

As we slowly descended the steep hill which leads into the town of Bushmills, a gentleman came up from the town and passed us. It struck me that this was one who would prove a brother, and who could give us some information. I sprang from the car, and, approaching him, found this was the Rev. W. Oliver, Presbyterian minister of Dunluce.

His work on 'Home Duties', has been reviewed in periodicals and journals, in terms of warmest commendation. Here, at all events, was one who was discriminative and cautious—one, moreover, who, at the beginning, looked doubtfully, if not suspiciously, on the Revival movement. But the Spirit of God came down on his people, and on the neighbourhood around, with such sudden and awful power, that he was bowed to the dust in adoration and astonishment. His church on the top of the hill had been the scene of glorious manifestations, and in our necessarily brief interview, information was given as to the spiritual resurrection of whole families together, and of the moral and social change, which (including the town of Bushmills) had passed over the district, such as caused us again to say, 'What hath God wrought!' I felt a yearning wish to have remained here over the next day (the Sabbath), but that might not be, and so we pressed on to the Causeway. In a written communication with which I have been favoured, Mr Oliver animadverts on the open and pertinacious opposition manifested towards the Awakening by certain ministers and professors of religion. He also says,

Christians are apt to test all by their own moderate standard. Feelings livelier than their own, tears gushing, the voice loud and earnest as if to pierce heaven, no matter who may be near us, the heart throbbing with a sense of sin, the whole frame convulsed as in a death agony, and then scenes of conviction followed by thrilling transports of joy, as if Jesus was seen descending, clothed with a garment of light, carrying a glorious pardon in his right hand,—these are deep and rapturous feelings that soar far above the languid joys of the dwarfish Christian, and lead him either to doubt the reality of his graces, or to asperse the work as the result of epilepsy, hysteria, or madness.

To those who, after calm consideration, believe the Awakening to be the work of God, Mr Oliver appeals thus: 'If you are convinced that it is a genuine work of God, why not carry out your convictions? Is it not the highest honour put upon man, that God takes him into his councils, and makes him his fellow worker?'

I shall not occupy the reader's time or thoughts with a description of that glorious scene, the Giant's Causeway. We might dwell on the boat borne over the long swell of the Atlantic billows, as they rushed on the iron-bound coast; or might tell of the lurid darkness of those giants' caves, where ocean's tides rave incessant, and into whose *chiaro-obscuro*[2] our boat was guided by the stalwart and hardy crew. One might become descriptive and semi-scientific in treading over again those hexagon and pentagon stones, hewn out so accurately, which might almost lead a Sir Roderic Murchison to doubt whether it was not after all man's art and device. But no; even at the Causeway, we could not dissociate our thoughts from that work of the 'Creator Spirit', of which we had already seen much, and before which the grandeur and sublimity of the material became comparatively little in our eyes.

And so was it at Dunluce Castle. There was here the recognized guide, an elderly man who rents the place from the Earl of Antrim. We listen, not uninterested, to his fluent rehearsal of the legends of the castle. He traces for us its different courts and chambers, and indicates

---

[2] *chiaro-obscuro:* the arrangement of light and dark parts in a work of art, such as a drawing or painting, whether in monochrome or in colour, *Ed.*

their probable design and original purposes. He leads us to the narrow bridge, over the fearful gulf below, and which we do not cross. Beyond it, on the topmost rock, are the chief ruins of the stronghold, including the banqueting-hall. There the Macdonalds and the Macquillan chiefs, long at deadly feud, were reconciled by a marriage union between the two houses—thus laying the foundation of the noble house of Antrim. But ere we leave, inquiries are made of the old man about the Awakening. He tells what a change has passed over the people's habits, and how many he knows who have been 'stricken'. Conscience evidently has been busy with him, and he yields assent to the duty pressed on him, of attending to his own salvation ere it be too late.

My friends, intending to spend the Sabbath in Londonderry, set me down near the town of Portrush, and press on themselves to Coleraine, to catch the train at five o'clock, P.M. I wend my solitary way for about the space of an Irish mile, and enter Portrush. It is a village watering-place, beautifully situated, and becoming every year more popular. Yonder, to the east, you see Dunluce Castle; and, further still, the bold majestic Causeway Head. Here, in front, the Skerries island rocks rise out of the water about a mile from the coast; beyond is the mighty Atlantic, and at your feet the gently flowing tide kisses the silver strand.

With a letter of introduction from an Episcopal clergyman at Newry, I soon find my way to the residence of one of his brethren here (the Rev. Mr Ffoliott), who was associated with the Rev. G. V. Chichester, in the cure of the parish. Both are perfectly joined together in the same mind and the same judgment about the Awakening. They had watched with interest its early birth in this parish, and speedily joined most heartily with the Rev. J. Simpson, Presbyterian minister, in hailing it as indeed the Lord's doing, and wondrous in their eyes.

These three excellent men have laboured together in season and out of season. The spirit of brotherly love reigned in the town and neighbourhood. It found practical expression in united meetings for prayer, and in the delivery of short addresses every morning, as well as in special Saturday evening prayer-meetings, convened to implore the Divine blessing on the services of the Lord's day.

Joyfully and thankfully, did I take part in this last-named meeting, as well as in another on the following Monday morning. I asked for 'prayer for London', and urged its claims for the myriads of its population, from the perishing condition and abounding wickedness of multitudes, from the dishonour done to God, from the consideration that if the 'mighty heart' of the world were purified by the Holy Spirit, all nations would realize the blessing and the benefit, and that the pulsations of spiritual life would be felt at the extremities of the globe. Very heartily was the appeal responded to, and it is pleasing for me again to remind the reader that in several places when social prayer is being stately offered in Ulster, the Lord's 'remembrancers' (*Isa.* 62:6) are pleading for an outpouring of the Holy Spirit on London.

The Sabbath which I spent at Portrush will always be memorable to me, as one of the happiest in my life. The weather was beautiful, the sea was calm, the sky was cloudless. A holy tranquillity marked the fair morning, only broken by the sudden and sweet outburst of psalms, and hymns, and spiritual songs, from the pious captain and crew, of a Welsh coaling vessel in the harbour.

It was my privilege to be present at three public services on the Lord's day. The first was in the church of the Rev. J. S. Simpson, whose guest I was, and whose venerable father (an elder at Coleraine) I had heard so clearly expound the Scriptures, and so earnestly plead with God in a congregational prayer-meeting, on the Friday evening before. Very sweet was it to sit among the worshippers this morning, and to join in their songs and prayers, as well as in hearing the word. Many strangers of the upper classes (visitors at the watering-place) were here. But the interesting part of the audience was that made up of the embrowned and stalwart farmers, labourers, fishermen, and their families. Many of them had recently received the truth in the power and love of it, and, with the hallowed earnestness of the new-born and newly rescued, they came to worship the Lord in the beauties of holiness.

The place was crowded to excess. Forms were placed in the aisles and vestibule, and were all occupied. The sermon (evangelical, earnest, and impressive) was preached by the Rev. William McCaw, of

Manchester (Moderator of the English Presbyterian Synod), from the words of our Lord, 'Except ye eat the flesh &c.' The minister of the place offered the closing prayer with great fervour and faith, like a man who had proved ofttimes in that sanctuary the power of believing supplication and intercession. And such had been the case. For example, during the first prayer offered here on a Sabbath morning (August 12th), two persons were brought under agonizing convictions, and were afterwards led to the Saviour's feet, and to an entire surrender of themselves to his blessed service. One of these persons was an old soldier, belonging to a regiment of militia, which was disbanded after the battle of Waterloo. He had lived a life of ungodliness. He was in the church that morning, and the arrows of the Almighty pierced his heart. There was no external agitation or outcry at the time; but very early on Monday morning his wife came into Portrush, and entreated the minister to come and see her husband, as he was in great distress of mind. Mr Simpson immediately went out to his residence.

'He was', writes Mr Simpson in his memoranda (as taken down by me at his house),

> in a most awful agony of prayer. He was sitting up in bed with hands clasped and tears falling from his eyes in torrents—tears which he made no attempt to wipe away. He at once grasped both my hands in his, and held me for a length of time. He exclaimed repeatedly, 'What a wretched sinner I have been!' And soon after relaxing his grasp, he poured out a prayer, of which the following are some sentences:—
>
> 'Oh, blessed Saviour of this world, melt this hard heart, this wretched heart. It *is* a hard heart, a wretched heart. Oh, blessed Saviour, pour out the Holy Spirit on every wretched sinner like me.' And then he said, 'Oh, a heart pressed down!' I asked him, 'What is it that presses down your heart?' He replied, 'Sin, Satan!'
>
> He then resumed his supplication thus: 'Oh, Saviour, free me! Oh, wash me in the fountain opened; oh, *plunge* me in it. I know that—
>
> > He will not put my soul to shame,
> > Nor let my hope be lost!
>
> Oh, blessed Saviour, I will not distrust thee one jot! Oh, dear Saviour—dear Lord and Saviour—forsake me not!'

Was not this a prayer of the Spirit's own prompting? Let it be remembered that this man was, and is, unable to read. He had, indeed, frequently heard of Christ, and of the way of salvation. When asked what enabled him to pour out such a prayer, his reply was, 'It is nothing but the work of heavenly love by the Holy Ghost.' He then exclaimed, 'Oh, heavenly Love, subdue me! Oh, he *will* be my friend!'

The minister, before kneeling at his bedside, asked what he was to pray for? He replied, 'For the abundant outpouring of the Holy Spirit on this wretched heart.' He then exclaimed in broken accents, 'Oh, relief!' and as if resuming his petition, and longing for the Holy Spirit, he added, 'and for all that desire him.'

Reserving further notices of Portrush Sabbath services (in the afternoon in the open air, in the evening in the parish church) at which I was present, I shall conclude the present chapter with the following record of the prayer of the second person brought under conviction on the 12th of August, at public worship. This was a young girl, and thus she pleaded:—

> Oh, Jesus, let thy Spirit come as a dove—let him fold me in his wings. Oh, blessed Jesus, didst thou not say in thy Sermon on the Mount, 'Blessed are they that hunger and thirst after righteousness, for they shall be filled?' Oh, Jesus, have mercy—oh, have compassion! My heart is empty—do thou fill it! Oh, thou wert empty on earth, but art full in heaven. Oh, give me of thy fullness! Oh, Jesus, if I perish, I perish at thy cross!

She then added—

> Rock of ages, cleft for me,
> Let me hide myself in Thee!
>
> I lay my sins on Jesus,
>   The spotless Lamb of God;
> He bore our sins, and frees us
>   From the accursed load.

And yet, prayers like these, abounding all over Ulster at this time, the *Saturday Review*, in its haughty ignorance of facts, and writers at the press, who neither knew what they said, nor whereof they affirmed, were ascribing to hysteria and epidemic fanaticism! As for the Irish Protestant press generally, it either sustained the movement, or regarded it—as the Earl of Carlisle expresses it 'with reverent watchfulness'. This is surely a most weighty fact, and comes out more distinctly when I add, that those Irish papers which have misrepresented, opposed, and ridiculed the Revival, are either under Popish or Unitarian influence.

Others, including the Romish priests, have said that the devil was the author of this movement. The best reply to this irreverent folly is to be found in the words of the Rev. J. S. Moore, of Ballymena, in his *History and Prominent Characteristics of the Present Revival*.

> Very learned and philosophical Christians ascribe many of the results mentioned to excitement, nervousness, and 'epidemic'. The Jews ascribed Christ's works to Beelzebub; and, alas! there are those now who, ignoring the all-sufficiency of Christ, and the existence and power of the Holy Ghost, proclaim the Spirit's work to be a work of the devil.
>
> Every honest inquirer after truth would examine before he decides; and he would form his opinions on the whole, not a part of the evidence. One who had witnessed much, and felt a little, of the salutary change, returning lately from an altar lecture, in which his satanic majesty got all the credit of the 'Revival', and its results, said to his companions—'My friends, all I have to say is, if the devil has done this, there must be a *new devil,* for I'm very sure the old one wouldn't do it at all!'

CHAPTER 18
PERSONAL OBSERVATIONS AND INQUIRIES

Sabbath at Portrush—meeting on Rathmore-hill—Revival sermons, Episcopal and Presbyterian—the Welsh sailors and hymn singing—Monday morning prayer-meeting—the English servant—summary of results—Mr Simpson's testimony—Mr Hanna's letter.

RESUMING our notices of Portrush, and Sabbath services there, I have pleasure in recalling the three services which were held in the afternoon, and during the evening. The first of these was at three o'clock, P.M., and had only been proposed and resolved upon late on the Saturday evening. But by the aid of a few written placards, and by announcements made at the Episcopal and Presbyterian churches, full publicity was given, and on the sides of the romantic hill of Rathmore, overlooking 'the sounding sea', about 500 persons were brought together. Amongst them were many of the upper classes of society, including several magistrates and barristers. The service occupied one hour and a quarter, and was commenced by the Rev. Mr Ffoliott, who delivered an address of ten minutes in length, argumentative and earnest. Addresses were also delivered by four other ministers of religion present, and singing and prayer were appropriately intermingled with those words of exposition and appeal which were spoken.

The weather was very fine, and the scenery around sublime. With the songs of praise mingled the deep diapason of the ocean, as its billows rushed in upon the rocky shore.

At five o'clock the evening service commenced in the parish church, and I was pleased to see the building entirely occupied. Here is always found a spiritual band of worshippers, led to the throne of grace by two godly ministers of the Lord Jesus. In this church some physical agitations have occurred, one person, for example, being struck down during the reading of the Apostles' Creed. But here, with and without such manifestations, the word has often been with power. So also has it been in connection with the Sunday schools of this parish. To this awakening among the young, in contrast with the past, the Rev. G. W. Chichester bears striking testimony in his weighty letter to the *Daily News*.

'However hopeless', he says,

> we may have been in our Sunday-school labours, feeling that all our attempts to impress Scripture upon the mind, have been only like writing on the sand; yet when the heart has been thus powerfully awakened, the conscience convinced, and the spiritual eye opened, how copiously do long-forgotten passages rush into the mind, and how many words and verses, which have hitherto only knocked ineffectually at the door of the outward ear, are received and welcomed within, from whence they soon pour themselves forth in prayer, or praise, or exhortation from the tongue.

Mr C. also refers, in the same letter in the *Daily News,* to marvellous beauty and fullness in prayer, on the part of those converts who have come under his notice—a beauty and a fullness of which we have given two examples, from among the flock of the Presbyterian pastor, the Rev. Jonathan Simpson. Mr Chichester's testimony is the following:

> The working of the Spirit is also evidenced by the wonderful power of prayer, and new gift of utterance which seems to be imparted, not only to the most illiterate, but also to young children. Those who are highly educated, and have long been habituated to such exercises, may well form a humble estimate of their extempore powers, when they hear such sounds as these proceeding from minds hitherto dull, and from tongues hitherto dumb.

But, returning to the parish church, the evening sermon was preached by the Rev. Mr Ffoliott, and to me it was both suggestive and profitable. It was founded on our Lord's parable of the unclean spirit—driven out of a man previously demon-possessed—'seeking rest and finding none', returning to his original abode, so that the last end of the miserable man was worse than his former condition. The preacher gave the text a threefold application and illustration:—first, the expulsion of idolatry from the Hebrew mind and heart, after or rather by reason of the judgment of the Babylonish captivity: for that was a sin to which they never returned; but in the days of our Lord, the evil spirit did return—the nation, 'possessed' with many devils, blasphemed the Son of Man, crucified the Lord of glory, and, because of this, 'wrath came upon them to the uttermost'. Mr Ffoliott applied the subject, secondly, to the case of the professedly Christian church, which had been exorcised of idolatry and superstition by the Reformation, but afterwards fell into corruption and heresy, and which (according to his estimate) is likely to become worse and worse in these last days, so that when the Son of man cometh he shall not find faith in the earth, save in a little remnant. But the third and last portion of this thoughtful discourse was what pleased us best, inasmuch as it was both practical and seasonable. It was a direct dealing with those who had either professed to be truly converted during the present Awakening, or who had been so awed and subdued by a sense of God's presence and power in the midst of the people around, that they had at least given up open sin, and begun with apparent earnestness to seek God in the sanctuary. Weighty were the warnings and solemn the appeals thus urged, and awful, it was shown, would be the doom of those who should appear to run well, and yet draw back to perdition.

A later service was held at the Presbyterian church. Hereafter finding a seat with some difficulty, so crowded was the place—I heard a striking sermon from an able and earnest young minister, the Rev. H. Osborne, of Rathfriland, County Down, on the words, 'Elias must first come.' The leading ideas of the sermon were, that conviction must precede conversion, and that as the ministry of John the Baptist preceded and prepared the way for that of Christ—so, as the Puritan divines have it, 'law work' must make the heart ready for the reception of the gospel of the grace of God.

The shadows of evening were falling, as I retired from the sanctuary, and accompanied a Belfast merchant and his family to their lodgings. Soon after entering the house, the sound of sacred song burst on my ear. I sallied forth, and passed rapidly round to the harbour. There

I stood on the shore, while side by side, the same Welsh captain and crew who had saluted the Sabbath morn with jubilant praise, hallowed its eve and filled the air with song, now plaintive, now joyous.

Mingled together (in a tongue unknown to me, but understood and heard and accepted by the common Father of his dear children) were the rich, full voices of full-grown men, and the soft sweet treble of a fine boy, who not long since had left his Welsh mother's side to begin his service before the mast. One thought, at such a moment as this, of coincident Welsh Revival and Irish Revival, and how also that (oh! that it may be soon) 'the abundance of the sea' shall yet be turned to the Lord.

And so passing back to the hospitable tea table of the worthy Belfast merchant and elder, we closed this happy day with reading, exposition, and prayer.

Next morning (Monday) brought a goodly company of the upper ranks to Lord Antrim's school-room. Here prayers were offered afresh for London and for myself, and I was permitted to say a few words to those assembled. These meetings, with their occasional addresses from strangers, have been divinely owned and blessed. It was only the previous week, that the simple exposition of the 53rd of Isaiah by a minister from Cheshire, was the means of arresting and converting the English servant of an Irish lady, sojourning at Portrush. In her case, there was bodily as well as mental agitation; although she did not cry out aloud, physical weakness oppressed her for a time. But her soul had been truly awakened from the sleep of spiritual death; and, ere long—visited, instructed, and led to the Saviour's feet—hers were the peace, and hope, and holy love of a new-born, trusting soul.

A forenoon visit was paid by invitation to the vicarage, and profitable conference with Mr C. and Mr F. was held. Thus were my latest hours at Portrush filled up; and early in the afternoon, departing from the hospitable Presbyterian manse, I bade Portrush farewell.

All round this neighbourhood, it is emphatically true that the word has been with power—that the Divine Spirit has put forth his might to awaken, convert, and renew—that sinners of every class have been blest, and that God has been abundantly glorified.

The Rev. Jonathan Simpson, at the time of my visit, had conversed with no less than 229 persons who had been brought under the conviction of sin. Many of these had been under physical agitation. Mr S. considered that by far the greater number of these persons truly believed, and had turned unto the Lord. He kept an accurate record of all the cases of anxious inquirers who came under his notice.

Mr Simpson, in a lengthened and most interesting written communication lately received, gives a striking account of the origin and early progress of the Awakening at Portrush, and closes as follows:—

> The number of cases of conviction coming under my notice, or which I have been called to visit in this neighbourhood, are close upon three hundred. Of these, a few have gone back, but they are, thank God, *very few*. The physical prostrations bear but a small proportion to the whole number. The evidences of real conversion are, increased attendance on the means of grace (our places of worship are too small), and the abandonment of vicious habits, such as drinking, swearing, &c. The worship of God is established in many families, and the blessed day of God is better observed.
>
> In my own church, I see in attendance on public worship, some who had been most abandoned drunkards, whom I never expected to see in the house of God. One man, a railway labourer, who when he came to me, under deep conviction of sin, said, 'There is no sin I have not been guilty of but murder and robbery', now can say, 'I obtained mercy.' His wife and grown-up daughter have been visited and blessed. He is now, with his daughter, seeking admission to the Lord's table. He worships God in his family, and a prayer-meeting is held in his house once a week.

Mr Simpson adds, 'The whole country is studded with prayer-meetings, and the *whole face of society is changed.*'

I insert here a letter, from the Rev. Hugh Hanna, of Belfast. It is all the more valuable, as the Romanist and Unitarian press in that town had from the first misrepresented the movement, and heaped abuse upon the ministers most active in its advancement. The reader will observe what Mr Hanna says on misrepresentations and bitter opposition, how that whatever is human and evil is made prominent, while the abounding good is concealed or denied:—

Belfast, Sept. 15th, 1859.

Dear Sir,—The work of the Lord goes prosperously on. The meetings this week have been very largely attended. A Roman Catholic convert appeared at one of these, and delivered his testimony for the truth of God, and against the errors of Rome. Three years ago he was unable to read; now he not only reads, but he is an intelligent young man, a very fair speaker, and is able to take up his Greek Testament and examine the original for himself. His presence excited great interest among the Romanists, and many of them attended. It is to be hoped that the seed of truth has not been sown in vain.

On Tuesday evening a Roman Catholic girl was brought under conviction. Her relatives are all Roman Catholics also. Most of the converts from Romanism have great difficulties to endure—many of them much persecution from their relatives. I visited this girl on the day after. She is fortunately a servant in a Protestant family, and enjoys their protection. She was happy and hopeful, anxious to enjoy more of Christ.

Another Roman Catholic convert, an exceedingly interesting girl, was moved the other evening to make a visit to an aged Romanist, who comes from her part of the country. The old man was furious. This bigotry burst out into a storm of fierce invective, but the girl remained calm and firm. He had heard she was afraid to visit him since her conversion, and he was quite determined to make himself a terror to such apostates. But no: she replied that she was not afraid. She would be happy to visit him if he retained his composure. She had done nothing but what was enjoined in the word of God. She believed the Bible to be the word of God, that it was her duty to read it and obey it. Therefore, she was a Protestant, and such, by the grace of God, she would remain. Her attitude and arguments were not without impression on the venerable bigot, and he at last relented, and even admitted that she ought to obey her own convictions of the right.

The Lord has done great things in Berry Street among the Romanists. Consequently, the priests and their sturdiest adherents are exceedingly mad against us. The press teems with the vilest productions that Romanism can engender. Many of them are grossly libellous—all of them abominably filthy, with the purpose of disparaging the Revival, and warning Romanists against attendance at any of the meetings. To a large extent they are successful in kindling the hatred of the masses, and I cannot traverse any of the streets without encountering insults, which evince the desperate demoralization of Belfast papacy. I believe it never was so bad. The devil seems to be preparing himself against the truth, by more mischievous efforts among the Romanists. But the Lord knoweth them that are his, and God's people shall hear his voice, saying, 'Come out of her, my people, that ye be not partakers of her plagues.'

We have now about forty weekly meetings for scriptural instruction and prayer connected with my congregation, and scattered over all the town. We have chosen the most necessitous localities for their establishment. They are working well. They are managed by the active and godly people, chiefly the young people of the congregation. The average attendance at each may be about fifty. I attended one of them the other evening, and I never breathed a more heavenly atmosphere than that which pervaded it.

The converts are maintaining their profession with hopeful consistency. Of many of them we have now three months' proof. I do not know, within my own sphere of observation, a single case of backsliding. The Lord is putting his seal on the work in such a manner as to call forth the gratitude of the churches. The testimony from all parts of the country is uniformly to the credit of the young believers. God has gotten to himself great glory by so marvellous a work.

Human infirmity will appear and somewhat mar the work in which God employs man as an instrument. Hence the irreligious press here makes a great outcry against a few evils that have arisen. It speaks as if there were nought but evil. It refuses to make honest acknowledgment of the mighty good that has resulted from the Revival. The good so vastly preponderates, that the evil is as nothing to the good. 'The Lord hath done great things for us, whereof we are glad.' Sincerely yours,

Hugh Hanna.

CHAPTER 19
PERSONAL OBSERVATIONS
AND INQUIRIES

Letter from a minister on furlough—conversion of Romanists—companions
in travel—Derry: its memorable past and 'glorious present'—meetings—
marvellous Revival issues—an exclusive spirit at Derry, and its contrasts elsewhere—testimony of the Rev. R. Smyth of Derry.

REFERRING to over-taxed yet willing workers, I found several
such, absent from their posts when I visited Ulster. But they
did not leave till compelled to do so, by being absolutely broken
down. The comfort of such toilers is, that they had already filled
their bosoms with the sheaves, and that they left behind them such
life, and zeal, and fire in the new converts, and such spiritual eager-
ness and earnestness on the part of all, that they had no grounds to
fear that the cause of Christ would suffer serious detriment by their
absence.

One congregation (that of Ballycarry, in the county of Antrim),
finding its pastor fast failing in health, insisted on his leaving for a time,
in order that by rest and change of scene he might regain his strength.
For this end, in the greatness of their love, they at once provided him
with ample means, and he left home accordingly. Little did I expect
him to turn his face towards the metropolis; but early one morning
in September, when passing the General Post Office, I suddenly came
upon the good minister of Ballycarry, the Rev. John Stuart. He was
sauntering round the building, and bore the plain trace of a bronzed
and veteran soldier, whose campaign in his Lord's service had well-
nigh cost him his life. His heart was still at home, although his footsteps tended towards France; and ere he left London he furnished
me with the following deeply interesting and most gladdening
account of what the Lord had done in a wide district of Antrim
County. Let this letter (and I write this advisedly) be received not

only as an authentic statement, but as furnishing a sample of what God has done, in wondrous grace, in many districts of Ulster. Mr S., has been for a quarter of a century an ordained minister, and is a man eminent for zeal, piety, gravity, sincerity, and conscientiousness. His communication is as follows:—

> I do not think that any locality has been more favoured with the out-pouring of God's Spirit than our own. Ballycarry is the cradle of Irish Presbyterianism. Here Bryce [one of the ministers of the Church of Scotland who followed the early colonists to Ulster] commenced his labours in 1613.
>
> Before holding our communion in May last, a feeling of solemnity pervaded the great mass of the people. Our week-day services were more largely attended than heretofore, and on the Sabbath we had one hundred communicants above any former occasion.
>
> Immediately after, as we then commenced prayer-meetings every evening, God poured out his Spirit largely on the people. In the course of about six weeks about one hundred and fifty persons were 'stricken down'. These were mostly young people, but since that time many elderly persons, some as old as seventy, have been converted.
>
> Of nearly three hundred persons awakened, I form the most sanguine hopes as to their future faithfulness. There have been no backsliders. Once I found it difficult to tell where family prayer was observed; the difficulty now is to tell where it is not.
>
> 'Oh, Mr S.', one woman said to me, 'if you knew how happily we (the family) live now! We have family worship morning and evening. John, or Isabella, or Jane, as the case might be, has conducted it.'
>
> Five Arian families have joined my communion, and also a considerable number of the younger branches of Arian families. All over an extensive district of fifty-four square miles meetings, attended by hundreds, are conducted by converts.
>
> And then such prayers! No circumlocution, no! Earnest crying and tears. 'Lord, give me the faith of the dying thief! Lord, give me the faith of the centurion.'
>
> Our Sabbath school has been quadrupled since June, and my Bible class contains one hundred and fifty converts. The church is filled—pews, aisle, vestibule, and pulpit stairs. I expect on my return nearly one

hundred candidates for communion in October. Truly a cloud of mercy, surcharged with blessings, has poured down a copious shower upon us. Oh! what love, what life, what zeal!

Some of my most gifted converts were men apparently on the broad way to hell. The females of the congregation have their prayer-meetings also. Their prayers are peculiarly beautiful, scriptural, and sublime. The first female convert, who was for three days under deep conviction, is incessant in her prayers for the conversion of a regardless father. In travelling over this extensive district, I have often seen girls turn off into some side path lest they should see me! Now they run to meet me, look me straight in the face, like educated females, and, their eyes sparkling with delight, are the first to introduce religious subjects, and tell me of their love to Jesus.

One young girl, a Romanist, whom her father brutally beat and turned out of doors, said she would suffer her body to be burned before she would worship saints any more.[3]

The Rev. Robert Sewell, Independent minister at Derry, was a sojourner at Portrush during the time of my visit there. He was obliged, in order to save his life, to abandon the field of delightful yet overwhelming labour which he had been called so unexpectedly to cultivate, in connection with the sudden influx of the mighty Revival wave upon that old Protestant city. To the results of the great Awakening at Derry, in connection with a visit thither, I shall have occasion immediately to refer. Pleasant and profitable was it to converse with this excellent man, who has testified his opinion as to the present state of the Irish Roman Catholic mind in Ulster in the following published statement:—

I have no fear of successful contradiction when I express my solemn belief that there have been more Romanists converted in Ulster—truly converted to God—since this Awakening commenced, than have been converted in Ireland for the last half century; and that the Romanists

---

[3] Since his return home, Mr Stuart writes me that the work of grace had progressed with marvellous power in his absence, and that not less than two hundred additional members have been added to his church. Drunkenness had ceased. At Ballycarry fair, not a single member of the church went into a public-house.

of Ulster are more willing to hear the gospel now, than they have been since the days of Bedell.

Bedell was a bishop in the days of Elizabeth, who at fifty years of age set to himself the task of acquiring a knowledge of the native Irish language (the mother tongue of the population, to which they clung, the use of which England foolishly proscribed), and preached to the natives with great acceptance.

Mr Sewell's statement, let it be observed, refers to 'the Romanists of Ulster'. It is strictly correct, save as to the Romanists of Belfast, whose 'desperate demoralization' and priest-produced rage against the Revival, was indicated by Mr Hanna in his recent letter. Mr Sewell could not say so much of the Romanists in the other provinces of Ireland. The Awakening among the Protestant population in Ulster first attracted the attention, roused the inquiries, and next impressed the minds, hearts, and consciences of many Romanists. They could not but see the social change; they acknowledged that *it,* at least, was good; some of them mingled in crowded meetings, the arrows of the Spirit pierced their hearts, and to 'Jesus only' they cried for mercy.

In the train which conveyed me, on a bright and beautiful afternoon in August, from Coleraine to Londonderry, I found myself in the same carriage with the excellent Mr Hargreaves (a well-known English Wesleyan minister), and also with Mr Budgett, of Bristol, son of the 'successful merchant'. I had previously met these gentlemen on their journey northward. On the morning of the day on which I was brought into their pleasant and profitable society once more, they had paid a visit to the Giant's Causeway. There they had *improvised* a little congregation in the open air, and had spoken to the people on eternal realities, and on life and salvation through a Saviour's name.

Mr Budgett expressed himself more than surprised with what he had already seen in Ulster, especially at Belfast. He very nobly and honestly acknowledged that he had been more than once staggered by attempts in England at getting up Revival excitement as a part of machinery and means—well intended, but dubious in their character and results. But with regard to this movement in Ireland, he considered that it was indeed Divine, and that human appliances had not been the means of kindling the flame.

The magnificent cliffs of Downhill are passed; the sea-shore, with its beautiful sands, is no longer nigh at hand; Malin Head, the northernmost promontory of Donegal, comes out into bolder prominence. Yonder is Lough Foyle, debouching into the ocean; and the river Foyle, up which the relieving ships sailed in 1690, during the memorable siege of Derry. That portion of the river, with its villa-crowned banks, is pointed out to us where the boom had been broken through by one of the ships, under the impetus of a broadside.

We at length arrive at the railway station. The 'Maiden City' is before us, pictorial in its culminating streets on the hill-side, and gloriously historical and heart-stirring too to every Protestant patriot, in the reminiscences of a successful struggle here waged by a handful of brave men against the army of the bigoted James II.

Yonder stands out against the luminous western sky the monument of Governor Walker, who, through famine and treachery within, and amidst onslaughts and incessant cannonades from without, rung out from day to day cheery words, which were to the besieged as the breath of the trumpet. And yonder, too, is the spire of the venerable cathedral, within whose walls, during the siege, Episcopalians and Presbyterians worshipped alternately, and in whose burial-grounds around, sleeps the dust of those heroes who perished. Let any Christian read Lord Macaulay's chapters on the siege, and he cannot but acknowledge that God's great power interposed there, to put an end to arbitrary power, and to secure to England the inestimable blessings of civil and religious liberty.

And has the 'Lord of all power and might' been visiting this place, by manifestations of his special grace? Is the great Awakening in Derry? Has the spiritual revolution—by which Ulster generally has been turned upside down—come hither also? 'Yes', we reply; 'it is even so, and the evidence and proof are at hand.'

I cross the bridge of Derry, and enter the city, under promise and engagement to supply the pulpit of the Rev. J. Sewell, whom I have left at Portrush, in enforced silence and necessary absence from home.

Here I am hospitably received by a Christian merchant, R. McCorkle, Esq., and afterwards make my way to the earliest daily evening services. The hour is a little after six o'clock, and, accompanied by a minister from Bristol, I enter the Victoria Market. Here I find a congregation of several hundred persons gathered under a covered roof (the place open at the sides), with the Rev. Dr Denham presiding on a platform, and Mr Hargreaves standing in front, and earnestly and affectionately speaking to the people. There is deep solemnity, as well as profound attention, but no visible excitement. At the close of the address, a psalm is sung—with what heart and voice!—and after prayer and the benediction, the people, according to nightly custom, hurry away to the various places of worship for additional services. Dr Denham carries off my friend, the Bristol pastor, while I repair to fulfil my promise to the disabled Independent brother, at his new and handsome chapel. Dr Denham's church is exactly opposite, and yet there is no antagonism here. Both places have been, during the summer, the scenes of marvellous mercy. Dr Denham has been one of the most successful, in the best sense, of the Ulster Presbyterian ministers; singular evangelical fullness and unction have marked his public career in Derry, and he has been made the spiritual father of many souls. And yet, compared with the present—the glorious present—the past was so dwarfed into littleness, that Dr Denham has deliberately declared that during the last summer he had seen more real conversions, a large number of sinners truly brought to believe in the Redeemer, and to walk in newness of life, than during the whole period of his pastorate in Derry, extending over twenty years.

As for Mr Sewell, by the blessing of the Lord of the harvest, he, too, had filled his bosom with sheaves. The chapel, where I officiated at night, was indeed 'holy ground'. There had been 'seen' Jehovah's 'goings in the sanctuary'. Under that roof the arrows of the Spirit had flown numerous and swift from the 'bow' of that great King, who goeth forth 'conquering and to conquer' (*Rev.* 6:2).

'The 12th of June', writes Mr Sewell,

is the time from which we date this great Awakening in our city. On that day, on the invitation of one or two churches, some of the newly

155

converted were brought from Ballymena to address meetings. A united
meeting was held in the First Presbyterian Church, when some of their
young men spoke. Many were moved to tears, while some had to be taken
into the vestry to prevent their disturbing the congregation. Next day
a general feeling of solemnity was manifested by all classes, and many
under conviction were spoken to in their houses or places of business.
United meetings were appointed to be held daily in the Corn Market
and Corporation Hall, to be conducted by ministers of several churches,
who all heartily joined, except Episcopalian ministers, who held aloof.
Besides these were meetings for prayer every night.'

Referring to meetings for prayer held at Derry, Mr Sewell men-
tions a half-hour thus spent at the dinner hour by working men;
and next the meeting held in the Corn Market at 7 P.M. attended
by numbers varying from 500 to 5,000 persons. This was succeeded
by meetings for prayer in the several churches, which continued till
10 P.M. ('the people would not leave sooner'), and then 'the anxious
remained for direction'. 'Seldom have I got out of the vestry before
twelve o'clock, and sometimes not without difficulty till long after
midnight.'

As to the effects on ministers, churches, and the world, Mr Sewell
bears the most striking testimony.

> Ministers are greatly quickened, realizing more than ever their interest
> in Christ, getting more confidence in the power of truth, the effects of
> prayer, the presence of the Spirit; and they preach if not better, yet more
> appropriately and earnestly.

And as to 'churches', we are told that there had been 'stirred up among
members, an anxious inquiry about personal salvation, and the prin-
ciple of purity of communion'; and 'the dormant energies of many
true Christians have been called forth. In not a few cases we have
persons leading in prayer, expounding the Scriptures, ministering to
the careless, and directing the anxious. These persons had been members of Christian churches, but previous to the Awakening had been
merely anxious as to *their own salvation.*' Alas! is not this the spiritual
condition of many Christian professors in all our churches at this
moment?

As to effects 'on the community at large', Mr Sewell said,

> they are equally marked. There is no class, from the highest to the low-
> est, whatever may be their creed, who have not been influenced to some
> extent. Even Romanists stand in awe, and many of them, to my own
> knowledge, have professed conversion; whilst among Protestants there
> are few persons who have not been arrested and brought to Christ.
> Our police-courts, our streets at night, and the comparative absence of
> drunkenness on our market-days, attest how widespread and powerful
> is the reformation. If need be I could adduce facts to prove this, and
> more.

Referring to the state of 'the streets at night', I have here to mention a remarkable fact as to the effect of the Revival on the 'great social
evil'. In the city of Derry, by reason of the famine of 1846-7 driving
many poor creatures to extreme want, and also exposing them to the
influx of foreign sailors coming with grain ships from the Mediter-
ranean, the social vice had become rampant.

There was up to a recent period a far larger proportion here of
'unfortunates' than is usual. But mark the effects of the Awakening as
related to me by a Christian merchant in Derry. 'One half of them',
said he, 'are in the penitentiary by their own desire, the other half have
almost all left the town!'

Mr Sewell's most interesting statement concludes thus:—

> I thank God for what is done at large, especially for what *I* have wit-
> nessed. At least 300 have been converted in my own chapel, or in con-
> nection with my own efforts. Many of them may not join my church,
> as they belong to other congregations. Some have joined; others would
> have joined had I been at home. The building up of a sect is to me,
> however, of less importance—much less—than to see Zion in all her
> branches prosperous.

Would to God that in Derry all Protestant ministers had shown
like catholicity of spirit; but it will be observed that Mr Sewell states
that the Episcopalians did not join the united movement. The Archdeacon of Derry published an address to the clergy, which was approved
of by the Bishop, in which the good work of the Spirit was clearly

acknowledged. But (alas! that there should have been a *but* in the matter), inasmuch that the Church of England clergy could not join other denominations, 'except on the principles' of the latter, he recommended that they should keep aloof, and hold meetings of their own.

The effect of this had been (as stated to me by several parties) damaging to the best and highest interests of the Church of England in Derry. Services were held in the cathedral and in school-rooms; but they were thinly attended, and there was little life. The law of love had been violated, and the result was that the Episcopal fleece is almost dry, while that of the Evangelical Nonconformists—who had asked for Episcopal co-operation in vain—was wet with the dew of Hermon.

Oh, how different in the parish of Portrush, where Mr Chichester and Mr Ffoliott went lovingly hand in hand with Mr Simpson. How different in the parish of Killinchy, where the Episcopal rector, the Hon. and Rev. H. Ward, co-operated zealously and lovingly with his Presbyterian brother, and where his family readily worship at times, on week-days or Lord's days, in the Presbyterian church.

And how pleasant and delightful to contemplate the beautiful union of mind and heart at the meeting of the Evangelical Alliance at Belfast! The Bishop of Down and Connor, Dr Knox, presided at the opening, and the Moderator of the Irish General Assembly delivered the inaugural address; its burden, 'a flock divided into many bands, and led by many under-shepherds; but fed in the same ample pastures—knowing, owning, and following the one great Shepherd of souls.'

At a subsequent session of the Alliance, the Bishop spoke thus of the Revival:—'I rejoice to think that this movement has taken nothing of a sectarian aspect, but that, like the dew of heaven, it has fallen on all the land, and blessed the increase.'

In my visit to Londonderry, I found one of its most valued ministers absent—his health having given way in consequence of overwhelming labours in connection with the Awakening. Subsequently I addressed some special inquiries to him, and I have now the pleasure of laying his reply before the reader. This letter traces the antecedents and precursors of the Revival in Derry, and furnishes a fresh glimpse of that preparatory work in Ulster, by which 'the way of the Lord' was made straight. It is emphatically true that the faithful and extensive sowing of good seed, accompanied by intense desire and by earnest and united prayer for a blessing, did precede and pioneer the Revival:—

Londonderry, Oct. 17, 1859.

My Dear Friend,—In the midst of very pressing congregational duties, I snatch an hour to reply to your letter, and give you what must of necessity be an imperfect sketch of the great religious Revival which God has graciously vouchsafed to us during the past summer. As you will most probably avail yourself of the experience of brethren in other parts of the province, I shall confine myself to that portion of the field where I have myself laboured and rejoiced. I shall thus avoid giving hearsay evidence on this momentous question, and by keeping within the limits of personal observation, I cannot be ensnared into any statement for whose authenticity I cannot vouch.

Perhaps the time has not come for writing a complete narrative of the Revival, as we are hardly yet out of the blaze of spiritual visitation; but sufficient time has elapsed to enable us to form a tolerably correct estimate of the results, actual and probable, of this marvellous movement—a movement without any parallel in the history of Ulster.

Ever since the news of the American Revival of 1857 reached our shores, ministers and people felt motions at their hearts impelling them to renewed earnestness at a throne of grace, that God would stretch out his arm for some great spiritual deliverance in this country. The pulpit sounded forth sermons on the work of the Spirit, on the necessity of a new birth, and kindred subjects, whilst the glories of the cross were set face to face with the consciences of the hearers. Presbyterians met for special consultation and prayer on the subject of 'Revival'; and at the annual meeting of our General Assembly in Derry, in 1858, two sessions were set apart for conference and addresses on this question. The addresses were listened to by an audience of two thousand persons, and the deepest solemnity pervaded the vast assembly. Members of all evangelical churches were present, and a very general impression was produced that there was something more in religion than mere 'bodily exercise, which profiteth nothing'. Nine months passed, and then we began to hear that an unprecedented earnestness pervaded certain districts of Antrim County.

The next news was that cases of sudden conversion, attended by strange, bodily affections, were taking place every day and every night, at prayer-meetings in churches, in private houses, in school-houses, barns, and even in the open air. It soon became a subject for newspapers. God used the secular press as a vehicle for the marvellous tidings, and before many weeks had elapsed, the Antrim Revival was the topic of conversation in railway carriages, in news-rooms, clubs, firesides, and streets; and even merchants laid down their pens in counting-houses, to talk of the wonderful 'manifestations'. Ministers and others visited the localities where the work was going on, and came back baptized and fired with fresh zeal for Jesus. The tide flowed northward, eastward, and westward, and early in June, the waters of life had reached us in the city of Derry.

The secondary agency employed by the Holy Spirit in commencing the work here was that of four young converts from County Antrim, brought here by the Rev. Jackson Smyth, of Armagh, all of whom addressed a united meeting in the First Presbyterian Church. Three persons cried out for mercy during the meeting. A thrilling sensation passed through the great assemblage, as these mourning cries were uttered, and the thousands present felt each for himself and herself, 'I have a soul to be saved.' God had touched some mighty spring at his own throne, and the vibrations were felt in our meeting that night. Hundreds went home with an arrow in their heart. The 'Revival' had begun in Derry. Perhaps never since Derry was a city,—and it has seen stirring and awful days in its eventful history,—did so many souls ache upon sleepless beds as on that mysterious night. They rose in the morning unrefreshed, with the hand of God heavy on them. Some have told me how they struggled during the silent watches; some wept for hours, others felt an awful petrifaction in their bosom, and others, in wild frenzy, muttered blasphemy upon their beds. Monday passed, and another united meeting was held in the First Presbyterian Church that evening. The building was crowded to excess. Several ministers addressed the meeting in calm and unimpassioned solemnity. The meeting felt still as a grave; the stillness was fearful: those who were present will never forget it. At length the silence was broken by unearthly cries, uttered simultaneously by several in different parts of the church, and in the course of a few minutes the vestry of the church was filled with individuals who lay in mental agony and absolute bodily prostration.

Socialists may talk of 'hysteria' and 'catalepsy'; but I can testify that, so far as I know, not one of those who were stricken that night, and who professed to have found peace in Jesus, has gone back to the world. If hysteria produce such results as these, then I pray that every man, woman, and child in Ireland may become 'hysterical' before the end of the year.

It would be impossible to enumerate the cases of conviction and conversion that occurred that evening. In one pew no less than four young men were stricken in soul, and afterwards found peace. One of these (a merchant in the city, and a man of good education, morality, and high intelligence) told me his experience. He thought he saw hell opened before his eyes, and that there was an irresistible power forcing him headlong into it. He looked round, and said to himself, 'I know where I am; this is the church where I usually worship; I am under a delusion.' But still he looked down, and there was hell. He rose from his seat, and convulsively seized hold of the back of the pew; but hell was sending forth its smoke in his very face. A shudder passed over him, and his heart sighed the awful words, 'My sins!—my sins! I am lost!' He staggered out of the meeting, and went homewards. In describing his feelings on the way home, he told me, 'Had anyone asked me, Where are you going? I would have answered, in calm despair, I am going to hell!' Making his way to his room, he sought relief in cries. This continued for an hour or two, and then a heavenly radiance overspread his soul, the promises of grace came flooding his now sanctified memory; he seized them joyously, and rose a Christian. His first race in the dark dead of night, was to his partner in business, to urge him to flee from the wrath to come. 'Tap, tap, tap', at his friend's door. 'Who's there?' 'I must come in!' 'Come in.' The door opens, and the happy convert cries out, 'I have found Christ, and I have come to tell you.' Prayer went up from that bedroom to heaven, and three days after, the other had fled for refuge, and laid hold of the hope set before him.

This is one case—the type of hundreds in the city of Derry. I could fill a volume with them. I am almost sorry I have given you this one case, for I feel such a desire to go on, and give you more. But I must deny myself, and have consideration for you and your readers.

Drunkards have become sober, profligates have turned into the fold of Jesus, worldlings have ceased to go on their knees to gold, and now worship the living and true God; swearers have ceased to burn their lips with blasphemy; some publicans have given up their unsanctified calling; altars are erected in families where no incense burned for years; ceremonial professors have thrown aside aids to family devotion, and refuse now to be hampered by forms of prayer, but give vent to the simple feelings of their souls at a throne of grace; our churches are crowded with eager worshippers, who now understand what we mean when we preach on Christian experience; prayer-meetings are frequented thrice a day still in the city; Bible-classes are now of unwieldy size, and are more like what our congregations used to be; our Sabbath schools are nearly doubled; and, in short, there is now everywhere a reality in worship and in life.

On Saturday last I was talking to an intelligent man, who was imbued with Unitarian principles, and he said to me, 'Mr Smyth, you know I did not agree with the doctrines of the *Westminster Confession,* but I have been thinking that the system cannot be bad that has produced results, such as I have witnessed during the last five months.' That is one of the most valuable testimonies I have heard in this city. This man attends the prayer-meetings, is honest and earnest, and I regard him as in a most interesting state of mind and soul.

I am, my dear friend, still wondering at God's great love to the city of my dwelling. My own soul has been watered, and now, when I preach, I feel that there are hundreds of hearts in unison with my own. God bless you, and your beloved people, and your great city.

Excuse great haste, as I have written this just before going out on Monday morning to pastoral visitation.

Ever yours, affectionately in the Lord,
RICHARD SMYTH.

CHAPTER 20
PERSONAL OBSERVATIONS
AND INQUIRIES

A morning visit to Derry's walls—the onward journey—Donagheady, and its pastor—the Wesleyan Chapel—Adam Clarke and his first sermon—district Awakenings—Strabane and Raphoe—Omagh and the Revival gathering—the Diocese of Clogher—Enniskillen: its Protestantism and prosperity—the work inaugurated—a missionary deputy, and a good report.

R ISING early, and having a lengthened day's journey before me, I emerged into the streets of Derry just as the smoke began to ascend from the peat-lighted morning fires, and as the small dealers and grocers were taking down their shutters. I passed rapidly towards the city proper—having slept outside the old historic boundaries—and ascended the hill up which pressed so often the surging wave of James's invading army, close to the famous 'Water Gate', from thence as frequently to be victoriously repelled by the indomitable garrison within. Soon I am *on* the city walls, commanding a delightful view of hill, and tower, and town, with the Foyle flowing onward through rich demesnes and villas towards the Atlantic. I pause at Governor Walker's monument, and look with a strange feeling of respect at 'Roaring Meg'—that piece of ordnance, which to every Derry Protestant is so suggestive of stirring memories, and which—silent and voiceless all the year beside—on the anniversary of the shutting of the gates, makes its voice to be heard in echoing thunder-tones.

Next, I pass onward towards the Cathedral. It is early, and the gates are shut; but I look through them, and see the piled-up mounds of human dust, and think how sleep there, the defenders who died because of 'the straitness of the siege', or from the hostile shot of the Papal foe without. But this day of grace, in August, 1859, tells me of *a glorious present* in Derry—

163

> No war or battle's sound
> Is heard the place around;

and yet here, during the last two months, a siege against a band of rebels against the Everlasting King has been successfully crowned, and multitudes of hearts have surrendered to the rightful claims of Emmanuel. For Protestantism political, there is now Protestantism living, loving, unselfish, charitable, earnest, and spiritual. True, the Romanists of this town are very numerous—as these sign-boards in the humbler streets testify, and as the very physical aspect and social squalor of many men, women, and children of the humbler classes declare too plainly; but yet even from among *these,* trophies have been won, while over the dry bones of an orthodox yet dead Protestantism, the breath of the Lord God has passed with resurrection power.

After a hasty breakfast, and the deposit of a goodly parcel of tracts in the hands of my host, R. M., Esq., who is just the man to dispose of them aright, I wend my way to the railway station, and 'Enniskillen', to the south-west, is my destination. Here I find myself once more with the Tottenham gentleman and his worthy pastor, in whose pleasant society I had visited the Causeway. As we sweep rapidly onward, Mr W., the pastor, points out to me an opening in the hills, to the left, where, the previous evening, with his friend, he had visited a Presbyterian elder, at his mansion, and where he found a glorious work of Revival in progress. The Presbyterian minister is the Rev. Francis Porter, and the congregation derives its name (Donagheady) from the district so called. Mr Porter is a man of much energy both of mind and body, and has always preached with ability and fullness; but, like others of his brethren, he has found a blessed illustration of the truth that it is not by might nor by power, but by the Spirit of the Lord of Hosts. Now, his hands were more than full of work, and we afterwards read with great interest his very striking appeal, addressed to the *Londonderry Standard*, asking for help to the Ulster pastors from those who have time on their hands. For, although visitors did, and do give help as they pass along from place to place, yet this is chiefly on what may be called the 'trunk line' of the Revival. There are very many other districts where the work of God has gone on with such power, and that silently, that the ministers are overwhelmed with toil. Are there not some, yea, many, in England, who are without pastoral charges, who have both time and means to respond to the cry from Ulster, 'Come over, and help us?' To give an Ulster pastor a holiday, would be a doubly seasonable service rendered to the cause of Christ by any English minister who has leisure on his hands. Mr Porter also argued powerfully in favour of lay agency, of which he was judiciously and wisely, making extensive use in his own district.

But—returning to my journey—what is that little building in the middle distance? It is a Wesleyan chapel, and memorable as the spot where Adam Clarke preached his first sermon. My fellow traveller has been there the night before, and has heard from the villagers how that chapel is now, to many, the house of God and the gate of heaven. On the Sabbath evenings, over those eastward hills, and from the region around, come troops of peasantry—including many who hitherto were utterly indifferent to Divine ordinances—and amongst them the arrows of the Mighty fly swift and fast, as, under the blue canopy of heaven, earnest prayers are offered, and there is addressed to them the word of life. Truly, Londonderry County, generally, has participated largely in the refreshing showers of the Spirit. The London Religious Tract Society has received and responded to many applications from that county. In the letters thus forwarded, was one from Faughanvale, as follows:—

> If you could favour me with a grant of tracts immediately, you would confer a great boon on this neighbourhood. Such anxiety about the 'one thing needful' was never manifested before. Hundreds in this place, who were hitherto careless, are asking, 'What must we do to be saved?'

In like manner, the Rev. Mr Smyth, rector of Errigal, wrote from near Garvagh:—

> I have been twenty-seven years rector of this parish, and never before witnessed even the most remote approach to what is now going on. Vice and immorality, of every sort, lessened to an incredible extent, and oaths scarcely ever heard, or drunkenness seen; the houses of religious worship well filled, both on the Sabbath and week days. Even the Roman

Catholics now seem afraid to speak against the work, which at first
they ascribed to the devil. I have witnessed persons of all ages, from five
years to nearly eighty, awakened to a sense of their sins, and calling for
mercy through a crucified Saviour; and in no instance have I seen one
backslider.

These are but specimens of what had been done in that favoured
county. Along the southern bank of the Lower Bann, through the
linen and agricultural districts of Aghadowey, at Garvagh and the
neighbourhood, and in the town of Strabane and Raphoe, as well as
in a wild mountainous district called Kilmore—where 'the people,
almost all Protestants', were 'stirred to the very depths of their hearts'
—the Lord had done great things.

And here—in our progress—we are at Strabane station, and there
is the town itself, on the left; and in the valley opposite, to the west, is
Raphoe, which helps to complete the ecclesiastical title of the Bishop of
the diocese, who is 'Bishop of Derry and Raphoe'; and of that town of
Raphoe I heard much that was very deeply interesting, but on which
I may not further dwell.

A few stations onward, we arrive at Omagh, and here the police
point out to us a large covered building, which, the previous week, had
been filled by a great congregation, gathered together to hear Revival
addresses, and to engage in prayer.

Omagh is the county town of Tyrone. There, in olden times, I have
been on deputation for the Bible Society, with one who is now a Dean
of the Established Church; and there Protestantism is strong. But into
it new life has been infused; and all over Tyrone, including Dungannon, Cookstown, and other districts, the Awakening has exercised more
or less influence. Thus, at Gortin, County Tyrone, a correspondent of
the *Derry Standard* reported;—

The good work is still progressing steadily in this locality. The meetings
are not, however, so large on week-day evenings as formerly, on account
of the harvest operations being proceeded with, and the Protestant population being sparely scattered over a large district of country. I am sure
that as soon as the harvest is over, the week-day evening services will be
better attended than ever, from the deep impression which the Revival

movement has made on all classes. The physical manifestations have decreased, but the great work of sinners turning to God is progressing as rapidly as formerly. The change effected on the great mass of the Protestant community is truly wonderful. As remarkable instances of this, there were two marriages lately in the neighbourhood, and the guests, after attending the wedding, in the morning, were at the prayer-meeting in the evening; formerly, on such occasions, the guests remained drinking all night. What is still more remarkable is, the change that has taken place at wakes. A respectable Protestant farmer died in this neighbourhood on the 28th August, and, instead of the disgraceful scenes which usually take place, there was praying, reading of Scripture, and singing; the religious services not ceasing for the two days and nights of the wake. The number attending this wake was so great, that on the evening of the 29th they had to go out to an adjoining field to sing and pray, during which time a young girl, a daughter of the deceased, was brought under conviction of sin, and it is hoped truly converted. This has been the means, I believe, of doing a great deal of good; the exclamation of all who attended was, What a change! Several families in the district between whom a deadly feud existed, and where the members would not speak to each other, were now on the best terms. In the neighbouring districts of Cappagh, Glenelly, Corick, and Newtonstewart, the work was progressing rapidly, and at nearly all the meetings in these districts there have been numbers of convictions, accompanied by prostration.

The number of persons brought under the power of the Holy Spirit in the County Tyrone since I passed along its western borders, has very greatly increased. In October last the Religious Tract Society received an application for tracts and books from an Episcopal clergyman in the diocese of Clogher, who stated that six weeks before a case of visible conviction was witnessed in his parish, and that fifty cases of similar physical agitation afterwards occurred during service on successive Lord's days. Throughout the parish 250 persons had been brought to Christ, and 'new life' was the clergyman's emphatic description of the blessed change which had been so suddenly accomplished.

Another clergyman writing from the same diocese stated, that there was a population of 5,000 persons in his parish, and that there was scarcely a family in which one person at least, and often more, had been truly awakened.

The hour of noon is at hand as we approach Enniskillen, a frontier Protestant town. Its inhabitants fought a successful cavalry action with King James's forces in 1690, and saved the place from plunder and massacre. Entering it we find all the appearance of temporal prosperity. With my Tottenham friends I make an excursion in a wherry-boat up the beautiful Lough Erne to the island of Devenish, and visit the ruins of an ancient abbey church. We also find one of those 'round towers of other days', which have so puzzled and perplexed antiquarians, in perfect preservation there. We inquired of the boatman about the Revival, and he stated that large meetings had been held in the town. Still we perceived that we are getting a little beyond the boundaries of the great Revival wave, and that as yet the people of County Fermanagh were not, as elsewhere in County Derry, 'stirred to the very depths of their hearts'. Since the period of our visit to Enniskillen, a special Revival meeting has been held in the pleasure-grounds surrounding the striking monument of General Cole—an East Indian officer of reputation, and the member of an ancient Enniskillen family. Of ministers of religion, there were present at this meeting, one Episcopalian, two Presbyterians, and a number of Wesleyans. One of the latter gave a narrative of what he had witnessed in Derry, previously to which the Rev. Mr Dill, Presbyterian minister of Dromore, addressed the people—about 1,000 in number—from Ezekiel 18:32, 'I have no pleasure in the death of him that dieth, &c.' In his introductory remarks he spoke as follows:—

> My dear friends, I have seen so much of the power of the Spirit of God within the last two months, that I am willing to speak anywhere and everywhere that I may be called upon to speak a word for Christ. My own heart has been revived. And if I ever had a failing of faith before, blessed be God I have none now; if ever I had a doubt in my mind regarding the power of God's Spirit, I have none now; if ever I had a doubt on my mind regarding the willingness and love of the Lord Jesus Christ to save the uttermost, I have none now; and if ever my heart was cold to Christ and his cause, there is no coldness now, but my feeling is

that, like the apostle, I am willing to spend and be spent, yea, even to die for the Lord Jesus Christ.

He then proceeded to address a few appropriate observations on the passage of Scripture selected by him.

To Enniskillen I was accompanied by a worthy young minister of the General Assembly at Sligo. He was returning from an extended tour on behalf of Home Missions, and after his return home—agreeably to my request—he furnished me with a letter introducing results, social and spiritual, which came under his notice, which cannot fail to be interesting to the reader.

Sligo, August 30th, 1859.

After spending some weeks in Ulster, I reached home a few days ago. Being one of a deputation appointed to advocate the claims of the Assembly's Home Mission, I had to visit many districts of the counties of Derry and Antrim. I set out, fully convinced that a work of grace was going on; but I soon found that the half was not told me. At some of the meetings which I attended, there were instances of bodily prostration. It was truly dreadful to see some of these. To hear at intervals the agonizing cries for mercy, and to see the terror depicted on every feature of the countenance, were truly awful. But how delightful it was to observe the sin-stricken souls resting on the Saviour, and finding all the promises of the gospel Yea and Amen through him! Words can convey no idea of the heavenly joy that beams from the eye, or of the calm assurance depicted on the countenance when Christ is realized as 'the chiefest among ten thousand', and 'the altogether lovely'. The physical manifestations are not now so numerous as they were. They seem to have answered the purpose of drawing attention to the Spirit's work. The cases, however, of conviction of sin and of conversion unto God are, I believe, increasing rapidly. The movement is extending to new districts, carrying with it floods of enriching blessing wherever it is felt. Thousands of God's people have been literally revived and refreshed by it. They are nerved with fresh courage and determination to carry on the Lord's work. All the persons with whom I had an opportunity of conversing, concur in declaring that so far as they are aware there are no instances of awakened ones relapsing into sin. On the contrary, in every case of which they are cognizant, a consistent walk and conversation are maintained. One of the most striking results of the Revival is the removal of long existing enmities between families and individuals. At the hour of midnight, faults have been confessed and forgiveness asked by men who a little before were sworn and irreconcilable foes. When the spirit of love and peace was poured out upon them, they could not rest satisfied until mutual explanations were given and received. The west of Ireland has not yet been visited with any of these gracious influences. Some of God's people here and elsewhere are anxiously awaiting them. They are pleading earnestly at a throne of grace for a blessing. Their language is that of Jacob, when he wrestled with the angel: 'We will not let thee go unless thou bless us.' 'Hast thou not a blessing for us—even for us, also?' is their plea at the mercy-seat. May Jehovah carry on his own work until every part of Great Britain and Ireland, and of the world, rejoice and blossom as the rose. May the time speedily come when the declaration will go forth that 'the kingdoms of this world are become the kingdoms of our Lord and of his Christ.'

Believe me, yours very faithfully,

MOFFAT JACKSON,
'Minister of the Assembly.'

My day's journey was not completed at Enniskillen; I visited both Monaghan and Armagh, ere I slept, and had yet to hear or witness much of deepest interest: but for the present I pause in the narrative of 'Personal Observations and Inquiries.'

CHAPTER 21
PERSONAL OBSERVATIONS
AND INQUIRIES

The Irish car-driver—wayside tract distribution, and cheerful acceptance—the autumn evening prayer-meeting—the minister and the Awakening—its early history at Monaghan—physical prostrations—'arrow-heads'—the 'hysteric note', and preaching in Ulster—from Monaghan to Armagh—evening meetings—Awakening in a school—Red-rock—the aged minister, and the might of prayer.

IT was on a beautiful afternoon that I left Enniskillen, in order to proceed on my journey. Through a populous and highly cultivated district the train swept onward. I passed by Clones and other places, where, as I had heard, the Awakening had begun to manifest itself, and left the train, whose destination was Dundalk and Dublin, at the station called 'Monaghan Road', because it was the nearest station, on the Enniskillen line of railway, to—the county town—Monaghan itself. Here I found an Irish jaunting-car, not so elegant in structure, or ornamental in harness and equipments, as you see in Belfast. A genuine Celt is the driver; the face and figure indicate that he has no affinity with the 'Black North', or its semi-Scottish population. For, this is debateable ground. Although Protestantism in this county, as well as in that of Cavan adjoining, is strong, and morally and socially dominant, yet Romanists are still very numerous. The *adscripti gledae*, the old Celtic adherents, who cling to the wilder and less cultivated regions, occupy small holdings, excavate the quarries, are farm-servants, car-drivers, *et hoc genus omne*.[4]

And so the car-driver is in his chosen place, and aspires after no higher post than driving to and fro through summer's heat and winter's rains and frosts, and gloomy nights, over those six Irish miles which separate 'Monaghan Station' from Monaghan.

---

[4] *et hoc genus omne:* and all that sort of thing, *Ed.*

On this occasion I am his only passenger, and we proceed onward, slowly but surely, across a semi-mountainous region. I have a parcel of tracts, including some of the *Monthly Messenger,* and others with large print for old people, and, Romanist though he is, the driver takes quite an interest in my distribution of them as we pass along. He causes the horse to go slowly as the children run after the car, and drives it close to the farmer's cart as he and his family return from Monaghan, so as to allow me to drop the little messengers of truth and mercy into the hand or lap of one of the party. And then he cheerfully stops altogether, as an aged woman comes along the road, and permits me to speak to her a few kindly words, and offer her one of my illustrated *Messengers* or large-typed tracts.

Nearly all whom I meet in the first half of that evening's ride are Romanists, yet none refuse the tracts. No sullen, priest-inspired scowl of suspicion falls upon me, Protestant and heretical propagandist though I be. One old woman is certainly taken a little aback by the address of a stranger, and, as she stands in the sunlight, gazing at me, she is quite a study, hesitating as to whether she will take the tract or not. But after a little parley and doubt whether she could read it, I tell her that some one can read it to her, if she was not able to do so herself, and she receives and takes it away.

My stock was nearly exhausted as I drew near to Monaghan. I was now coming into a more cultivated district, and the Anglo-Saxon type of countenance, as well as farm-houses of a better order, and Lord Rossmore's magnificent demesne, now began to present themselves to my eye.

I was passing a road-side cottage of the more comfortable class, and as I offered some of my few remaining tracts to a little girl, there emerged from the cottage two or three young women neatly dressed, and each with Bible in hand. I began to feel at home, and felt that I was once more within the blessed scenes of the Ulster Awakening.

These young persons, I said to myself, are going to some schoolhouse, where a meeting for prayer and scriptural exposition is to be held. And when I asked the question whether it was so, I received at once an affirmative and smiling reply.

'Is the Rev. Mr Blakely, of Monaghan, at home?'

'Yes, he is coming to the school-house this evening, you will likely meet him on the road as you go towards the town.' And so it was. This venerable minister of Christ, nearly seventy years of age, for many weeks past has been incessantly engaged in public and private labours in connection with the Revival. When absent in Dublin, in the first week of July, during the sitting of the General Assembly, he was suddenly summoned home by tidings that the work had begun. And with rare prudence, and with a very abundant blessing, had he been enabled to guide the movement so as to avoid undue excitement, and to gather fruits most precious. Mr Blakely arriving from Dublin on a week-evening, found his church crowded to excess, and the greatest possible spiritual anxiety and earnestness pervading the throng. During the address and devotional services, physical manifestations—similar to what had occurred elsewhere—showed themselves. The people remained in the church 'till near morning', and they included all denominations.

Mr B., in a letter which soon after my wayside interview he addressed to me, wrote thus as to the further early development, as well as to the judicious measures adopted by him:—

> I announced a prayer-meeting for nine o'clock the next Sabbath morning, and at four in the evening. At these I delivered addresses recommending that the stricken should be kept calm, should pray by themselves, and that no singing or loud praying should be allowed. I referred to Saul's three days by himself at Damascus, with only a promise which he was permitted to plead and pray, and not till after that time did he appeal in the church or speak to others. This meeting was largely attended. I believe it contributed much to the quietness of our after operations. Anyone stricken afterwards, was removed quietly to the session-room, and only one or two friends or judicious Christians being admitted, we had no after confusion.
>
> I may add that not one of those affected the first night, belonged to us; being mostly, if not all, of the Established Church.
>
> Our weekly and Sabbath prayer-meetings continue to be largely attended, although now there are many others.

The Wesleyans have adopted the same hours on Sabbath morning and Friday evening. They have also a meeting every evening.

The Established Church has service on Wednesday evenings. Mr Rankin has a meeting at the Second Presbyterian Church on Thursday, and I understand that next Sabbath he will also have a similar meeting at nine, A.M.

I have for these three weeks preached every evening in the country to crowded audiences, always taking some place, distant from the regular prayer-meeting of any other church. With regard to prostrations, so far as I have seen them (for there have not been many among my own people), they have been confined to the ignorant; I should rather say to the ill-instructed in the doctrines of the gospel. The cases of deep prostration and loss of consciousness for hours have all been of that class.

With others, there may be for a season, an hour or two, deep distress, from a sense of sin, and then, gradual trust and bright hopes of salvation—agonizing prayer passing into adoring praise.

Mr Blakely then goes on to tell of the marvellous illustrations furnished him of the convincing power of Scripture truth, when accompanied by the agency of the Holy Ghost. It appears most clearly from this narration, that the shafts of the mighty Archer had been lodged and were rankling in the consciences of many, long before the Revival movement began. One and another now came and told the minister how in such a sermon, and in such an address, at the Lord's table or elsewhere, such and such texts had been brought home with power, and how these had never ceased to agitate their souls, until at length, when the Spirit was poured out suddenly, they had been led to the Saviour, and had found joy and peace through faith in his name. Mr B. is wont to call such texts 'arrow-heads', and is making a collection of those passages of the Bible, which the Holy Ghost has specially employed in the conviction and conversion of sinners.

He also wrote me that there was scarcely one of his household who had not been more or less physically agitated, in connection with solemn and saving impressions made on their minds and hearts. This included his servants and the labourers on his farm, and also the young lady who accompanied her father to the prayer-meeting on the evening when I met him.

Mr. B. is the Presbyterian chaplain of the jail at Monaghan, and is, besides, thoroughly competent, from long knowledge of the people's habits, to give an accurate and trustworthy account of the social change that has come over society in this district. His strong testimony on that subject will be found in its proper place, near the close of this volume. Mr Blakely specially refers also in his letter, to the alleged use of the 'hysterical note' employed in preaching by Ulster ministers. He emphatically declares that, so far from this being the case, the manner of the ministers, as a body, was more subdued than usual. The people needed no artificial stimulus like this, and the simplest truths, spoken in the most quiet tones, were received and relished as the very food of their earnest and hungering souls. Oh, what a blessed thing is it to preach and teach among such a people! For, multitudes know what that scripture meaneth, 'Thy word was found of me, and I did eat it; and it was the joy and rejoicing of my heart.'

After the interview detailed in the present chapter, with the respected minister at Monaghan—unable to accompany him to the country school-house in which he was about to preach, or to accept his proffered hospitality for the night—I hurried to the railway station, and thence proceeded by the latest evening train to the city of Armagh. I passed by the various stations of Clontibret, Tynan, &c., and I was reminded by what I had read, and from what I heard from a fellow-passenger, that the work of Revival had spread wide and far in these localities.

It was at a comparatively late hour that I reached Armagh. As I passed from the railway station into the city, through one of the oldest and most populous streets, I could plainly discern that the majority of the young people and others seated at the doors, in the soft light of parting day, were Roman Catholics. But even here, there was a witness for the Revival, who, amid jibes and scoffing laughter, was courageously asserting his faith in it as truly of God.

On arriving at the house of a beloved brother, the Rev. J. McAlister, about nine o'clock, P.M., I was told that he was at a meeting in the

Second Presbyterian Church, and that such meetings were now held nightly at Armagh in different places of worship: and so after a little rest and refreshment, I proceeded to the place of assembly. Here I found a numerous congregation, which increased as the night advanced, until, when I was retiring about ten o'clock, I found many persons of the humbler class standing in the vestibule and near the door. The minister of the church, Mr Henderson, presided on the occasion, and the Congregational minister was also present, after having conducted a separate service of his own. The Episcopalians (Mr Wade, the rector, is Evangelical), while they stood apart from other sections of the Church of Christ, held occasional meetings of their own. But to return to my narrative. A Scottish minister of great earnestness and piety was delivering a solemn address on 'things revealed to us and our children', and concluded by fervent appeals to the ungodly and undecided. Then my friend Mr M. ascended the pulpit, and informed the people of a manifestation of Divine grace which had appeared in the forenoon of that very day among the children of his day-schools. It appeared from his statement, and from what I more fully learned from him afterwards, that a scene similar to what had been realized at Ballymena and Coleraine among school-children, had occurred that day at Armagh. The pious monitor of the girls' school had previously noticed an increasing tenderness and solemnity of feeling among the children, as she spoke to them of sin, of Christ, and of eternal things. The Spirit was preparing the soil for a special shower of blessing, and that morning a little girl came into the girls' school, and with joy sparkling in her eyes she threw up her arms and exclaimed, 'I have found Jesus!' Instantly an electric sympathy ran from heart to heart, and a large number of the children fell down on their knees weeping over their sinfulness, and crying to the Saviour for mercy. Mr M. and his Scottish friend came speedily, calmed, instructed, and comforted the children. Some of them were heard ere long, pleading with their parents to repent and turn to God. Since that period Mr M. has written me to say that they hold prayer-meetings of their own, when supplications are offered up by them with affecting earnestness and beauty.

The Revival had but begun to display its energy in Armagh when I visited it, but in the country districts around, at Moy, at Markethill, at Richhill and Red-rock, great numbers had been brought under alarming convictions of sin, and many truly converted.

The name of the latter place, Red-rock, vividly recalled to my mind a solemn scene (years before) when, at a Synod meeting in Coleraine, an Ulster Presbytery solemnly 'licensed' a student, according to the forms of the Church of Scotland, to preach the everlasting gospel. On that occasion the preliminary examination was conducted by the Rev. J. Hervey, a man of primitive and Puritan mould. He afterwards offered up a prayer on that young man's behalf, remarkable for its unction and fullness—such as he can never forget. This man, all his life—and he is now verging on four-score—has been mighty in prayer. At one of the Revival meetings in his own church—as Mr M., of Armagh, informed me—he had poured forth a torrent of importunate supplication for a whole hour. The kingdom of heaven was besieged and taken—large numbers over whom he had long watched, and for whose souls he had apparently cared and toiled in vain, were now as 'a willing people', submitting themselves to their rightful King. Methinks such an aged Simeon as Mr H.—with two godly and gifted sons in the ministry, and with his church filled with living worshippers, formality gone, love, and light, and song abounding—may well exclaim, 'Lord, now lettest thou thy servant depart in peace, according to thy word, for mine eyes have seen thy salvation.'

CHAPTER 22
PERSONAL OBSERVATIONS
AND INQUIRIES

Spurious 'statistics'—the true state of things—false statistics about lunacy in Ulster—Mr Hanna's letter—great prayer-meeting at Armagh—the Hon. and Rev. B. W. Noel's address.

I SHALL here prefix to my continued narrative of 'observations', the result of 'inquiries', addressed to the Rev. Hugh Hanna, with regard to statements made and published on the 'immorality of the Revival'.

Certain 'statistics', so called, published by the *Northern Whig*, were copied into *The Times*, with the remark that they were sufficient 'to stagger the staunchest Revivalist'. The result of the alleged statistical inquiry was, that the number of criminal cases brought before the Belfast magistrates during the four months of the Revival, beginning with May and ending with August 1859, were considerably larger than in the corresponding period in 1858. The true reply to this statement is as follows:—1st. A large number of the cases adduced as 'criminal' were not of that character, being mere actions for wages and other 'civil' matters, including also desertions from the army. 2nd. It was found that there had been added over and over again the cases of notorious offenders, drunkards, &c., who almost every week were brought up before the magistrate. In this way the array of figures was made formidable. 3rd. In a populous commercial town and seaport like Belfast there is a large class still remaining whom the Awakening has not yet morally affected, as a whole, although many of the worst class have been converted and morally transformed. 4th. The Roman Catholic population of Belfast is very numerous, amounting to 40,000; and as a class they continue, in contrast with the Protestants, to drink freely, and thus they furnish a large quota to the numbers brought before the Petty Sessions as 'drunk and disorderly'. 5th. It is known that up to the period of the Awakening, offences against the law had been rapidly increasing in Belfast. This period did not begin with the month of May, as alleged, but in the middle of June in Belfast. As the result of the Revival, the Clerk of the Peace stated in September, that there 'was little crime now in Belfast', while the criminal calendar of the Quarter Sessions in October was the smallest known for a long period. 6th. From that district of Connor, where the Revival first manifested itself, and once somewhat notorious for crime, there had not been a single instance of a person charged with criminal offences being sent to the county jail. 7th, and most conclusive of all, there had not been one person of those 'convicted' or 'converted' at Revival meetings, or who had attended such meetings, who has ever been brought before a magistrate. It is a painful fact, that while some of the journals have copied such 'statistics' as those now exposed and contradicted, they have not admitted into their columns any counter-statements as to the real facts of the case.

While correcting misrepresentations, I may also refer to allegations as to the number of cases of lunacy caused by the Awakening. No less than twenty-two persons were said to have been admitted from the neighbourhood of Larne alone, into the county jail and Belfast lunatic asylum. Accurate information furnished by the *Banner*, shows, that instead of these statements being true, only five cases were admitted from Larne into the lunatic asylum, and 'it was not clear in any one of those cases that the disease was traceable to the Revival movement.' And whereas it had been affirmed that twelve were received into the county jail as 'dangerous lunatics', only seven, and five of them from Larne, had been received during three months and somewhat longer, labouring 'under religious delusions', not at all an unusual proportion, nor at all distinctly traceable to the Revival movement. More than this, it was asserted that 'within the space of three months, sixteen persons were committed to the jail as dangerous lunatics, in a single town'— Belfast, of course. 'The plain and indisputable truth is, that not one single case of religious insanity in Belfast, from religious causes, have been admitted within the time specified into our county prison.'

As to the social results of the Awakening in Belfast, the following letter from Mr Hanna is important. He writes thus;—

Belfast, Sept. 20th, 1859.

Dear Sir, —I am not able to refer to any statistics of undoubted character, and constructed on any considerable scale, to show the social results of the Revival. I am able only to inform you of such facts as have come under my own observation, or have been attested to me by reliable authority.

1st. Drunkenness was a prevalent vice. The use of distilled spirits was very general, and the custom was fast recruiting the wasting ranks of the confirmed drunkards.

Our temperance societies were numerous and active, but they made small progress in reclaiming the masses. But the gospel has annihilated the temperance societies—not all, but many of them. A higher argument and influence than they can wield, has regenerated the masses, and the absence of drunkenness from our streets—in markets, fairs, and on fair-days—is as marked as it is gratifying. You rarely see a drunken man now; brawling and disorder are consequently rare; and our police hardly know what to do with themselves. An officer in the county prison here, remarked the other day on the extraordinary decrease of prisoners for trifling offences.

The Revival has elevated the moral character of the whole community, and the social effects must necessarily be equally gratifying.

I am myself aware of four publicans who abandoned their trade, partly from the fact that their sales had fallen off so greatly that it was not worth their while to continue the trade, and partly because they considered that such a trade is a sin against society. In other parts of the country, similar facts are reported. Where worldly prudence and conscience regulate the spirit-seller's occupation, he will exhaust the time covered by his license, and sell off his stock. When that is done, I expect that many publicans over Ulster will renounce their licenses, and betake themselves to callings more consistent with the public good.

On our social relations the Revival has exerted the happiest influence. The party feuds of Ireland have been exceedingly mischievous. The anniversary of the battle of the Boyne stirred up all the bad blood of the country, and Protestants and Romanists were disposed to engage in bloody strife. But on the last 12th of July there was not a blow struck over all the country. Perhaps since that important historical transaction itself, there was not a more peaceable anniversary of it in Ireland; a new spirit animates the Protestant mind. Love (the fruit of the Revival), has taken the place of rankling enmity, and although the Romanists do not reciprocate in the same spirit, they are quiescent from the utter absence of all provocation. Ulster is now the most peaceable province in the British empire.

2nd. There is a marked change in the homes of the working classes. Many of them were thoughtless and improvident. Many of them were destitute of any very commendable notions of domestic comfort and taste. A great change for the better has taken place. I attended yesterday evening several classes open for instruction in the lowest parts of the town. About 750 persons were present in these classes, and the neatness, cleanliness, and appearance of comfort which marked them, were most gratifying.

3rd. The thirst for education is another feature in the results of this movement. A larger number of people unable to read, has been found than was supposed to exist among us. They have laid aside the habits which prevented them from learning, and you now see the old men sitting in the class with children, spelling out the precious truths of the Bible.

4th. The great social evil, the unblushing profligacy that infects the streets of large towns, was felt in Belfast, as elsewhere. It was a great affliction to contemplate it. Christian people did not know how to deal with it. But this movement has entered the haunts of the worst wickedness, and many a Magdalene has come to sit at Jesus' feet. Ministers will now, in such places, get a congregation of attentive and tearful listeners. About fifteen of these unfortunate women have, to my own knowledge, abandoned their evil ways, and have returned to the paths of virtue. Other ministers can speak of similar results. Sincerely yours,

'Hugh Hanna.'

A man of business, writing me from Belfast, Oct. 13th, after stating that the Revival meetings were still kept up, and that the united weekly prayer-meeting was very largely attended, added: 'There can be no doubt that a great improvement has taken place all over the country in the morals and conduct of the people, and one that seems likely to be permanent.'

I also received information, at the same period, of many publicans throughout Ulster giving up their licenses, or simply asking for a temporary renewal, in order to make final arrangements for giving up the trade. In the town of Crumlin no less than ten publicans had given up their licenses, and 'others made a final application for renewal, simply with the view of winding up what they considered was a ruined trade.'

On Wednesday, 16th September, the second day after I left Armagh, a multitudinous meeting was held there by the friends of the movement in that and in the adjoining counties. In order that a concentrated effort might be made for full attendance, there were special trains from Monaghan, Dungannon, and Belfast. While the crowded train was on its way from Belfast, the sound of voices singing well-known hymns arose from almost every carriage, while at the several stations, large numbers of tracts were extensively circulated.

The meeting was held in a capacious field near the Armagh railway station. Very many laymen from England and Scotland were present, as well as clergymen and ministers from different districts of Ireland. Two of the chaplains of the Lord Primate were on the ground. The chair was occupied by J. M. Lynn, M.D. The chief speakers were the Hon. and Rev. B. W. Noel, his son, Ernest Noel, Esq., and the Rev. J. S. Moore, of Ballymena. The *Banner of Ulster* gives the following outline of the Hon. and Rev. B. W. Noel's address:—

> He took for the basis of his address the fact that the Lord Jesus Christ was ready to save the immortal souls of sinners, and that they only were to blame, if they did not ultimately obtain salvation. Upon this topic he spoke with an amount of fervent simplicity which we have rarely heard equalled. He expressed the great delight which he felt in being privileged to attend such an immense meeting as that was, and he thanked God that the souls of the people had been awakened to a sense of their position. If in the multitude (he said) that was before him there was one unconverted soul—and he was sure there were many—now was the time to approach the throne of grace—now was the time to approach to that heavenly Father, who, through the intercession of the Saviour, was willing and ready to forgive the transgressions of their past lives, if they only appealed to him in the true spirit. He addressed himself to the young and to the old—he addressed himself to those who were upon the noontide of life, and to those who were upon the brink of the

grave; and he earnestly besought them to avail themselves of this glorious opportunity to make their peace with God. He trusted that, with the blessing of God, this movement would not be confined to Ireland; that it would spread itself among the great intellects of England, and that men would see, at length, in a true and sincere spirit, that they had souls to be saved. It might be a strange thing that the north of Ireland, and its people, should become the great heralds of this movement; but he believed that, if they exercised their influence, they might do much to extend the cause of God's kingdom and glory. He prayed that the mind of this country might be made to thrill with the name of the great Evangelist, and that Ireland might really become, in the sight of Heaven, the 'Isle of Saints'.

The *Banner* adds of 'an English clergyman' who was present: 'He informed us that a member of the constabulary force, who attended the meeting, stated that in the constabulary station at Armagh there had been no less than seven cases of conversion, and that all of them bore evidence of a truly permanent character.' It is pleasing to know that similar conversions have taken place among the constabulary elsewhere. For example, two of the constabulary at Lisburn, in County Down, on Sabbath, the 18th Sept., stood up before the minister and congregation in the Wesleyan chapel, and avowed themselves Christ's loyal subjects and servants. This came under the personal observation of Benjamin Scott, Esq., Chamberlain of the City of London, who has in private conversation related it to me. I cannot help adding that the Christian public are under obligations to Mr Scott for those valuable public addresses and lectures in which he gave the results of his own personal observation in Ulster, and in the face of multiplied misrepresentation, testified to a 'reality' of life and power, which exceeded all his anticipations.

The Times' 'Special Correspondent' was present at the Armagh meeting. While writing respectfully of the addresses of Mr Noel, Mr Moore, and others, he found fault with parties who, in different parts of the field, harangued separate bands in a vehement manner. The *Banner of Ulster* also deprecated some things which occurred on the outskirts; but, on the whole, the meeting seems to have been attended

with real and lasting benefits. A Presbyterian minister, from Roches-
ter, was present on this occasion, and wrote thus:—'At Armagh I
attended the great gathering (upwards of 20,000), and took part in the
service. Truly it reminded you of a field of battle, so many were the
slain by, the "sword of the Spirit".'

CHAPTER 23
PERSONAL OBSERVATIONS
AND INQUIRIES

Return to Belfast—second Union prayer-meeting—Dr Edgar's address—visit to
Berry Street—intercessory prayer a special feature of the Awakening—specimens and illustrations at Berry Street and the Music Hall, Belfast—cottage
prayer-meetings—social prayer the special feature of the Ulster Revival.

I RETURNED from my long circuit to Belfast a day too late to be
present at the second Union prayer-meeting, held in the Royal Botanic Gardens. The first of these meetings was held on the 29th June,
and the second on the 17th August. The *Banner of Ulster* stated that at
one period of the day there were 20,000 persons present:—

> From remote portions of Antrim, from far away districts in Down,
> from portions of Armagh, where the sickle was busy, from Tyrone, were
> seen numerous groups, all apparently earnest in the cause which had
> concentrated them at the same point. These consisted mostly of young
> people, respectable in dress and demeanour, evidently of the better class
> of tenant farmers' families, attended by fathers, brothers, or husbands.
> A better, a fairer, or more honest specimen of the descendants of these
> Scottish settlers has never before been presented upon a field in Ulster,
> or upon an occasion when they could be seen to such advantage.
>
> There were numbers of persons present from Scotland—ministers
> and laymen of various congregations. Some of these took part in the
> devotional exercises, and all expressed themselves delighted and aston-

ished by a work which is now sowing its seeds in the motherland [Scotland], producing, we trust, good fruits.

There were also present Episcopalians and Wesleyans, Presbyterians and Independents, (including Geo. Pritchard, formerly missionary at the Sandwich Islands, and afterwards British Consul at Otaheite),[5] with Baptist and other ministers and laymen from every part of the United Kingdom. The Rev. Robert Knox discharged the duties of president. The Revs. Messrs Seaver and Hanna, and Mr McQuilkan—a convert from Connor, whose addresses have been so signally blessed— together with Dr Edgar, addressed the people. Dr Edgar spoke as follows:—

> Brethren, I am very desirous of impressing upon the minds of all here, that by such meetings as this, by the news of these revivals, which has been spread through the newspapers, we have brought upon ourselves great responsibility. For example, I have recently been visiting about twenty meetings in the south and west of this country, and wherever I have been, it has been my anxiety to hold out you and the people of this province as furnishing an example worthy of imitation. I have been told that such is the wonderful change that has been exhibited in Ulster, that, in one single Presbytery, conversions have been computed at no less than 1,000 persons; that in one single congregation sixty young men have been brought in a few weeks to God; and that, in another congregation, out of 209 families, 207 now regularly observe family worship. Now, I tell you, you are pledged; we are before the world, and we must show to the world that our actions are equal to our words—that this is not a mere evanescent movement. I believe that now there is a greater demand for gospel truth than there ever has been in our day—that there is a greater demand for Bibles than we have heretofore known—that our colporteurs never had their labours so much called upon. It is our duty to keep this work going on; to endeavour especially to supply Bibles with Psalms to your brethren. I have told how, during the course of this movement, members of one family felt for the conversion of others of the same family—how sisters have sat up all night praying for the conversion of a brother. It is your duty

---

[5] Otaheite: the island of Tahita in the South Pacific, *Ed.*

to see that such statements as this shall not be made in vain; and that to take care the work of sobriety, which this movement has so singularly encouraged, will continue to progress. I have said that where this work has gone on, spirit-sellers have been compelled to abandon their trade; and I trust this principle will be established to still greater extent, and that your band of union will be still greater than before.

The Rev. Duncan Long, incumbent of St Paul's, Bermondsey, London, forcibly expressed the great happiness which he experienced in attending that meeting, which was so eminently calculated to extend God's kingdom. This clergyman was present at many of the united prayer-meetings held at Belfast and throughout the provinces, and always asked for special intercessions on behalf of his 'new parish' in the metropolis.

Agreeably to previous arrangement, I proceeded on Wednesday evening, August 24th, to Berry Street Church, to deliver an address to the assembled congregation. The Rev. Hugh Hanna began the service; and before offering the first prayer, called on the crowded congregation to engage in silent prayer. The stillness and solemnity were most impressive. I observed that very many of the people turned round and fell on their knees, instead of standing at prayer, as has been usual in Presbyterian churches in Ulster.

Immediately before the prayer, Mr Hanna read out a series of requests for intercessory supplication. This was usual at every service held in the church, is not infrequent at Ulster prayer-meetings generally, and was a marked feature of the Union prayer-meetings held in the Music Hall, Belfast.

One of the requests intimated by Mr Hanna was 'prayer for London'; another was from 'a soldier', another from an 'aged and anxious inquirer and his family', another from 'a voyager', another asking prayer for 'Scotland', another for 'Pentland'. Such requests for prayer are so very suggestive, that I subjoin some of those presented by Mr Hanna, on the evening when I occupied his pulpit. Here is a request forwarded from Canada:—

Rev. And Dear Sir,—Knowing the sympathy and love which, as a Christian and minister of the gospel, you have for *all* men, especially for those who are, or are seeking to be, of the household of faith, I feel that you will forgive the liberty which I, an entire stranger, and living many hundred miles away from you across the sea, take in addressing you this letter. Having read with longing interest the accounts of the wonderful work which God is carrying on in your district, and in others near and around you, I have prayed that it might please the Lord to begin such a work here, in this part of this country—here, where there seems to be 'no truth, no knowledge of God'; and on reading in our *Witness of Montreal* the last accounts, the thought suddenly occurred to me, 'write and ask the converts to pray for yourself and your family.' Longing to know God again, and to worship him in spirit and in truth, I eagerly took the advice thus suggested, and now, perhaps foolishly, but respectfully and earnestly ask, if the spiritual interests of those among whom you labour do not forbid, that you would kindly lay our case before some one of your dear converts, who, having tasted of the mercy and exceeding grace of God, desires and prays that others may receive of his fullness also. We are a family who have, indeed, the 'form of godliness', but, alas! 'deny its power.' We are far, very far, from God, but we (at least several of us) who have a faint idea of the work, long to be brought nigh through Jesus Christ. O then, dear sir, lay the matter before some of God's people, that they may supplicate him for us and all around us. Trusting that you will pardon this intrusion of a stranger upon you, and praying that God may continue to pour out upon you all the precious gift of His Holy Spirit, I am, reverend and dear Sir, yours in wishes God wards,

'* * * * *'

REV. MR. HANNA, Belfast.

The next letter was from a person living in the neighbourhood of Greenock:—

REV. SIR,—Permit me to address to you a few lines on a very important subject; that is, to request the prayers of your congregation for myself and my wife, that God, in his infinite mercy, may be pleased to convert our precious souls, as we feel ourselves to be still in the gall of bitterness and in the bond of iniquity. I went to Ireland lately for a few days, and was in your church on Sabbath, the 14th inst.; I was also in the Botanic Gardens on the following Tuesday, and felt convinced that God is working mightily among you by his Holy Spirit. I was at the same time much impressed with the happiness enjoyed by all true Christians, and the fearful danger of all who are still out of Christ; and as I am an old hardened sinner, who have long resisted the strivings of the Holy Spirit, I much fear he has withdrawn altogether, and that my heart may become more hardened than ever, after the solemn scenes I witnessed in Ireland. It is also my misfortune to live in a dry, barren part of the country, under a cold and formal ministry, so that my case is a very critical one, being now above fifty years of age, and having a young family to provide for, and ought to train up for God's service. My business also (that of a merchant) is too engrossing for the welfare of my immortal interests.

Will you, therefore, remember me and my partner in your meetings at a throne of grace? Nothing is impossible to him, who has our hearts and our future destiny in his Almighty power.

Hoping that the Holy Spirit will answer your fervent petitions, and make you the honoured instrument of bringing many souls to find rest and happiness in the blood of the Lamb, I remain, Rev. Sir, yours sincerely,

'* * * * *'

Since my return, Mr Hanna has sent me the originals of two other written requests, presented at a period later than my visit. The first runs thus:—

The prayers of God's praying people are earnestly requested for Scotland, and especially for the town of Paisley.

The second is from a lady, intensely longing for the conversion of her kindred:—

Rev. And Dear Sir,—A stranger from the south of Ireland, who has heard of and rejoices in the great things which the Lord has done and is doing amongst you, and how he specially manifests himself as a prayer-hearing and answering God, earnestly solicits the prayers of united Christians on behalf of herself and her family, her father and mother, her brothers and sisters, that the God who delighteth in mercy will show mercy on each of them, by renewing them in the spirit of their mind, and giving them the power of godliness instead of its form; that he will vouchsafe to unite them in the love and service of Christ, and make them instrumental in bringing others to him; that, if it be his holy will, he will be pleased to restore bodily health to one of that family now lying apparently very near to death, but that, if not, he will vouchsafe to prepare him for that great change which seems so near, and will give him repentance unto life. Oh, dear Sir, do not cast aside the prayer of a stranger: it comes to you in the name of Jesus—that name so precious to all his people; and if you know (as I believe you do) the happiness of loving him, will you not ask him that we may love him too?

I have prayed these things myself, I do pray them; but all my prayers seem so cold and heartless, I never feel to get a bit nearer to him: still the veil between us; still the hearing of the ear, instead of seeing him for myself. And in connection with this family, your prayers are besought for an old man of eighty-four, who, as far as man can judge, seems unconscious how much he needs the Saviour's blood and righteousness. As a stranger I feel an apology is due for this intrusion on your notice; but as one anxious for the saving knowledge of Christ for herself and family, I hope I may meet with sympathy, and that you will not refuse to remember us in your meetings for prayer; and may God's blessing and presence be with you.

And here let me again record my joy and thankfulness at the glorious spectacle of fraternal love presented in that weekly united prayer-meeting in the Music Hall, which three times I had the privilege of attending. There, as elsewhere in Ulster, the spirit of intercessory prayer prevailed; prompted into daily exercise and earnestness by written requests laid before the chairman, this spirit of intercession continues. My excellent friend, the Rev. Charles Seaver, incumbent of St John's, Belfast, joint secretary with the Rev. Dr Morgan, of the united prayer-meeting, has forwarded to me the following specimen of requests thus presented:—

> The prayers of the meeting are requested for the conversion of the eldest son of a clergyman, placed in circumstances of temptation. Also for the conversion of a Roman Catholic female, on whose behalf special exertions have been made.

> One who loves Jesus desires the prayer of the meeting on behalf of three

brothers, whose case is described in 2 Timothy 3:4—'Lovers of pleasure more than lovers of God.'

A daughter asks the earnest prayers of the meeting for her mother and four members of her family, that they would feel their sins and live closely to Jesus.

The prayers of all the Lord's children in attendance on the Union prayer-meeting, on Wednesday afternoon, are earnestly requested for an outpouring of the Holy Spirit on the several sections of the Christian Church in Newcastle-under-Lyme (England).

The prayers of this meeting are requested for a family, that each individual of it may experience the quickening power of the Holy Spirit, that they may be awakened and stirred up to see and feel more deeply the love of Christ, and follow him more closely.

A person requests the prayers of the meeting for herself, all the members of her family still unconverted, her unconverted Sabbath school children, also for her minister, that he may 'be strong in the Lord, and in the power of his might'.

A lady, a widow, asks the prayers of this meeting for the conversion of her son, a youth exposed to temptation; and she would ask the Lord to choose for him the profession in life that will be for his glory. She refers this to God, and asks his blessing on it.

The reader will observe how suggestive are the whole of these requests, and will be reminded afresh that Ulster is now 'studded' (as one minister expresses it) with daily and nightly meetings at which the weapon 'ALL PRAYER' is wielded with power.

Some of these meetings are held in cottages, and a clergyman of the Church of England at Portrush (the Rev. H. Ffoliott) writes me with regard to one of them, which he says is usually conducted entirely by the labourers or small farmers themselves.

The exercises consist of—1st, a few verses of a psalm, sung with great fervour; 2nd, prayer by one of the young men; 3rd, a chapter of the Holy Bible, read by all present, *verse about;* 4th, each verse is taken up and made the subject of conversation or inquiry; 5th, psalm as before; 6th, a concluding prayer by one of the older members.

'This', adds Mr F., 'appears to me a rational, calm, and profitable mode of spending the evening.' Verily it is so. Oh that it were prevalent in Great Britain! Mr F. goes on to say:—'It may help one in judging of the extent to which religious feeling prevails, to know that within a circle of a mile from John's cottage'—where the clergyman had been present at a meeting—

> there are ten such meetings in the week, *not* including those held on the Sabbath. I know of these ten, and there may be others of which I have not heard.
>
> Although there was another meeting within a short distance last night, there were as many present as the cottage could contain, i.e. from forty to fifty. Cases of strong impression often result from these simple readings. One young man a few weeks ago was so much stirred up, that on returning home he commenced family prayer, and has continued it ever since. Twelve months ago nothing but a dance, or one of their rustic 'singings', could have induced these men to leave their homes in cold and wintry nights, such as we have had the last fortnight, and walk a mile or two after their day of toil.

Let me then leave the distinct impression on all English friends whom my communications reach, that prayer is the grand characteristic, the life and essence of the Irish Awakening. With it also, be it remembered, are always associated holy song, and the exposition and study of the word of God. The cottage meetings are emphatically 'fellowship meetings', such as in times of spiritual declension in Ulster the Covenanters—the straitest sect of the Ulster Presbyterians—have always kept up, and by reason of which their singularly intellectual, vigorous grasp of theological truth, as well as their healthful piety, have been secured and maintained. Little did my esteemed friend, the Rev. Dr Houston, of Knockbracken, Belfast, when he published his excellent work on *Fellowship Meetings* a few years ago, expect to see the day when Ulster would night after night abound with such gatherings. Well may he and all good men there, and here also, exclaim, 'What hath God wrought!'

CHAPTER 24
PERSONAL OBSERVATIONS
AND INQUIRIES

'Stricken' cases at Berry Street Church and a marvellous change—the Pastor sowing in tears, and reaping in joy—conversion of a hardened transgressor— farewell visit to Townsend Street—homeward bound—song and prayer on the Quarter-deck.

THE address at Berry Street was hortatory in its character, and especially addressed to converts, urging upon them the duty of 'following on to know the Lord', in humility, self-denial, watchfulness and prayer. Nothing exciting was said on this occasion; but near the close of the service two persons were removed from the church to the vestry, crying out in wailing tones. After the service I repaired to the vestry, and found there a young girl, in a prostrate condition, not able to speak, and with eyes closed. Persons, however, in this condition are not unconscious; 'awfully conscious', as one of them said, they generally are, under a sense of guilt and peril. There was also a boy, of about twelve years old, sitting on a form, and leaning against the wall pallid and ghastly. His eyes were closed, but I put my ear to his lips, and heard the words repeated again and again, 'Jesus, have mercy!' Both were afterwards removed to their homes, and I found it impossible next day to visit either of them, as I had wished to do. But ere they left, those who were present—including some ladies from Scotland—united in singing and prayer.

Great and tender care is taken of all such 'stricken' cases, both in reference to physical restoration to health, and their instruction in the things pertaining to the kingdom of God. Mr Hanna has a large staff of visitors, as well as of elders, who are most diligent in ministering to those under physical and mental distress, as well as in instructing converts in the way of God more perfectly.

At the house of a friend, in the neighbourhood of Belfast, I met the Rev. Dr G., the able and esteemed minister of C—h. Three years before I had found him anxious—so many and peculiar difficulties were in his path, and such was the apparent deadness of the great mass of the people. But now, what a blessed change! It is as life from the dead over the whole district. His church is overflowing, a minister's manse is about to be built, and all is spiritual prosperity.

Since my return from Ireland I have received a letter from Dr G., detailing the spiritual results of the Awakening in his congregation. The following extract strikingly indicates the power of the Holy Spirit in the moral transformation of a stout-hearted sinner:—

> I met him on the road, and although on many a former occasion he had passed me with a cold bow of recognition, or an angry look, this time he was determined not to let pass. As soon as I approached him, he took off his hat directly, and began to pray. Persons were near at hand, or passing, but he did not mind that. The earnestness of his manner, and the fervency of his petitions, were remarkable. His oft repeated cry was, 'Lord, have mercy on me, a sinner! Lord, take away this hard and stony heart, and give me a heart of flesh.' Turning to me, he said, 'It is the Lord that has wrought this change in me—such a careless man as you know I was.' By his desire I had prayer with him on the road-side. Next day, being the Sabbath, he was amongst the first I observed coming to church after many long years of sinful neglect. The same night he felt the pardon and peace he had been seeking. The Saviour thus overtook him in his carelessness, and saved him from his sins. For several months I have never missed him from the Sabbath and week-day services. His conduct and conversation adorn the doctrine of God our Saviour. Everyone that knew him marks the change. This was the *first* case of conversion in my congregation. Thank God, very many have occurred since then, some of them in public, others in private, all of them I believed truly genuine.

I was induced to remain in Belfast a day or two longer than was (in point of convenience in reaching home) in itself desirable. But ere I left I felt desirous of paying a visit to the people of Townsend Street Church, where, amid the many changes by death or otherwise which had taken place in twelve years since I left, there was still many remaining to whom I had ministered the word of life.

This congregation is mainly composed of the artisans who are employed in forges, foundries, mills, and factories, and of their families, as well as large numbers of young persons engaged in the flax-spinning mills which abound in that particular district of Belfast. Its numbers have been always great; the results of the gospel ministry among the people have ever been encouraging. Here for at least sixteen years the work of daily and Sunday-school teaching—during the pastorates of the late Josias Wilson and myself, as well as that of my zealous successor, the Rev. William Johnson (who is son of tbe Rev. Dr Johnson, Ex-Moderator of the General Assembly)—has been most diligently and successfully pursued. Hugh Hanna (now the minister of Berry Street Church, Belfast), when at the head of the Townsend Street Congregational day-school, raised its reputation very high, not only in respect to a sound and practical English education in all its branches, but also as to the habits of diligence, thoughtfulness, and cleanliness amongst the children; fancy needlework and useful sewing being practised under an excellent female teacher, who remains still in charge of her own department. Best of all, scriptural instruction, both on week-days and the Lord's day, accompanying intellectual instruction, were crowned from year to year with a special blessing. The intelligence of young persons passing from the Bible-classes to the communion-table was always marked and gratifying. In connection with the public preaching of the word, there was always a greater or less degree of the presence and power of the Holy Spirit manifest; and it might be justly said that this congregation was gathered together under the saving and sanctifying power of a true Revival preacher in the best sense of the term, the lamented Josias Wilson.

But it was reserved for the year 1859 to manifest a more enlarged bestowment of spiritual life than had been realized at Townsend Street before. For a time the pastor was laid aside by a severe illness, which threatened his life. Previously, he had written me that all the ministers of Belfast were visiting persons brought under conviction almost night and day, and that not until a late hour on Saturday night was he able to sit down to make a hurried preparation for preaching on the Lord's day. But in his case, and in all such cases, 'the joy of the Lord' was the minister's strength; his heart was filled, and therefore his pen indited and his lips gave forth 'good matter', and as all the people pressed on the Master to hear the word of God, so was it now—so is it still, thank God—with regard to his servants. 'Oh, what a heaven', writes one of them to me, 'to minister to a revived people!' Yes! it is so indeed; would to God that it were so everywhere, in this London, this England of ours! Surely all the ministers of Christ should wrestle with God, night and day, for such a 'revived people'!

I shall not dwell on the address delivered at Townsend Street, the affectionate greetings of old friends, and the tearful eyes of a dear little orphan girl, whose father and mother I had known so well, and towards whom my heart yearned. I look back to Townsend Street, to Belfast itself, to Newry—my first choice and scene of toil—with 'fond affection and recollection', not only in remembrance of old times, but also of my recent visits to them; and for all who love and labour for Christ and souls in Ulster, be they Episcopalians, Presbyterians, Independents, Wesleyans, or Baptists, I earnestly desire and crave the continued outpouring of the Spirit of life, light, comfort, love, and holiness.

Even on board the swift steamer, that bore me away from Belfast and Ulster homeward, I still saw the traces of the Revival. Seated in the cabin with a London merchant, I suddenly heard the voice of song. We found that it was sacred song, and speedily repaired to the quarter-deck, whence it proceeded. Here we found, dimly discerned in the shadows of night, a band of men whose hearts God had touched, and whose lips his Spirit had made vocal with praise. The leaders in that harmonious singing (for all the parts were given with accuracy and fullness) were Primitive Wesleyan gentlemen from Manchester. One of them was a merchant, aged and venerable, another a minister. They had been two days before at the great united prayer-meeting at Armagh. Their hearts were full of gladness by reason of what they had seen and heard.

Other passengers gathered round them—English, Irish, Scottish—and we poured forth together to him who sits King for ever, as the ship glided swiftly through the calm and star-lit waters, songs of rejoicing. Some of the crew and second-class passengers, with the steward and stewardess, drew near. At last we said, 'Why not pray also?' 'Oh', said the old gentleman, 'the captain does not like it. We came over last Monday night, and he forbade our praying, and shook the minister by the collar in order to stop him.' And then the old man went away to try and talk over the captain to give his consent. Fresh hymns were sung, and again the question was put, 'Why not pray?' to which it was added, 'We talk quietly we can pray quietly. Let us pray.' And so hats were taken off, and without waiting for or asking leave from any man, our joint supplications ascended to heaven.

So ended a three weeks' visit to my native province—now dearer to me than ever, because the footprints of the Saviour are everywhere visible, and the land is full of life, and love, and praise. Oh, what a marvellous display have I been privileged to witness, in connection with the Ulster Revival of 1859, of the might and grace of him who 'ONLY DOETH WONDROUS THINGS!'

PART THREE
MATTERS ARISING FROM
THE REVIVAL

CHAPTER 25
THE 'PHYSICAL ACCIDENTS' OF
THE AWAKENING

Difficulties and objections considered.

THE physical manifestations which have appeared in connection with the Ulster Awakening, although already noticed
and virtually accounted for in our narrative of facts and incidents,
seem to demand separate consideration. For, not only have these
physical affections been adduced, by writers who are the avowed
foes of evangelical religion, as proofs that the entire movement in the
work of Ireland is nothing better than fanaticism and extravagance,
but they have awakened doubts as to its reality and genuineness in
the minds of many sincere Christians. These last are wont to feel
and say, that inasmuch as the American Revival of 1858 was quiet
and unattended with nervous excitement, that doubts may well be
entertained with regard to the genuineness of the Awakening in
Ireland.

Leading articles in medical and other journals have appeared on this question, and most of our reviewers have 'pronounced' on the subject. Thus the *Lancet* has used such language as the following, which, from its most calumnious charge against honourable and upright men, it is difficult—for one who knows how unjust it is—to quote without indignation:

> All means are employed by *the organizers of the agitation* to increase its violence. The *blasphemous ravings* of half-mad girls are quoted and recited, and *the utmost excesses of language and demeanour* are favoured as the special evidences of peculiar inspiration.

The readers of the *Lancet* are also told of 'insane and indecent follies', which are held to be *'indicia'* of conversion'; that these are 'such as evidence a temporary unsettling of reason among the *duped,* and *a high degree of rascality among the knaves* who encourage the evil.'

In like manner, a 'Special Correspondent' suddenly landing on the shores of Ulster in the month of September, 1859 (very speedily, however, silenced and withdrawn by his employers), denounced, what he called, 'dangerous agitation'. On the faith also of statements made by enemies of the movement, a London morning paper, professedly Protestant and Conservative, 'thanked God' that 'our Church' [the Church of England] 'had been saved from a corrupt Revival'.

A daily liberal journal, of large circulation, after having admitted that *if* what the Earl of Roden had testified as to the social changes in his own district of Ulster were true, that the Revival should be spoken of 'with respect', a few weeks later so far forgot its admission and its self-respect, as to speak of modern Revivals—that in Ulster included—as but the resurrection of 'the monstrous absurdities and impious jargon of the Anabaptists'; as 'disgraceful exhibitions invading one part of the empire after another, rendering women forgetful of the modesty which belongs to their sex, and men of the reason for which they ought to be distinguished.' The journalist classed these Awakenings with the 'superstition' of which 'corpses and human bones are the insignia', which loves above all things to mark its track by slaughter', and as precipitating a 'reaction to infidelity' and 'libertinism'!

'The foaming preacher' also—we were told—was the means of awakening 'the lowest emotions of our nature'; the subjects of the Awakenings are classed with the 'Adamites who grazed the fields, &c.'; and the conclusion arrived at was, that what 'in the nineteenth century is called a religious Revival, is in truth only a revival of the Isiac mysteries, of the festivals of the Bona Dea, and of the orgistic extravagances of the Bacchanals'; and that it is to be 'reckoned' with those 'abominations' which have 'debased multitudes of men and women to the condition of the maspausan and chimpanzee.' *'It behoves society, therefore, to put a stop to them in time.'*

It is a significant fact, that on the day after the appearance of this article, a virtual apology, in the shape of a modified defence, was made for it, coupled with the admission that 'more than one hundred letters' of remonstrance had been received. But, unhappily, ere this second article was concluded, the outrage on truth and decency was repeated. 'Outbreaks of paganism' were 'now in operation in Wales, in Ireland, and to some extent in England.' And as for Scotland, 'they [these outbreaks] have been domiciliated there for ages.' A hint was given in conclusion, that after the example of 'the most tolerant of governments' [the Roman Republic], 'the *magistrate* should interfere!'

Language, if not as coarse, yet virtually as unjust and bitter in spirit as the foregoing, has been employed by various public writers on this side of the Channel. It is well to remember that they have written *without a personal examination* of the facts of the case, and that they have presented the melancholy spectacle of confounding a glorious spiritual movement with its mere 'accidents'; that the ministers of religion and others, who have identified themselves with this movement in Ulster, are accused as a body of what they are altogether innocent; and, in a word, that a position has been taken by many English writers at the press, such as in Ireland is occupied by Unitarian and Romanist organs only.

Corrections of 'statistics' as to the alleged 'immorality of the Revival' have been also refused admission into the columns of the same journals which copied them; and so it has come to pass that the English public is misinformed. Thus, like the Rev. William Arthur (whose letter was shut out of a leading journal), I too, 'who knew the people, and believed my own eyes', had to come back to London 'to learn that all that had been told me in Ireland of the improvement going on, was all a conspiracy of friends, strangers, and appearances to deceive one!'

The physical agitations, in the estimate of many who claim to be philosophic to a degree, are 'hysteria' or 'epidemic'—the nervous excitement, and its reaction, of popular fanaticism: nothing less, nothing else, and nothing more. But what if true philosophy, while recognising nervous excitement and its reaction, can by a Baconian induction of facts, trace in a large majority of cases, the *cause* to powerful internal emotions of which the Divine Spirit is the author? What if there should be still occasion to apply to 'the spruce philosopher' of our own day, the language of William Cowper to the socialist of his own time?

> He has found
> The source of the disease; our good town feels
> Hysterics, nervousness, clairvoyance. Hence
> He bids the world take heart, and banish fear.
> Thou fool! Would thy discovery of the cause
> Suspend the effect, or heal it?
> Go dress thine eyes with eye-salve—ask of Him,
> Or ask of whomsoever he has taught,
> And learn, though late, the genuine cause of all.

There are also those who avow themselves to be the friends of Evangelical religion, and of the 'work' of genuine Revival, who yet maintain that physical agitations are the 'counter-work' of man, and if so, it follows of Satan, acting through him, a prominent agency. Among these, and pre-eminent, is the Archdeacon of Meath.

Now, that 'the cries, moans, and other inarticulate sounds of hysteria are merely expression of diseased physical feeling' is a statement of Archdeacon Stopford's,[1] which no 'observant person' can dispute. It is equally true that 'the words and expressions used in these hysterical affections, upon the most important topics of religion, require care and thought to discriminate their real value.' It

---

[1] *The Work and the Counter-work* (Dublin: Hodges and Smith).

is also cheerfully granted to the Archdeacon that it is not true that in the cases of persons 'stricken', conviction of sin has been universally expressed, or the cry for mercy universally raised; still let it be remembered that the Archdeacon says, 'I acknowledge that the burden of sin is bemoaned and the cry for mercy offered, and the shout of victory and thanksgiving raised, in a *great majority* of cases by these bodily affections.'

Here then, with this acknowledgment, comes the vexed question to be grappled with, 'whether these expressions indicate the real affection of the soul?' Here the Archdeacon, treating of, and calling, each of such cases a 'paroxysm of *hysteria*', takes ground which I respectfully submit cannot be maintained. First of all let us inquire what medical authorities who have carefully examined such cases, say on this subject. In so far as their counter-reasonings and adverse conclusions are valid, then, the Archdeacon's statement—that words which have been used in that (a hysterical) state, even while expressing 'real sorrow and mourning for sin', are worthless as proofs of genuine feeling—is found inapplicable in many cases of persons who have been 'stricken' in Ulster. The following statement of an eminent physician, Dr Motherwell, of Castlederg, County Tyrone, was read at the meeting of the Evangelical Alliance in Belfast;—

> Like many other medical men, on reading of the 'cases', or hearing descriptions of them, I thought they were hysterical, and that close rooms or meeting-houses, exciting language, sympathy, imitation, &c. &c., had much to do in producing the physical manifestations. Observation, however, soon dispelled such an idea. In the first place, the more prominent and distinctive symptoms of hysteria were not present. There was no '*globus*', and many more of the usual hysterical symptoms were absent. As to epilepsy and catalepsy, out of the dozens of cases I saw, there was not one that any medical man could for a moment mistake for either of these affections. In many of the cases the countenance was pale, in others flushed, being a dull or dusky red, the voice feeble in speaking, or attempting to speak, the pulses low and weak.

Dr Motherwell, remarking the great muscular relaxation which attends the 'cases', states that this, with 'slow, weak pulse, pale or dusky red face, indicates deficient action of the heart'. Then as to the complaint of the 'load' of sin, as the stricken say, at the region of the heart, on which the patient's hand is often placed, the falling down, the scream, &c. &c., Dr M. says, all seem more analogous to nightmare than any other affection. The scream seems to be the instinctive effort of the respiratory organs to supply air to the blood, which is insufficiently aerated, apparently from the partially suspended action of the heart. Let the reader mark what follows:

> When I say that the heart seems the organ most affected, you may say—expect me to say—*what causes the diminution of its action*. Now this is not easily done. I must say, and say truly, that it is owing to a diminution of a portion of the nervous power, essential to the nominal action of the heart. But then, what *withdraws the nervous power?* In fact, he who would ascribe the physical phenomena, and the whole religious movement to *merely physical and ordinarily moral causes*, would place himself very much in the same dilemma as the Hindu mythologist, who said the world was supported by an elephant, that the elephant stood on a tortoise, but what supported the tortoise he could not say ...
>
> *Although at first, before I saw any cases, I was physiologically sceptical, especially respecting the physical manifestations,* after making all due allowance for other influences, I think any logical mind must come to the conclusion that *the present religious movement is owing to a direct outpouring of the Spirit of God,* and whatever doubt may have existed is, I think, removed by the good effects that have been so universally observed and acknowledged.

Archdeacon Stopford declares, in reply to those who assert the universality of the conviction of sin, the cry for mercy, and the feeling of peace as a proof of the spiritual origin of the affection, that 'in a great number of cases it is already proved by the lives of the persons, and the subsequent confession of the persons themselves, that there never was any real influence of the Spirit of God in their hearts.' 'And this', he says, 'I have to account for from what we know of hysteria.' Whereupon he proceeds to show how hysteria produces what is called 'self-feeling'; and argues that because 'guilt has been felt in some small degree by all, and suspected to a still greater extent as a possible cause of unknown suffering', accompanied, moreover, as it is, by a popular 'expectation of a new form of distress arising from this very cause, a cry for mercy suggests itself as its remedy.'

But what if the statement—made by one who spent only ten days in the north of Ireland, and whose inquiries were only confined to Belfast—that it is 'invariably acknowledged', that 'in a great number of cases', and 'in very many instances', stricken persons turn out to be unrenewed, stands opposed to other more matured and more extended observation? I have the solemn testimony of a minister, even in Belfast itself, both by personal assurances and by letter, that 'five out of six of all the cases' (400 at least) 'which have come under his personal observation and examination, have manifested tokens of genuine conversion, and are 'such as may well *gladden the church of God.*' Now, admitting that 'hysteria' might account for *one-sixth* of these cases, or that such proportion of cases indicated mere 'conviction' without 'conversion', what can Archdeacon Stopford say of the *five-sixths?* Let himself give the reply.

'The existence of such real feelings [of sorrow and mourning for sin] can only be believed in evidence of *previous feeling or subsequent conduct.*' Let us then test the *cases* by the Archdeacon's own standard. Granting, as we do, that animal emotion has nothing in it of a religious character, yet if 'previous feeling' and 'subsequent conduct' both attest that there has been something more than the physical in a vast majority of cases of prostration, can the Archdeacon deny that a Divine influence has been present?

We do admit, with him, that *'words spoken while in that state'* (hysteria), namely, 'of sorrow and mourning for sin, afford no proof that such feeling is genuine or real, however sincerely it may be believed in by the patient at the time'; and we grant, moreover, that in *some* (*not* 'very many') it has subsequently appeared that 'there never was any real influence of the Spirit of God in their hearts', even after professed conviction, and cries for mercy. But what if 'real feelings' are proved to exist on 'evidence of *previous* feeling or *subsequent* conduct'; must not the effect correspond with the cause? Can 'the paroxysm of hysteria' account for the *'antea'*, or the *'post hoc'?*[2] And if not, where is the 'counterwork' in those physical affections which are preceded by genuine conviction of sin, and followed by real conversion? What have such cases to do as parallels with 'sympathy', or 'self-feeling', or 'the *expectation* of a new form of distress', or with the case of a child in its *first* illness, crying out again and again under a new and strange form of physical distress, 'I am very hungry?' Are such cases of real conversion but 'a re-adaptation' of the child's case 'founded on mere experience'? The Archdeacon himself says no; he also qualifies, in the Appendix of the fourth edition of his pamphlet, the statement that 'all the cases he saw in Belfast were unmistakably hysterical', and that such, so far as he could judge, was every case described to him. He did not mean to say 'that all the bodily affections *in the Revival movement* are hysterical'. Yet, even after a medical friend in Belfast had assured him that he was *forced* to look on them as something different, the Archdeacon still defends his position as tenable with regard to 'the great majority of cases'. He declares that he 'did not see one of the "non-hysterical affections"'. He also appeals to 'inductive philosophy' to support his views.

Accepting, therefore, this Baconian standard of inquiry, we proceed in another chapter to inquire what have been the general spiritual results of stricken cases throughout Ulster.

---

[2] *antea:* before, formerly; *post hoc:* after this, after the event, *Ed.*

CHAPTER 26
THE PHYSIOLOGICAL AFFECTIONS,
AND THEIR SOLUTION.

WE have already given one authority as to Belfast itself, and that testimony could be indefinitely multiplied. The Archdeacon's examination did not extend to the province at large, and here 'facts' become 'stubborn things' indeed. In his former parish in County Tyrone, a mighty work of Awakening has been in progress, accompanied by physical manifestations. The correspondent of a public journal, in sending an account of the movement for publication, remarks that if the Archdeacon paid a visit to his former scene of labour, he would find mighty *spiritual* changes there in connection with nervous agitations.

The Hon. and Rev. H. Ward has given his solemn written testimony that in nearly all the cases of 'striking down' in the parish of Killinchy, in Downshire, has issued a real conversion; and has in my own hearing, at a public meeting at Newry, in very solemn tones, condemned those who attempted to account for these agitations on the 'hysterical' theory. The Rev. G. V. Chichester, curate of Portrush, in a letter written to me after he had read a review, with extracts of the Archdeacon's pamphlet, says, 'I think some counter statement is absolutely needed.' He says of the tendency of the review, and of the extracts from the pamphlet, that he fears it is 'calculated to shake the minds of many who live at a distance, and lead them to resolve the whole thing into that wonderful disease, hysteria.'

'I have seen', he adds, '(and the other clergy of my neighbourhood) very little of such hysteria as Archdeacon Stopford describes, *though I have seen whole parishes in which a work of grace seemed apparent in one or more members of almost every family "visited".'* In like manner this clergyman virtually sets aside the Archdeacon's statement that Presbyterians 'struck' are often little else but 'Presbyterians turned Methodist; class-meeting is their future worship.' Mr Chichester points out to me the error of the *English Churchman,* when it asserts that one effect of the Revival is to divert the people from *public* worship, and to depreciate our Christian ministry. I myself can also testify from wide observation that the very opposite is the case. Never were places of worship in Ulster so crowded as now, or ministers so honoured as now. One brother, writing me from Boardmills, County Down, on the 26th October, expresses the universal feeling among the Presbyterian people, 'NEVER WAS THE MINISTERIAL OFFICE SO MAGNIFIED AS NOW.' Mr Chichester, also, in a letter to the *Daily News,* dated Sept. 12th, says,

> I cannot but feel, in conjunction with *the great majority* of those who, like myself, have personally witnessed and shared in the movement, that Archdeacon Stopford's pamphlet is calculated to leave a wrong impression on the public mind. It is quite incorrect to say that sensitive women are the only [Archdeacon S. speaks, however, of 'men capable of becoming hysterical' also, but they are not the *'strong men'* of Mr. C.] subjects of the change, for there are *a great number of strong men* affected in every locality, and sometimes more violently than the women. It is also unjust to give the impression that all the cases of conversion can be reduced to hysteria. By far the greater number of cases are either without hysteria, or soon lose the symptoms; and the genuineness of their religion is proved by its fruits.

Another Episcopal clergyman writes from the county of Antrim, of 'some men openly *"stricken"*, and almost without exception these have continued *steadfast,* notwithstanding that the antecedents of some of them were such as would not bear the light.'

The Rev. Flavel Cooke, incumbent of Millbrook, Devonport, writing to an officer at Woolwich, after saying, that with the exception of one woman and one man, we 'found next to no excitement' in Ulster, refers to the woman physically affected, as one in whom, along with the nervous agitation, was clearly to be discerned 'a line of spiritual operation affecting her soul'. He pertinently asks, 'Can hysteria alone leave, as an after effect, faith in Christ? Can hysteria sweep over the frame of a sinner, and develop in its passage the fruits of the Spirit?'

The Rev. Charles Seaver, incumbent of St John's, Belfast, after referring to cases of persons physically affected, says:—'Undoubtedly there is not any necessary connection between the bodily ailment, whatever it be, and the spiritual work; but neither is *it to be violently deprecated, as if its direct and necessary tendency were evil.'* He remarks, first, that the number thus affected bears a small proportion to that of those aroused to spiritual things; secondly, that the 'cases' are divisible into two parts: one, and the much larger, those who are excited to tears and trembling; the other, and smaller, in which complete prostration of the nervous system ensued; thirdly, that bad bodily results seldom ensue, unless under injudicious treatment, or prolonged and improper excitement. He then adds—'We see, then, no cause for the alarm pronounced by some. With prudence and caution, *such* as we *believe* and *know* are used by the great majority of those engaged in the movement, evil effects are guarded against, *while we see clearly the plainest and happiest results in countless instances';* Let the reader observe that Mr Seaver has been referring solely to persons stricken, and also weigh well what follows:—'*The impressions on the individuals themselves have been deepened and rendered lasting, and the careless have been awakened to deep spiritual anxiety.*[3]

These are 'facts', which, on the principles of 'inductive philosophy', warrant a general conclusion.

The twofold result also thus produced—first, on the converts themselves, and, secondly, on the ungodly around—is specially worthy of thoughtful attention, as suggesting reasons why the physical affections should have been permitted to accompany the Ulster Awakening. In particular, the *striking down* of the wicked, I was assured by two of the town missionaries of Belfast, was the means of arresting the attention of the *very worst* of the population. On this class of men and women, continued persuasions and entreaties had been tried in vain; but when one of their number was prostrated before their eyes, when

---

[3] A paper read by the Rev. C. Seaver before the Evangelical Alliance at Belfast, September, 1859.

his agony and despair found vent in loud cries, they were filled with awful apprehensions of the reality of Divine wrath, of judgment to come, and of hell; and gathering, moreover, around the stricken ones, they heard—it may be for the *first* time—those gospel statements which, applied by the Holy Spirit, brought them also to the Saviour's feet. In direct confirmation of this, I have to submit the following extract of a letter addressed to me by the Rev. Hugh Hunter of Bellaghy, in the county of Londonderry, on the 25th of October, 1859:—

> I think about two months ago the prostrations in this place ceased. I don't regret the absence of them. We were glad to take the blessing in any way the God of grace was pleased to bestow it, but the physical sufferings which were evidently the unavoidable accompaniments of the great movement are, in themselves, considered by no means desirable.
>
> *They were sent by God to serve a special end, and when that purpose was served they ceased. They were sent—in my mind—fully as much for the benefit of others,* as for those who were the subjects of them. *Every prostration I firmly believe was a sermon, a thrilling appeal to the profligate and a solemn warning to those who were at ease in Zion,* who, because they had a name and a place in the church, seemed to think that all was well with them for time and eternity.

To the same effect a sober-minded Christian layman writes me from Banbridge, County Down,—

> We have still occasionally some cases of 'prostration', but they are becoming less frequent, and this we do not regret. They appear to have served the purpose of arousing the minds of the ignorant and careless to think of their salvation in a way which no other instrumentality (humanly speaking) could have done.

As to genuine fruits following in the cases of persons thus stricken, a medical gentleman, in the same town, writes:—

> A very large number have been visibly affected, and so far all have persevered in the right way. All have been influenced by it more or less, even those opposed to it. We have scarcely any drunkenness or quarrelling. Vice of every kind has hid its head, or been altogether banished. The

public-houses are empty, and in place of drunken brawlings or noise in the streets, the singing of psalms and prayer.

In the preceding narrative I have given the testimony of many ministers and others as to great numbers stricken, whose cases had turned out well. Witness the statements of the Rev. J. Stuart of Ballycarry, of the Rev. Messrs Adams and Buick of Ahoghill, of the Rev. H. Hunter, the Rev. James Rogers, and the testimony of ministers at Ballymena and Coleraine, and elsewhere—all personally known to me. All these Presbyterian ministers entirely accord with the Episcopal clergy already quoted from, and whose language so strongly contrasts with the views and statements of Archdeacon Stopford. While, therefore, the value of his pamphlet, as a warning against extravagance, excitement, and attempts to *create* hysterical emotion, is not to be despised, yet it undoubtedly leaves a *wrong impression* as to the *results* of stricken cases in Ulster, considered in a moral and spiritual point of view. We leave to his severe denunciations any *one* Presbyterian or other minister who has *prayed* that persons might be stricken, and also denounce, as he does, any preachers who have 'given countenance to the persuasion that they are persons all safe and right, because they have gone through a diseased state of physical feeling'. Let the guilty parties at Belfast, or elsewhere, bear the blame. Let Methodism, which, as 'a system', says the Archdeacon, 'needs the warning more than any other', take the warning if it has transgressed. Let the *'saeva indignatio'*[4] *not* be written on our tombs, but go forth in righteous denunciation *now*. But while follies have doubtless been committed by *a few,* we deny that any preacher (such as that one described by the Archdeacon) ever intended by his preaching to perpetrate 'an outrage on the moral nature of woman'; and also refuse to believe that the result (of hysteria) is *very commonly intended,* with deliberate premeditation of the means. I also protest against the description of a professed mill-girl convert, who was *dressy* and vain, as at all applicable to that class of converts, at Belfast. From having been nearly two years the minister of a Belfast congregation, containing a large body of 'mill-girls', I can confidently say that 'showy bracelets,

---

[4] *saeva indignatio:* fierce indignation, *Ed.*

several rings on the fingers', do not characterize them as a class. Nor yet could I say—after having visited the house where one young girl, who fell into 'sleeps', and who related, on her awakening, supposed 'visions' (the supernatural character of which I totally reject)—that 'the company were highly amused', and that, 'from first to last, there was not one trace of anything like reverential, religious feeling.' I saw parents and acquaintances stand by solemnized and awe-struck. The joy of true conversion, after severe agitations of body, and terrors of soul, had in that young girl's peculiar nervous condition so acted on her imagination that she really believed she had been in heaven, and had seen the Saviour there.

I believe that those who have countenanced the idea that the gift of prophecy was revived, have no sympathy with the expression of an eminent minister, that however the Miriams might fret and fume, in a certain town, 'a very large number of the people were turned into *prophets* and precentors', if that was intended to mean anything more than as afterwards stated, that the converts 'ministered to the religious instruction' of persons who had been stricken, and 'were the readiest and most efficient agents for the diffusion of religion'.

I know also that ministers generally in Ireland discourage as much as possible all physical manifestations, and are thoroughly in accord with Archdeacon Stopford, to 'direct emotional feeling according to the will of Christ'. I *did* indeed hear in Ireland of *one* minister who seemed disappointed after an address given by a friend that no cases of 'striking down' had occurred, but that this is common there is no good reason to believe; certainly not. And then as to 'the sermons in frightful contrast to the gospel of love', which Archdeacon Stopford 'heard',—sermons wanting in 'any appeal to reason and to conscience, and divested in their application of any connection with the love of God through Christ', all Ulster will rise up and say, that not one such sermon has been preached among a thousand.

The Archdeacon's design to warn against encouraging or *creating* nervous excitement is praiseworthy; but unhappily the impressions left by his pamphlet, as a whole, on the mind, to anyone who has not seen and examined the real state of the Ulster Awakening, are most unfavourable. Enemies of all religion have eagerly seized upon it, and not all the explanations, alterations, and apologies in a fourth edition can undo the mischief. His main position, moreover, is untenable. Hysteria does *not* account for those physical prostrations so numerous over the north of Ireland, in which—although *quiet* conversions have far outnumbered them—as attested by fruits following, the Spirit of God *has* been working in his irresistible might and glorious majesty.

Giving, then, full credit to the Archdeacon's desire to write in the cause of truth as his sole object, and acknowledging that abuses have been committed, the repetition of which may have been prevented by his counsels and warnings, yet we respectfully submit that the true theory of physical agitations remains yet to be explained. That explanation I shall not attempt in language of my own, but submit it in the weighty words of men of great sobriety of mind, and men also of remarkable philosophic acumen, who have written on the subject. Bishop M'Ilvain of Ohio, in a letter to the Bishop of Down and Connor, says:—

> At the great Revival in the parish of Cambuslang in 1742, in which Whitefield took part, and at which, among others, the eminent mathematician, and also the author of the *Cross of Christ*, Maclaurin of Glasgow, was present, cases of prostration or 'falling' frequently occurred, and profane persons called it 'the falling'.

One feels as if reading a chapter out of the history of the present Revival, and finds also a true solution of the similar prostrations, in the following language employed by the historian of the Cambuslang Revival:—

> As for what these young men termed 'the falling', it was a way of speaking among scoffers at the time, occasioned by the bodily distress, which in many instances accompanied conviction. *The word was much objected to in consequence;* but when the intimate connection of soul and body is considered, it will not appear surprising that *great outward agitation should mark the emotions of a soul fully awakened to the dread realities of judgment and eternity.*

The loss of a dear relative and many of the other painful vicissitudes of life, when suddenly forced on the mind, affect the bodily constitution so powerfully as, in some instances, to occasion even death. And if such is sometimes the effect of things merely temporal, need we wonder that a vivid sense of a sinner's salvation out of Christ, with nothing but the brittle thread of life between him and everlasting destruction should over-power the body? The wonder rather is that the preaching of the solemn truths of God's word is so rarely followed by such consequences; and we can account for this only by supposing that the Spirit of God does not make the sinner at once alive to all the terrors of his condition.[5]

In the *Evidence of Revivals,* furnished by ministers of the Church of Scotland in 1840, the Rev. Robert M'Cheyne of Dundee gives the following testimony:—'I have myself frequently seen the preaching of the word attended with such power, that the feelings of the people could not be restrained. I have heard individuals *cry aloud as if pierced through with a dart.'* And when 'tender gospel invitations' have been given, 'every sentence has been responded to by the bitterest agony. At such times *I have seen persons so overcome that they could not walk or stand alone.'*

Dr Merle d'Aubigné, in an address delivered on the 3rd of Oct-ober, 1859, at the opening of the School of Theology at Geneva, spoke as follows:—'We would ask', he said,

the adversaries of this movement if it is surprising that a strong emotion of the mind should also act upon the body? Are, then, these two parts of man two separate beings? Are they not, on the contrary, most intimately united? Psychology teaches us the different systems invented to explain this close union. Whether we subscribe to that of a pre-established har-mony, or to some other system, it matters little; according to them all, the mind and body form one and the same being. And yet some are now to be found who would affirm that one part of this being cannot, and ought not, to feel that which passes in the other. What! is it not a fact, that an eloquent orator, a great actor, a skilful physician, sometimes even the simplest person, can in certain cases work upon those who are quite

[5] *Narrative of Revivals of Religion in England, Scotland, and Wales,* (Glasgow: W. Collins, 1840), p. 7. 'With regard to the Revival at Cambuslang', says the writer, 'the greater number were not under bodily distress'—in exact accordance with the Ulster Awakening now.

strangers to them, and affect them with the most powerful emotions; and is this influence to be considered inadmissible when it refers to the mutual action between two parts of the same being?

I was present lately at a meeting in an important continental town where several learned doctors, as well as many fervent Christians, were assembled. I brought before them the principal features of the Revival in Ireland. One of them, a man of great experience, said, 'The influence of the mind upon the body is a palpable truth which ought to be recognized by everyone. I can give an example to prove it. About forty years ago I was a young man of twenty-five years of age, full of strength and vigour. I had been separated by the sea from my father for about sixteen years, but had reason to hope that he would soon come to see me, or that I might go and visit him. One day the servant entered my room, saying, 'Your father is here.' The sensation produced upon my mind had such an effect upon my body that I fell powerless to the ground. Ah, if that joyful announcement, 'Your father is here', could make such an impression, what might not be produced upon a newly awakened conscience by the double tidings, 'Sin is in thy heart—thou art lost!' Then, 'Behold thy Saviour—thou art saved!'

After he had done speaking, a pious layman asked leave to relate an incident from his own experience. 'I had been converted', said he, 'about fifteen years, but had become cold and indifferent. One day, my conscience accusing me, I shut myself up in my room, and falling on my knees, I reviewed my life during the past fifteen years. This retrospect brought my sins vividly before my mind, and I was so terrified at the thought of them that I fell down insensible, and remained in that state for some time.'

I myself remember, gentlemen, having been, thirty-five or forty years ago, at a Swiss village on the Rhine, of which the excellent Spliess was pastor. That learned and pious man died not long ago Antistes (President) of the church of Schaffhausen; his biography, which has lately been published in German, I beg to recommend to your notice. His preaching produced, at the time I speak of, a remarkable Awakening, which was accompanied in many cases by physical affections, even more extraordinary than those which are witnessed in Ireland. The converts were sometimes seen passing their hands rapidly over their body, as if to drive away the evil spirit. Well, after forty years that work still subsists, in the canton of Schaffhausen, free from all excess, and is manifested—amongst other ways—by charitable institutions of the most interesting character. This last objection, therefore, which has arisen from the state of those who have been stricken in Ireland, cannot, any more than the others, be brought forward as a charge against the Revival. *The bodily affections only prove one thing—the existence in the soul of a deep and powerful feeling.*

The Rev. G. V. Chichester says, 'All attempts to account for this great movement on natural principles are futile.' He then adds :

Is it an epidemic—something working in the air? The 'prince of the power of the air' does not usually produce such orthodox results from his atmospheric experiments. But it may easily be resolved, it is said, into sympathetic excitement. Are souls saved by , sympathy? Is a change equal to that of the creation of light, or of calling a world out of chaos, produced merely by one nervous mind acting upon another?

Again, we are told that such a movement has its origin in nothing more than the natural excitability of the Irish character. If this be so, why has it originated in that especial part of Ireland where the population are half Scottish? Not in the south or west, or in those places where they are purely Celtic, but in the extreme north, where, owing to the reason mentioned, they possess a larger amount of the unexcitable element of character than in any other province.

And if it be said that exciting scenes, and sermons, and prayer-meetings are the producing cause, how then are we to account for such cases as these? A person was struck down during the reading of the Apostles' Creed in the Church of England service. There is nothing very exciting in the Apostles' Creed, nothing very much calculated to evoke hysteria. And this is only one out of numberless instances of cases daily occurring during the Church of England service. Many are affected in the quiet Sunday-school class, many on the road-side, in the field, and in their own houses; and at a small religious meeting in a cottage in a mountainous parish of the county of Derry, no less than nine persons were struck down with deep and genuine convictions, while the rector of the parish, a sober-minded and experienced Christian minister, was cautioning his hearers against identifying bodily manifestations with the work of conversion.

That there are painful circumstances attending this movement it is impossible to deny. Pamphlets have been published—clever, and eloquent, and scientific; letters have been written, and sermons have been preached, especially by persons at a distance, in order to enlighten the public mind on this great subject. We read of hysteria, for instance, and hear many strange and interesting things about it, especially its counterfeit symptoms of religion. But whatever of important and cautionary truth such treatises may contain (and I do not at all depreciate them), yet I only turn away from them as much confirmed as ever as to the reality of the movement. Does it disprove the fact that the tide is going out, or coming in, because a counter-current may be pointed out along the shore? or are we to conclude that there is no good money in the Bank, because there are a number of bad notes, and light sovereigns, and copper shillings to be found there?

So in this instance, supposing that we meet with false cases, fanatical cases, cases of paralysis, of derangement, of hysteria, of catalepsy (and these are only the exception), what do they prove, even if they were more numerous than they are? Nothing but the truism, that evil will always be found mixed up with good.

In reply to the statements of the *Saturday Review* and the *Lancet,* a very able writer, in the *News of the Churches* for September, 1859, says:—

The *Saturday Review* is evidently ignorant of the details of the work which it caricatures. It rushes into the subject with brilliant daring, but in its reference to facts, it shows that it has no acquaintance either with the Irish Revivals, or with those earlier Revivals to which it refers. In its comparison of the movement to the excitement of a great public assembly, such as that at Ephesus, when the people cried out about the space of two hours, 'Great is Diana of the Ephesians', it shows that it regards it as proceeding from great camp-meetings at which multitudes have become suddenly prostrate after being wrought up to a high pitch of excitement. The great meetings, such as those in the Botanic Gardens of Belfast, have, however, been the consequences, and not the cause of the movement. The movement has originated in the quiet work going on in individual souls, and, amidst all its extent, there is no man who has stood forth prominently as a Revival preacher. It has been pre-eminently, as in America, a work of the people themselves, and has manifested its power chiefly through the instrumentality and by the desire of prayer. The writer displays striking inaccuracy when he says that this Revival arises from 'the tendency which exists in all crowds and large assemblies to act upon sympathy, quite apart from reason and conviction'. If one feature more than another has characterized this Revival, it has been the mental action which has been apparent in almost every case. Even the Roman Catholics have been able in general, though attaining to previously unknown or distorted truths, to state explicitly the causes of their violent emotion, viz., the sense of the burden of sin in the presence of a just and holy God, and the recognition afterwards of Christ as an all-sufficient Saviour. There is not one of the converts who does not state positively, that the physical effects produced in what is called the 'striking down' did not proceed from a mysterious bodily impression, but from the oppressive burden of a mind agonized under the over-whelming sense of guilt in the sight of God. Nothing, therefore, could be more contrary to the truth than to speak of this as a movement in which reason and conviction have had no part. The *Review,* in accepting the medical explanations of the *Lancet,* shows again that he has thought it of no importance to investigate the facts of which he treats. *Medical men who have examined the symptoms on the spot, are, as far as we know, unanimous in regarding with contempt the theories of the* Lancet. *We have seen it stated in numerous letters written by them, that the account of the phenomena adapts itself in no measure to the facts.* Nothing, besides, could be more unguarded than to make, without support from the previous evidence, the assumption that catalepsy is a contagious disease, and may at once spread over large districts of country. The *Saturday Review,* in depending on such precarious support, gives an example of the bias which affects even ingenuous minds when dealing with facts on which *conclusions had been previously formed.*

Peter Bayne, Esq., the philosophic editor of the Edinburgh *Witness,* after stating his desire to discuss 'the matter' (of physical agitations), 'divested as far as possible of all evangelical phraseology', thus grapples boldly with the question:—

> The point now requiring our attention is that of the bodily appearances which have accompanied these admittedly great changes upon the con-

duct of these people. We assume at once that, as the effect, so the cause, is a work of God; for to suppose that the actual results in question are from either the devil or man, each or both together, is in direct contravention of all reasoning. Nay, more, we affirm that it is God's work in a *direct, special* way. Everything is admitted that can be arrogated to the side of natural causes; and full indulgence is granted to that sort of shirking compromise,—ripe and plenteous in these latter days of mechanics' institutes and constitutions of man,—which tries, with all imaginable self-complacency, to hold at once by Scripture and by a philosophy altogether anti-scriptural. Notwithstanding all this, we at once affirm it to be a psychological impossibility to reconcile the phenomena referred to by any other than distinct evangelical theory. We rather suspect that the scriptural theory of conversion obtaining now-a-days, among some of our younger preachers especially, is deeply tinctured by certain vague notions on *intuition* and *secondary causation,* and that the work of God's Spirit, as disclosed in the Scriptures, is very quietly glossed over, if not altogether ignored; and further, that a very similar state of things exists among men who would feel high offence if they were recognized as belonging to any other than the class of sound orthodox Christians. For our own part, we are satisfied to abide by the old landmarks of the inspired word; and find them amply sufficient to guide us in this, as in all like difficulties. It is quite true that God acts in the *natural* world by natural causes; but, as we are told by admitted authority, the conversion of a sinner belongs *not* to this natural world, but is a *supernatural* act, and therefore demanding supernatural means to produce it. On either the Calvinist or the Arminian theory, *this* act requires the *direct, special* agency of God. Now, starting from this ground, we are ready to take up the operation of secondary causes: their existence has not been denied, but only the necessity of keeping them in their proper sphere asserted. As in the primordial act of creation—to borrow an illustration—the direct, special work of God was essential (for clearly there could be no secondary causes in operation *then*), while his after-work was carried on according to the operation of causes, the nature of which he had by his primordial act defined; so in our present case, *the primordial act in the effectual conversion of a sinner is the work of God's Spirit on the intellectual and emotional parts of his nature; and as these, along with the other faculties of his mind, hold a very distinct relation to his nervous system—the brain*—we at once perceive how this system must be influenced under the circumstances referred to. Between the brain and the mind there is an intimate state of action and reaction, whether we admit this to proceed the length which some physiologists hold, or only to a modified extent. This being the relation, it is evident that, *other things being equal, the greater the mental cause so much greater will be the consequent nervous effect, and vice versa.*

Now, admitting, on the very lowest explanation, that the cause acting on the converted man was, though moral in its nature, an altogether humanly produced conviction of sin, it will still be seen how terrible must be the effect that is wrought upon his nervous system. *This effect will, of course, be vastly modified in its external features by the peculiar idiosyncrasy of the man. And more abundantly will this effect be expected to appear outwardly in the case of a poor, ignorant man, when we recollect the every-day fact that mental emotion is always the most powerfully indicated in uncultured minds.* It is not necessary, neither is this the place, to state fully the enormous extent of that influencing cause of mental, and hence of nervous, manifestation which the case under discussion supposes; but if every page of the Scriptures, the every-day preaching from the pulpit, and all our missionary exertions, be not a mere farce and a sham, then surely *that* cause were enough, and more than enough, to produce all the phenomena in question. We very much fear that men who are immersed daily and hourly in all the harassing cares of worldly business, but dimly realize—with rare exceptions—man's present state and future prospects, as involved in the phrase 'conversion'. *But here, among these persons, has this realization been effected; and strange would it be if such realization did not show itself by outward signs,* too obtrusive, perhaps, to please fastidious tastes or rose-water sentimentality. It is, of course, quite true that these bodily manifestations, *as such,* prove nothing more than that an all-pervading and overwhelming emotion has been produced; but it does prove that. *The nature of that emotion remains to be inferred from its after-consequences. And here the conditions of the question granted are fully up to the demands of the argument,—the after-life, so far as it has gone of these people being, with perhaps but few exceptions, in sound accordance with the assumed cause and origin of their conversion.*

As to those instances reported where disease of the nervous system has been the physical result,—*the moral result being quietly left out of view*,—such melancholy results are perfectly explainable on the theory we have ventured to lay down. The act of God's Spirit in 'conversion' influences the mind, and thus reacts on the very delicately organized brain; and if that brain, either by self-inflicted or by hereditary causes, be in an abnormal state, that is, over-sensitive or otherwise diseased, then clearly such a brain cannot receive any powerful shock whatever without suffering more or less in its integrity.

Without attempting here to give explanations, consistently with our present theory, of every fact connected with these religious Revivals, it may be well, before concluding, to notice one objection which has been made by even the friends of the movement. Respecting these cases of disease, they either deny the fact of disease being produced, or affirm that the agency at work has not been really and truly Divine. Now, we object to this one-sided view of the whole fact; and maintain that the agency may be Divine in the strictest sense of the word, and yet the result *physically* be disease. These timid friends should remember that God does act confessedly in this manner. In the thunder-storm, the hurricane, the tempest, the famine, and the pestilence, we have instances to show how inseparable is the connection between his work and the operation of these secondary causes, so productive of misery and afflic-tion. Doubtless it will be found in the case now under our review, as in all others, that out of seeming evil he ever educes good.

Finally, we refer to the masterly paper, read before the Evangelical Alliance by the Rev. Dr McCosh (a distinguished philosopher, author of *The Method of the Divine Government*), on 'The Ulster Revival, and its Physiological Accidents'. He commences by observing—'A strong prejudice has been entertained against the Revival, because it has been accompanied by bodily manifestations in the case of some. I am first to address myself to that prepossession which is keeping many from acknowledging it to be a true work of God.' He then tells how for-merly as a minister on the eastern coast of Scotland, and standing on the shores of the German Ocean,[6] he saw a ship trying to make the harbour during a furious storm; how the ship struck on a rock and rebounded; how a mother who had a boy in that ship suddenly

---

[6] The German Ocean: the North Sea, *Ed.*

fell down convulsed and prostrate; how, carried to her dwelling, she continued long, now unconscious, and anon in terrible agony, till her son—saved—was brought to her. He then adds—

> Suppose that this mother, instead of fearing that her son was about to be drowned, had been led suddenly by the truths of God's word, applied by the Spirit, to apprehend that her soul was about to perish because of sin, I am convinced that the very same bodily effects would have taken place, and I believe she would not have found peace, until Jesus, the Son of God, had been presented to her.

Still more suggestive as to the *class* of temperaments who manifest bodily agitation under strong mental emotion, and as explaining philosophically the true cause of physiological prostration in connection with the Revivals, is the following:—

> At one part of my life, it was my painful duty to intimate to many a poor woman, who thought herself a sailor's wife, that she was a widow, for that her husband had perished in the waters of the Baltic Sea. I laboured to convey the sad intelligence in the most delicate manner. I sought to prepare her mind for its coming, and often began a long way off, but whatever the plan I took, I had at last to speak plainly, and as the awful truth did burst upon her, what a scene had I to witness! The effects differed in the case of different individuals. Some struggled with their terrible emotions, and kept themselves wonderfully composed, and this not because they did not sorrow, but because they controlled their feelings. Some could not shed tears nor utter a cry, but felt like a tree struck with lightning, and withered on the instant. Others gave way to frightful cries, tears, and convulsions, ending in bodily prostrations, and to such it was useless to speak for a time; I committed them to their friends, and returned after an interval to administer to them the consolations of religion. Now, suppose that these same persons had been assembled to hear the preaching of the word, and that by a gracious movement of the Spirit of God, they had been led to see their sin in its true colours, *I apprehend that precisely similar bodily—or, as they should be called, physiological—effects would have followed, and that these would have varied according to the nature, and depth, and intensity of the sorrow for sin cherished,* AND ACCORDING TO THE PECULIAR TEMPERAMENT

OF THE INDIVIDUAL.—This was expressed to me by a simple-minded woman, who had never attended any Revival meetings, but who was one day struck down with a sense of sin in her own dwelling. When she had recovered her composure, she said to me—'I am not a strong woman in body. I have been in this same state of body before, but on former occasions it was because I had lost a child, or suffered some temporal calamity; now I trust it is because I have been led to see my sins and my need of a Saviour.' In this present state of things, mind and body are closely connected; and whatever deeply affects the mind, be it from the earth or from above, must also affect the bodily frame, Man cannot think without the co-operation of one part of his brain; and as little, I believe, can he have a mental feeling or emotion, without an action in another part of his brain. It would be out of place in such a paper as this, to enter into minute physiological discussions. It will be quite enough to state, that it is the opinion of eminent physiologists, that as thought acts on the higher parts of the brain, so feeling of every kind acts on organs towards the base of the brain. These organs are near the place where all the nerves of the five senses terminate, and near the place whence the delicate nerves start toward the face, chest, and heart. Wherever there is strong feeling, there is action in this part of the brain, which produces an effect on the nerves, reaching over the frame. But it is not necessary for my purpose to enter into such discussions. Everybody knows that strong feeling produces certain effects on the body. In particular, a keen fear of approaching evil, or sorrow for evil arrived, agitates the nerves, and through them certain parts of the body. Man is fearfully and wonderfully made; and the general fact to which I have referred, while an evidence that man must suffer because he has sinned, may also be a provision for good, as a warning of danger, and an outlet for feeling which should not be for ever cherished. But we have not the full truth unless we add, that all feelings which contemplate the good—such as love, confidence, faith, and hope—have no tendency to agitate or prostrate the body, but have rather a stimulating, bracing, and health-giving influence. On grounds which I am immediately to state, I believe that this work of Revival in Ulster is a work of God. It has been characterized by deep mental feeling. Now, I suppose that the fear of the wrath of God, will produce the very same effects on the body, as any other deep fear, and that the sorrow for sin will have the same influence on the bodily frame, as the sorrow for the death of a son or a husband. This I apprehend it must do, unless God were to interfere to prevent it by special miracles—that is, to interfere with his own laws, which he is not wont to do in ordinary circumstances.

Then with discriminating wisdom Dr McCosh says—

'But I do not found my belief in the work as a genuine work on the bodily manifestations. This would be as contrary to Scripture as to science; Scripture sets no value on bodily exercise, and nowhere points to any bodily effect whatever, as a proof or test of the presence of the Spirit of God. *Nor have I ever heard anyone who takes an enlightened interest in this work, even appealing to any such evidence.*

All that these bodily affections prove, is *the existence of deep feeling.* As to whether this feeling is genuine or not—as to whether it is spiritual or not—this is to be tried by far different tests; it is to be tried by the truths of God's word. The Bible and science, truly so-called, are in this, as in every other respect, in beautiful harmony. Physiology can say this is a proof of deep feeling; physiology cannot say whether the feeling is spiritual or carnal. We are brought back to the law and the testimony; by them and by nothing else are we to try the spirits, whether they be of God.

Dr McCosh then proceeds to show that 'the galaxy of graces' (*Gal.* 5:22) have *all* been realized in cases of persons physically affected. To these spiritual as well as to *social* results, we shall refer in another chapter.

CHAPTER 27
SPIRITUAL AND SOCIAL FRUITS
OF THE AWAKENING

Letters of the Bishop of Down and Connor, and the Rev. T. Campbell—
drunkenness disappearing—spiritual fruits in Ulster—varied testimony—
increased missionary zeal and liberality.

THE Rev. Dr McCosh, referring to the *spiritual fruits* of the
Awakening, asks:—

On what, then, it will be asked, do I found my conviction that this work
is divine? I answer, on the fact that I have found everyone of the blessed
effects which are represented in Scripture as being peculiarly the fruits
of the Spirit. Everyone who has taken but a cursory glance at the work,
has noticed the conviction of sin—sharp, and penetrating, and deep;
and everyone who has at all looked beneath the surface has seen how
the persons thus impressed will hear of only one object. Talk to them
of anything else, very possibly they will not understand you—certainly
they will feel no interest in what you say; but *speak of Christ, and their
attention is gained and their heart is won. This has always been to me an evidence that the work is a genuine one, as it so powerfully draws men's regards
to our blessed Saviour.* This preparatory-work has issued in a vast multitude of cases in yet better, and riper, and richer fruits.

Let us look at that galaxy of graces set before us (*Gal.* 5:22-24):
'The fruit of the Spirit is love, joy, peace, long-suffering, gentleness,
goodness, faith, meekness, temperance: against such there is no law.
And they that are Christ's have crucified the flesh with the affections
and lusts.' I have rejoiced to recognize in not a few all of these graces,
glittering like the stones on Aaron's breast-plate; and in everyone who
possesses them I acknowledge a genuine priest of God, who has been at
the mercy-seat, and is entitled at all times to enter into the holiest of all,
to commune with God.

As to love, that man cannot know what love is who has not seen it flowing forth like a flowing fountain from the hearts of our genuine converts—flowing forth towards God and towards all men. The embrace of the mother and son, as the son is in the mother's arms after years of separation, is not closer nor warmer than I have seen the embrace of two strong, stalwart men, as they met for the first time after each had passed through the trial of triumph, and rejoiced to find that his friend had done the same.

The joy of converts has in very many cases been, truly, the joy of the espousals of the soul to Christ; and this, in most cases, has terminated in a settled peace, clouded it may be at times, but yet a peace with God, in which his love is ever shining, though the person may not at all see it.

With what long-suffering have the converts usually borne the scoffs and jeers with which they have been assailed, seldom answering back or returning reviling for reviling! Some of the bitterest scoffers have been won, as they found all their reproaches answered only by prayers. Many a mother blesses God for the gentleness which they have discovered in a son or daughter, so unlike their former character; and I have known impetuous blasphemers, and bold female viragos, the terror of the neighbourhood, made gentle unto all, and struggling with every rising temptation to passion.

A spirit of goodness or benevolence has been one of the characteristics of the work, leading the converts to do good to all men as they have opportunity; and I trust it will grow in fervour, till it burn up and destroy all uncharitableness of man to man, or sect to sect. I do trust that all sectarian bitterness is being consumed in the glowing heat of this season.

As to faith, it was by it they were led to Christ, and by faith they stand. Many are not only daily, but hourly, feeding on the word, and calling on God in prayer. They are, therefore, meek and submissive to whatever God may be pleased to send.

It is, I trust, temperance, in the Bible sense—that is, the government of the passions—which is leading to the careful abstinence from intoxicating drinks; they avoid them as temptations by which the inhabitants of this province have been led into terrible evils; and this Revival has cured many drunkards who have stood out against all temperance societies.

Whatever men may say for or against bodily excitement, I am sure that against such there is no law. I believe, in regard to many at this time, that they are Christ's, because they seem to me to be crucifying with all their might—God giving them grace so to do—the flesh, with its affections and lusts.

I speak of numerous cases in this great town in which I usually reside, and in a quiet country district in which I preached and laboured for two months in summer, and I am fully persuaded in my own mind that I have seen, in great numbers, these gracious fruits. I confess that sometimes when I attended public assemblies and heard foolish statements, made in an indelicate spirit, by men who seem to have no awe of tenderness on their spirits in the midst of such awful scenes, I have been tempted to doubt of the work; but these doubts have ever been dispelled when, without seeking out the cases which the neighbourhood were wondering at (but rather carefully avoiding such), I mingled freely with those who were cast in my way in Providence, and got into their confidence, and had their experience poured into my ears and bosom.

But the physician of wide and diversified experience tells me—'Oh! I have, in my visits, seen precisely similar bodily effects, and these have no connection with religion.' I freely, and without reserve, admit all this to the physician, and I would feel ashamed of myself if I appealed to these physiological phenomena as proofs of this being a work of Revival. But let the physician look beyond the bodily affection to the spiritual experience, and he will discern in many, I do not say in all, a mental and spiritual effect which he may not have been in the habit of meeting with in his ordinary patients. He may *discern a faith, a newness of life and conduct,* which must have proceeded from far other sources than from nervous affection.

The Bishop of Down and Connor subsequently addressed the following letter to an English gentleman, who had been present at the Belfast meeting of the Evangelical Alliance. The bishop had informed the Christian Knowledge Society that his 'confirmations for the year would be more than four times the average. Before this', he adds, 'the young men would have spent their evenings in public-houses.'

Palace, Holywood, Oct. 3, 1859.

Sɪʀ,—I beg to acknowledge the receipt of your letter, and will offer a few suggestions, which, I trust, will be deemed a satisfactory explanation of the returns to which you allude.

Presuming that the police returns, quoted by *The Times,* are correct, and which I see no reason to doubt, still the deductions drawn from them against the happy results of the present religious Awakening are most erroneous.

In the first place, there are in Belfast about 25,000 Roman Catholics, a large proportion of whom are of the lower class, and as the 'Revival' has not, I regret to say, affected them, it is no lack of charity to presume that to the same extent that they furnished the criminals at the police-courts before the 'movement', to the same extent they do so now; and this should be borne in mind in the absence of all religious criminal statistics. Again, the religious Awakening has been most marked, and attended with the happiest results, among a larger class of the nominal Protestants of the different denominations, who were before careless and ungodly persons, accustomed too often to spend their Sundays in the public-houses, or drinking at home, but still seldom criminal drunkards in the eye of the law, as they committed no public breach of it. Now, their reformation—and I thank God that a great and salutary change has been wrought among many of them—did not in the slightest degree affect the police returns.

But the most gratifying change wrought under the 'Revival' by the awakening influence of the Spirit of God, is among the young of both sexes just growing up into maturity. Their seriousness, deep religious impressions, anxiety to read the word of God, and to attend public worship, all testify to a change of heart, and 'by their fruits ye shall know them.' Now, as few of this class were brought before the magistrates for an open violation of the laws, here again the police statistics are uninfluenced by the religious improvement which has taken place among them. Nor must it be forgotten that many of the committals at the Sessions in Belfast, are of the same parties who are again and again brought before the bench, and among whom, I fear, little good impressions have been made. Besides all this, a town with a population of 120,000 inhabitants, with thousands of strangers and sailors coming and going each day, does not afford so correct a field for tracing the social and moral improvement of the people as the country districts supply, and which Chief-Baron Pigot distinctly admitted in his observations at our last Assizes, and which the testimony of various country magistrates fully corroborates. Still there is a marked improvement in the character and conduct of the inhabitants of Belfast since the 'Revival' appeared; and can I prove this better than by pointing to the total cessation of those disgraceful party riots which were of frequent occurrence, and which were the subject of a Government Commission of Inquiry? My own experience in the discharge of my official duties gives me *abundant evidence of the great and holy work now leavening* my diocese, and points it out too clearly to be mistaken for natural causes, but leads me to recognize the source from whom and through whom 'all holy desires, good counsels, and just works do proceed'. I am, yours faithfully,

(*Signed*)   ROBERT DOWN AND CONNOR.

The second testimony is from the Rev. Theophilus Campbell, a highly esteemed Episcopalian clergyman, well known to me, who writes as follows:—

With regard to the social evil, some of the unfortunate women have come to my house imploring me to do something to take them off the streets. One woman of herself specified the Revival as the cause; and a companion (a Roman Catholic) joined her in this. They are both of them so far reclaimed. I know of six others who have given up their unholy calling. I have been requested to go to a house where three young women of this class lived—one a Church girl, and the other two Roman Catholics. I have visited them more than once, and, when speaking to them of the gospel, the tears have flowed down their cheeks. One has left the house, another has nearly made up her mind to follow her example. Indeed, she says she would, if she had any certain means of support. This is, I find, the difficulty. I have helped a little in this way, but great caution is necessary. I rather object to gratuitous aid, unless under very peculiar circumstances.

A young woman who was living with a man, having one child, her mother and a foundling being also supported by him, has within the last month dismissed him, thus depriving four individuals of their sole means of support. She was led to this by the text introduced into a sermon of mine: 'He whom thou hast is not thy husband.' It came like an arrow to her conscience, and now, after weeks of penitence and reading of the Scriptures, she is able to look up to him who did not spurn the woman of Samaria, as her Saviour.

As to profanity—I inquired of the proprietor of a large mill what results he could witness from the Awakening, among the workers in the mill. His answer was, 'From one end of it to the other you will not now hear an oath or an indelicate expression.' Another mill-owner has borne to me a similar testimony. A third was compelled to think favourably of 'the movement', from the effects he perceived among his people.

It is a gross calumny to say that either directly or indirectly the Revival has led to drunkenness, prostitution, and profanity. I know the reverse. I have seen it in all its phases; I have watched those who came within the sphere of my duty who have been affected by it, and I have been unable to detect aught to which the finger of morality might point as objectionable. I do not connect the gross imposition practised by sleepers and others with the movement, any more than I do the unchristian opposition of the infidel and the worldling.

The Rev. Hugh Hanna has written a second letter on the same subject as follows:—

Whatever difficulty may attend the exposition of the Belfast police returns, I am thankful to be able to state that a decided check has been given to ungodliness. Sixteen outcasts have to my own knowledge been reclaimed. I do not say that they have all been converted; I believe that several of them have been converted. I have seen them, like Magdalene of old, weeping tears of penitence and joy at Jesus' feet. But some of them have told me that they were constrained to think of amended lives and return to the paths of virtue, by the distress to which they had been reduced. The wages of unrighteous-ness would no longer adequately sustain an ungodly life. Some have returned to employment at manufactures; others have consented to go into a reformatory until their re-established characters shall recommend them to domestic service, to which they were accustomed.

The Protestant population of Belfast exceeds eighty thousand; they contribute but very few to the police returns; they are industrious and moral. But we have a Popish population of nearly forty thousand; *the vast majority of our paupers and criminals are Romanists*. The adverse press has conceded this fact. The Revival has had a wide field of operation amidst the eighty thousand professing Protestants of Belfast, and its results have been of a very prodigious and varied character. Our churches are crowded with attentive and earnest worshippers. Our Sabbath schools are crowded. Prayer-meetings are held on every evening of the week in all the Protestant parts of the town. The Bible and religious books have supplanted the corrupting trash which, scattered over the land by certain periodicals, were too largely read in Belfast. Attendance on worship is increased greatly, society has a new aspect; the church is baptized with a new spirit. It is like life from the dead.

At the October sessions for Belfast, the total number for trial was seven; last year, fourteen. At Connor, the birthplace of the Revival, the constabulary prosecuted thirty-seven persons for disturbances; in the ten months of this year, only two of the Connor people were brought before the magistrates.

In 1857, Connor had one-sixth part of all the paupers in the Ballymena workhouse; in 1859 it had only the thirty-third part! At the Ballymena quarter sessions, October, 1859, the assistant barrister said there were only four cases, all of ordinary description, on the calendar, and congratulated the grand jury on the high moral tone which *now* pervaded the district. So much for the revived north of Ireland. Contrast with this the charge of Mr Serjeant Howley, at the Thurles[7] quarter sessions, in October; the offences consisting of nine grievous assaults and burglaries. Intemperance was increasing every day; human beings were being savagely beaten. At three funerals there were twelve, seventeen, and forty gallons of whiskey consumed; and in one case they fought over the dead body. *'Public demoralization had increased to a painful extent; the Roman Catholic clergy did what they could'* [how morally powerless is popery!] 'to check the growing evils: *their power had been unavailing,* and the law must now step in and punish the offenders.'

As to spiritual results, the *Banner of Ulster* says:—

It gives us pleasure to turn aside from this view of the question, which mainly concerns the moralist and the social reformer, and to direct

---

[7] Thurles, a town in Co. Tipperary, in the south of Ireland.

attention to another class of facts, which the religious world will appreciate. We know, for example, that in one Presbyterian Church of Belfast, no less than 340 persons have been added to the membership of the church in four months, and in other churches the membership has been increased by 250, 150, and 100. The Scottish minister, to whom we have already referred, reports to us that, in Coleraine, he found seventeen persons in twenty houses who professed to have received peace, and he was assured that one-fifth of the whole population of the town had been converted. In Newtonlimavady, he was informed by one of the Presbyterian ministers that he could now procure a hundred persons to conduct prayer-meetings, while formerly there was a great lack of persons competent to such a work. A gentleman in Ballymena told him that he had come in contact with upwards of 300 persons who had come under Christian influences, and there were only three or four—if indeed so many—with regard to the reality of whose impressions there existed any doubts.

The Rev. W. Arthur, in a letter which was refused admission to the columns of *The Times*, and which appeared in the *Daily News*, makes the following weighty statement of facts, as an 'eye-witness willing to vouch for them by his name':—

During three weeks spent in the midst of the Revival, it was my conviction that, after having travelled in the four quarters of the world, and used some care to observe moral symptoms, I had never witnessed anything to be compared with what I found from Coleraine to Belfast, in evidence of a great and sudden improvement in the lives of a population. I was not a stranger to the district, and, as your special correspondent said, 'ought to know something' of the people.

My favourite informants were not parsons, religious men, or new converts, but boys in the street, working-men, car-drivers, policemen, and strangers, picked up here and there. As to all other things connected with the Revival, I found much difference of opinion; but as to the moral results, none, except that some would ask—will this reformation last? Many Roman Catholics spoke of it with dread and aversion, but all took it as a settled point, that the love of whiskey, and the habit of cursing the Pope and 'Papishes', had got such a check as never was known in Ireland. In the electoral district of Kells, where it first began, I was told on the spot by Mr Robert Brown of Greenfield, that last year they had twenty-six paupers in the Union, and this year only four. He also said that he had, a few days before, asked a policeman if he was 'of any use at all now?' and the reply was that they had sometimes to 'march on' a prisoner. In Ballymena a carman told me that whereas before the Revival 'a dacent man couldn't walk the streets of a Saturday (the market) night, for fellows drunk and cursing', now, on the last Saturday, he could count only four men, and on the Saturday before, five, the worse for whiskey. The very day before he spoke to me he had pointed out to a gentleman whom he was driving, and who, he said, 'knew them as well as I did', two of the worst women of the streets, 'going to the fields to earn their bread honestly by work'. In Belfast, a friend of mine, who had sent his servant for change, received this answer: 'I can't get it, Sir; at the public-house where I always used to get it, they say since the Revival came they don't get any.' No topic of conversation seemed more common, in the second and third class carriages, than the wonderful change in the country. 'Do you really believe', I asked a woman from Ahoghill, 'that the Revival has made any change for the better?' She replied, 'I've lived there ten years, and it's no more like the place it was, than this is like Africa.' A policeman in Sandy Row, Belfast, the hotbed of mischief, told me that now there is not a quieter place in the world.

The way the 12th of July passed over astonished the most sanguine; and to anyone who knows the people, it must appear, beyond comparison, the most striking effect produced upon national manners in our day, in these islands, by the sudden influence of religion. I saw people coming away in streams from a fair (at Craigbilly), where before they would have been reeling by dozens, and I could only discover one man who walked unsteadily. I attended a prayer-meeting in a public-house. I heard masters tell of the change in their men, boys of that in their comrades, women of that in their brothers: heard gentlemen, doctors, merchants, shopkeepers, tailors, butchers, weavers, stonebreakers, dwell with great wonder on the improvement going on amongst their neighbours. I knew the people and believed my own eyes; but I come to London to learn that it was all a conspiracy of friends, strangers, and appearances to deceive one.

Our national condition can tell much of the moral effect of Revivals, if properly interrogated.

What were the mining districts in Cornwall before the great Revivals there occurred? Now, where is any mining district to be compared with them in point of morals or of respectability, in proportion to the people's earnings? Some light might be obtained if two districts were selected from each of four classes—urban, agricultural, manufacturing, and mining—in one of which Revivals have been known, in the other unknown, and the present moral condition of all compared.

There are vast masses among the population of the great metropolis, as well as in our large towns and rural villages, whom hitherto the gospel has not reached at all. City missionaries and Scripture readers have co-operated with Episcopal clergymen and Nonconformist pastors in seeking to evangelize these 'baptized heathens', but with comparatively small success. Even the *'aggressive'* Christianity which a Chalmers pleaded for, and a Guthrie illustrated in the Grassmarket of Edinburgh, has left many still callous, criminal, drunken, and vile. A *great Revival*, however, would supply the remedy. Thus a gentleman writing me from Ulster says, 'The class from whom the drunkards and criminals formerly came are now crowding to the places of worship which before they never attended; they were rude and wicked before, but now they are quite kindly and civil.' He adds that *'more has been done by the movement for the masses through the Divine energy of the gospel, both as to spiritual and social effects, than could have possibly been produced by all the appliances of secular philanthropy.'*

A minister at Boardmills, County Down, the Rev. G. H. Shanks, has also written me. He was from the first sternly opposed to the encouragement of 'sleeping' cases, and 'visions', and he condemns emphatically 'the indiscretion of some over-zealous friends, who by writing and publishing most silly things about the "sleeping cases", and the "spiritual potency of somnolency", do more harm than avowed enemies could do.' This gentleman tells how a public-house, notorious as a scene for drunkenness, cock-fighting, and quarrelling, is turned into a shop, and that the people hold large prayer-meetings there. He specifies the case of a drunkard completely reformed, who had often been before the magistrates. He dwells on the comparative absence of sickness and mortality, the decent and comfortable clothing of the poor, and their persons and dwellings as clean and comfortable. Sectarian bitterness has been swept away. There is an insatiable 'thirst' for tracts, books, and Bibles,[8] and an increasing love for sacred music. There is also a general desire for mental improvement. Young men (who were ignorant) have contrived to get to school. Several catechetical classes are held every day. One is taught by a married woman, and in her class is a young mother who is learning to read.

And then, as to family life, 'mothers are happy with their kind, obedient children; wives with their kind, sober husbands; and husbands with their wives'. The refining as well as elevating influence of the Awakening on the manners of the people is strongly dwelt on: poor peasants are now truly 'gentle', and understand the home application of the apostolic lesson, 'be courteous'.

The Rev. Edward Maguire, the incumbent of the parish of Muckamore, near Antrim, and brother to the incumbent of the parish of Clerkenwell, London, thus replies to queries which I took the liberty of addressing to him:

> 1. Party spirit? None at all. 2. Criminal offences. Never more free from such. The chairman of the county congratulated the community of Ballymena (nine miles from hence) last week, on the almost total absence of crime. 3. Family bickerings? I do not know of a single instance in my parish. 4. Strife and feuds among neighbours? None; all quiet. 5. Intemperance? It is many months since I saw a case here, though formerly it was a common sight. 6. Dishonesty and fraud?—No complaints. 7. The great social evil? Three cases of reformation since summer last; two of them I believe to be sincere penitents.

Mr Maguire, in a separate communication, writes me as follows:—

> My parish is *very small* in every way: a diameter of two miles and a half would take in the entire districts. The population is entirely rural, with the exception of two linen-bleaching establishments, which, however, are not sufficiently extensive to create even a village in our midst.

---

[8] The circulation of the Scriptures has immensely increased during the Revival period. In four months the editions published with the Scottish version of the psalms were sold to the extent of more than 14,000 copies, being an increase of 9,000 over the four corresponding months in 1858.

> *Old Stone* is a very ancient village: it is waxing old, and ready to decay, so far as the houses are concerned. It comprises about twenty-four cabins—*none good*—most of them extremely bad.

After referring to vices that had 'from time immemorial' prevailed, and saying, 'in my own time I have seen and heard of all these things', Mr Maguire adds:—

> At the commencement of the present gracious *Revival,* I began to hold open-air meetings on Old Stone Hill, and they were *numerously* attended. I then and there spoke earnestly and faithfully (I trust) to the people—told them what had been so often reported about them, and urged the necessity of becoming *new* creatures, and getting a new name. I even suggested that the place should take the name of *'New* Stone', &c. And, I can call God to witness, most earnest were our prayers—both in public and private—that the Holy Spirit would visit *us,* and revive *our* spirits, as in other places.
>
> In the course of the summer, many found great comfort and benefit from these meetings. Some were openly stricken, and, almost without exception, these have continued steadfast, notwithstanding that the antecedents of some of them were such as would not bear the light.
>
> Up to the present, though the weather is inclement and the nights extremely dark (and you must make great allowance for a scattered people in a rural country, where no *gas*-lights were ever seen), my Tuesday evening meetings are *very* numerously attended, and the people *take delight* in attending them. Several *Arians* have left their heresy, and have united themselves either to my congregation, or to the orthodox Presbyterian.

The Rev. H. Venn, rector of Hereford, writes to the *Daily News* as follows, after a month's visit to Ulster:—

> My impressions, or rather firm convictions, are as follows:
>
> 1. Within the last five or six months vast numbers of men, women, and children, have been truly converted to God, and become, new creatures in Christ Jesus.
>
> In all the places I have visited, those ministers and Christian friends with whom I conversed, spoke of 'hundreds' whom they could name as having been lately converted, and as having given satisfactory proofs of their conversion by their altered life and conversation.

2. A very general interest in the subject of religion has been lately awakened throughout that whole district.

The attendance at the regular places of worship; the multitudes of prayer-meetings held in the towns and villages, both in public rooms and in private houses and cottages; the prayer-meetings held, in several instances, exclusively by children; the readiness with which numbers would assemble together at almost any time, and at almost any inconvenience, on any special occasion; the earnest attention with which all—even children—would listen to any serious address; the numbers and the ages of those who attended the Sunday schools; the formation of so many adult schools and Bible-classes; the increased sale of Bibles, and the interest with which those whom I casually met with everywhere entered into conversation upon religious subjects; all indicated a general Awakening to the importance of things unseen, but eternal.

3. Crime and open immorality have been exceedingly diminished.

At Lisburn, the inspector of police assured me, that from Saturday afternoon till late at night, there used to be incessant disturbances from drinking and quarrelling: since the Revival, however, everything, he said, had been comparatively quiet.

At Belfast, a policeman told me that whereas in his district there used to be several cases of drunken and disorderly persons every night, during the last fortnight there had been scarcely a single case. The same policeman assured me, that one morning he saw fourteen women of bad character going in a body to the penitentiary. They had attended a prayer-meeting the previous evening. There were twenty other women also, he said, of bad character, who were being supported in private lodgings by the congregation to which he belonged, until they could be received into the penitentiary. I had every reason to give credit to the assertion of this experienced and Christian policeman.

The stipendiary magistrate for the county of Antrim told me that there were twenty-three petty sessions with which he was connected; and that the number of cases brought before them had most materi-ally decreased since the Revival—especially cases of assault. He knew, he said, of some instances in which Orangemen, who had been struck down, had gone to some of their Roman Catholic neighbours whom they had ill-used, and begged them to forgive them.

In Ballymena and Coleraine, in Portrush and Armagh, the cases of drunkenness were so very rare, that the decrease could only be accounted for on the supposition that a feeling of awe had come over the whole population, and had restrained them from all gross and open excesses.

The following are the weighty testimonies as to the fruits of the Awakening, which have been borne by the Earl of Roden and George Macartney, Esq., late M.P. for Antrim County:—

Hyde Hall, October, 1859.

It affords me extreme satisfaction to bear my testimony to the effects which have been produced in my neighbourhood—at Tollymore Park—since God has been pleased to send this wonderful Revival into Ulster. A solemnity pervades the population which is most remarkable. The general subject of conversation in the cottages is the great blessing which has come upon so many, and an ardent desire for the extension of these effects to the whole of their neighbourhood. In many parts the public-houses are nearly deserted. I am told that some are shut up. I visited one where the occupant had washed out over his door the words 'Licensed to sell Spirits' from the board, and declared that 'another drop of spirits should never be sold in his house.' Many quarrelsome characters are anxious to be reconciled to those with whom they have long differed. Prayer-meetings are established in many of the houses of the most respectable farmers on the mountain side, attended in great numbers by their neighbours, who, in their turn, have similar meetings; even those who are not subjects of the movement are astonished at the change they witness, and are silent. But those who have been awakened, give the praise and glory of these things to him to whom it is due, and who alone could have effected them. The ministers in our neighbourhood of all denominations are using their best endeavours to suppress undue excitement, and are anxiously leading their flocks to the word of God, as the only infallible guide to real conversion. I hear that the bodily affections have almost entirely ceased amongst us, without any diminution of interest in the important work. We ought indeed to be most thankful for having been permitted to witness what we have, and more especially *those fruits which have sprung from this Revival, and which have appeared in the moral effect produced upon all who have been brought under its influence.*

I am, &c.,

RODEN.

Lissanore, Ballymoney, October 24th, 1859.

MY DEAR SIR,—Confining my observations to the parishes of Loughguile, Kilraughts, and part of Ballymoney, I have no hesitation in stating my conviction that a great social moral and religious improvement amongst the small farmers and labouring classes has been the result from about the month of May last, and of which I find no abatement after an absence of two months from the district. The use of ardent spirits almost entirely abandoned both in public and private; frequent meetings after the hours of work in one or other of the neighbours' houses to hear a chapter in the Bible or Testament read and explained; occasional prayer-meetings in the Presbyterian places of worship, where the minister or one of his brethren presides; and some public-houses about to be closed, the owners not seeking a renewal of their license.

GEORGE MACARTNEY.

In further illustration of the results of the Awakening at Ballymoney, to which Mr Macartney specially refers, I have the pleasure of submitting the following letter, addressed to me by the Rev. Robert Park, Clerk of the Irish General Assembly, and minister of the First Presbyterian Church, Ballymoney:—

Ballymoney, November 3rd, 1859.

MY DEAR SIR,—I can assure you, first, *that the religious movement throughout Ulster during these last six or eight months, and in my own district particularly, has been a great reality,* to be ascribed gratefully to the special outpouring of the Holy Ghost.

Second. *That God's sovereignty has been most strikingly marked in the subjects on whom the Holy Spirit acts;* often the most profligate, most reckless, most opposed to religious things before their first affection—the young and the ignorant. God, almost literally, 'out of the mouths of babes and sucklings' has perfected praise.

237

Third. *The mode of the Spirit's acting has been varied.* In some scarcely discernible; in others quiet, yet marked; in others, great nervous excitement, striking down, &c., with all the excitement of great muscular energy; these all appearing more the accidental, than the essential portion of God's work.

Fourth. The immediate consequences are, almost invariably, liberty from a heavy load over the region of the heart; freedom in prayer; love of praise; expressions of thankful dependence on the Saviour, and devoted attachment to Christ and to his truth.

Fifth. *An intense love for souls, and anxiety for the salvation* of immediate relations, connexions, acquaintances, friends, *first,*—extending also to *all* within their reach. No labour too great, no sacrifice too severe; no opportunity to be slighted or neglected to proclaim to perishing souls around them the love of Jesus.

Sixth. *A most marked change in the countenances and appearance of the people;* no levity, no jesting nor foolish talking. One subject appears to occupy thought and to engage attention. Even where there had not appeared the special working of the Lord, the tone and manner of society is more serious, thoughtful, and anxious about spiritual things.

Seventh. *A most decided improvement in the habits of the people.* More progress in temperance than since the beginning of 'the temperance reformation'. Sabbath sanctification greatly improved; personal and family enmities subdued and removed; comparatively few offences requiring the aid of the civil power. No blasphemy nor profane spirit—all serious and solemn.

Eighth. *Religious ordinances more loved and attended on;* family prayer *in almost every house;* prayer-meetings in every district, sanctuary crowded, communicants much increased. The Bible prized and read, and its high and holy doctrines believed and maintained.

Ninth. *The intercourse of the minister and his people is delightful;* warmth and interest mutually felt, leading to more unreserved, more profitable communion, *profitable to both sides.*

Tenth. *The style of preaching has undergone a complete change.* Appeals to the *mind,* plain, personal, *home.* Ministers *alive* in manner, I had almost said, in matter. The great doctrines of the gospel are now made to take their proper place in the ministrations of the pulpit, and are pressed home with earnestness, faithfulness, and affection. Quite corresponding to all this is the attention of the people. Most cheering and encouraging to see the eyes fixed, the countenance attentive, the earnest desire not to lose a word, making the minister to know that what he had brought before the people had formed the subject of conversation, was meditated on, prayed over, and pressed home on souls around.

In one word, *I have had more real enjoyment, and more cause of grateful acknowledgment to a kind God, for what I have seen amongst my people for twelve months past, than for all the preceding past, of my now lengthened ministry.* The well-instructed, steady, church-going people have had a quickening truly deserving the name of *'Revival'*, whilst the *outliers* from ordinances have been brought to their right mind, and a large number have been, I believe, truly 'added to the Lord'.

Our Assembly meetings, both in Dublin and Belfast, afforded opportunities to tell and hear of God's doing in the length and breadth of our northern province. There was no difference of opinion as to the *fact* of the Spirit's work, though opinions varied as to the mode of his operation; and each member appeared anxious to encourage and strengthen the hands of the others to carry on the glorious movement.

Doubtless there have been some in every district who have gone back, or some who have relapsed into drunkenness and coldness; doubtless, too, the great excitement has more or less subsided, but there is still a going on of *'cases'*, and a rich harvest is being reaped of many truly converted, of hundreds changed by the grace of God.

Mr Park subjoins to his letter a copy of the resolutions adopted by the General Assembly of the Presbyterian Church in Ireland, held at Dublin, July 6th, 1859:—

I. That we desire to express profound thankfulness to God that it has pleased him to pour out his Spirit on so many of our congregations; and that we magnify with reverence and awe, and at the same time with inexpressible joy, that sovereign and infinite grace, which, notwithstanding our shortcomings, has bestowed on us such evident and abundant tokens of the Divine favour.

II. That in the new and unprecedently solemn circumstances in which the Church is placed, this Assembly deeply feels the need of having direction by the wisdom from on high, and would therefore now call on him, who giveth liberally and upbraideth not, to bestow the spirit of power, and of love, and of a sound mind, that we may know what we ought to do in this time of special visitation.

III. That while the Assembly leaves to ministers to deal in Christian wisdom with individual cases as they arise, we would earnestly remind the brethren of the necessity of guarding, on the one hand, against cherishing undue suspicions of the reality of the work of the Holy Spirit; and on the other, of adopting any course of procedure whereby our people may be led to mistake bodily impressions, or even convictions of sin, for genuine conversion to God.

IV. That whilst gladly recognising as one of the most marked evidences of the genuineness of this work, the fact, stated by all the brethren, that it has been originated and promoted by means of that system of saving truth, set forth in the standards of this church, we would earnestly entreat all our ministers and members to watch against the introduction, from any quarter, of error, either in doctrine or practice, lest Satan should get an advantage over us, and the Spirit of truth be provoked to withdraw.

In the course of my tour of observation in Ulster, I visited Monaghan, and from a venerable man, the Rev. John Blakely, who has been not only a pastor there for nearly half a century, but also one of the chaplains of the county jail, I have since received the following communication, dated September 26th, 1859:—

You ask what are the social effects? 1. Universal sobriety. The police state that the most troublesome of their duties, the taking up of drunkards who are either quarrelsome or incapable, has nearly ceased. Two publicans near my own residence have taken down their sign-boards and have given up the trade. They have done so from the belief that the traffic is sinful. Others will soon follow their example, finding the trade unprofitable.

2. Crime is very much diminished.

3. Party feuds have ceased, just because Protestants feel that they ought, as much as lieth in them, to 'live peaceably with all men'; and partly because there is a kind of awe upon the minds of Romanists, felt, though perhaps not acknowledged.

On the 12th of July, the Orange Lodge No. 1., well known in the history of our unfortunate party fights as one of the most determined, as also the earliest formed, held a prayer-meeting, and raised a subscription for the Bible Society. Similar prayer-meetings have also taken place in other lodge rooms.

4. Quarrels have ceased. Reconciliations have taken place where enmities had long existed. In many families, whence, from this contentious spirit of husband or wife, or perhaps of both, comfort had fled, there are now harmony and affection.

Of such results I hear every day. I have conversed with intelligent men from different parts of the country, and from different grades in society, and the same is the testimony of all. That such a change in so short a time, and from such silently operating causes, should have occurred, they could not have even fancied in their most sanguine imaginings, and they can hardly believe it even though it is now before them, the experience of every day.

The steward of a neighbouring demesne says he has no trouble with the labourers; the Protestant portion of them are so quiet, so orderly, and so faithful, that the others seem influenced by their example.

Today I was in conversation with two magistrates: their statements were very similar. One said that near his residence were two public-houses, where, on Sunday evenings especially, there was much drunkenness, followed by quarrellings, and waylayings, and that he had been obliged to direct the attention of the police to them. Now there is perfect quietness in those places, no drinking, no disorder.

My own field of observation extends over four or five miles around Monaghan, and such a state of kindly feeling towards Roman Catholics on the part of the Protestant population I never witnessed before. I often hear prayers offered up for them; indeed, the persons known as 'converts' scarcely ever conclude a prayer without a petition for them.

Mr Blakely has favoured me with a second letter, dated October 18th, 1859:—

The work is going on here steadily; no great excitement, but the same crowded attendance on the preached word, the same breathless stillness during the service, the same anxiety for books of earnest devotional and religious instruction.

Fifty copies of the *Anxious Inquirer* were sold in one morning. Many persons of mature years, who had not in youth learned to read, are diligently learning to read now, and are patiently surmounting the first difficulties.

Of the anxiety to hear preaching, I may give you one evidence, and I could give many similar. I had the week before last announced a service at Lydavenet, about four miles from my residence. A day or two previous to the day appointed a respectable farmer, living a mile or two nearer than the place fixed on for the service, called to ask me at what hour I would pass his residence. I said, 'about four o'clock in the afternoon'. The day was fine, and it was the hurry of the potato-harvest, yet on arriving at the farmer's house at four o'clock, I found a large congregation assembled.

They said as my appointed service elsewhere was at seven o'clock, I could surely stay two hours with them.

After preaching in this place, the greater part of the congregation went forward to the other preaching station, and waited there for a service which was to continue till nearly ten o'clock.

There is an interest deepening and extending among the gentry, and even our highest aristocracy. Of this I have many proofs most encouraging. This shows not only that the converts are commending the truth, but that the blessings of this Revival are being diffused in spheres which at first it did not reach.

In many cases, without any public notice, the change in families and neighbourhoods goes on so extensively, you could scarcely believe they were the same people.

Among the eminent services to the cause of religion rendered by Mr B., not the least has been his training at his classical Academy many youths who now preach the gospel, not only in Ireland, but in various parts of the British empire. It is delightful to find that a real work of grace is now going forward among his present pupils. On this point he says:—

Among my young people (you know I still conduct a boarding-school) a most blessed and delightful change has taken place. No prostrations, no crying out; but deep earnestness. Every leisure hour is given to reading the Bible or some religious book. On going round the dormitories, after bed-hour, I have found a little cluster of boys kneeling together, or seated on one of the beds, round a candle, each with some religious books.

I have used no authority as a master. I have not even requested any boy to go to the weekly prayer-meeting on Friday, or to the meeting of the young on Sabbath mornings at nine o'clock (still largely attended), until the expressed wish came from himself. Yet now nearly all are up and dressed early on the Lord's day, in order to attend, and have lessons all prepared in time to go to the church on Friday evenings.

Would to God that similar outpourings of the Holy Spirit might be realized in every public school throughout the United Kingdom!

The Rev. Alexander Strain, D.D., an experienced and sober-minded minister, and intimately known to me for many years, after detailing the origin of the remarkable Awakening at Cremore, in the county of Armagh, where he is pastor, in describing the results, both social and spiritual, writes as follows:—

A marvellous change has taken place in the habits of the people, in almost every house family worship is observed. Some of the people who never crossed the threshold of the house of God are now regular in their attendance. As to the number in this locality impressed and truly converted, taking in Tullyallen, Markethill, and Mount-Norris, I should suppose they would exceed 1,000.

The Sabbath schools are now crowded; psalms are sung in the public roads, the sectarianism of the neighbourhood has got a marvellous shock. A Roman Catholic girl, who at the first was 'stricken', has been a regular hearer with us on Sabbath days. Multitudes of ungodly sinners, who were living without God and without hope in the world, have been brought to bow low before the all-conquering power of the Spirit, and God's own children have had their Christianity intensified. This is the Lord's doing, and marvellous in our eyes.

The Rev. J. P. Wilson, writing me from Cookstown, County Tyrone, says:—

The Belfast distillery is for sale, and cannot find a purchaser. In Coleraine district, the duty on spirits has fallen fully one-half. The consumption of spirits in the Cookstown district is less by one-half than it was last year.

The cases of drunkenness that come before the bench of magistrates are only about *half the usual number*. Public-houses are closed on market days (i.e. Saturdays) two hours earlier than formerly, the people leaving the town *so much sooner than formerly*. Many are now regular attendants on public worship who formerly never entered a church. Some have been received as communicants, who up to this year were utterly careless. Those who have been 'struck down' are acting *far better* than was generally expected. We have very little *party spirit* in this locality.

The Rev. G. H. Shanks, writing me on the 16th November, says:

Since I wrote you I have no reason to change the opinion then expressed, as to the social and religious results of the Great Revival. So far as my observation extends, these are *good,* and *increasingly good*. Last Lord's day we had a communion here—the second since the Revival began, I call it my 'second Revival Communion', for I feel disposed to date now from the Revival, it has seemed such an epoch—a sort of moral resurrection. I saw two ministers meeting just after the Revival had broken out in their congregations, and their congratulations and joys resembled what I could suppose will take place when brethren shall meet on the morning of the Resurrection day. Theirs were resurrection joys and resurrection congratulations.

At the communion in August last there were seventy additional communicants, and on last Lord's day, there were thirty more, although on both occasions more than ordinary care was taken in selecting, and several were recommended to wait. My congregation is a small one. In large congregations the increase in communicants and church-goers has been much greater. In the first Presbyterian congregation of Ballynahinch there were 200 additional persons at the Lord's table, and the number at Kilmore was nearly doubled.

Two or three miles from this place, a dilapidated school-house has been repaired, and is lighted with paraffin lamps—a weekly prayer-meeting is held in it, attended by 250 persons. My congregation has built a capacious and elegant school-room, and is repairing the place of worship. A woman from this neighbourhood lately returned from Scotland, says, that she had heard much in Scotland about the Irish Revival, but the report came far short of the reality. We are praying for you, and for the great metropolis.

The Rev. Charles Seaver, incumbent of St John's Church, Belfast, and one of the secretaries of the united prayer-meetings, has kindly furnished me with valuable and important information in the following letter:—

St John's, Belfast, November 2, 1859.

My Dear Friend,—I am glad to find that you intend publishing an account of the Lord's gracious dealings in Ulster; many such have appeared, but all will be useful, and may be instrumental in leading to Awakenings elsewhere. I have written so frequently on the subject before, that I will not repeat what has already appeared, but rather give the aspect of affairs now.

In the united dioceses of Down and Connor, and Dromore, comprising the counties of Down and Antrim, the gracious work has made considerable progress, commencing in the month of January last, and continuing to the present day. I am in a position to state that above *seventy parishes* in these dioceses have felt the power of the Holy Ghost. Vice and immorality have greatly decreased, Sunday-schools have had the attendance nearly doubled, the houses of God have been crowded, and the communicants greatly increased; this state of things continues, very few of the persons seriously affected having relapsed. I may state that I have met many persons who entered on the investigation of this work prejudiced against its reality and truth, but who, on their return from a tour of inquiry have declared to me that these prejudices had all disappeared, and that the half had not been told them. In Belfast we had confirmations recently, and in consequence of the numbers coming forward, as well as for other reasons, the bishop held them in each church, instead of all in the parish church, as in former years. In Trinity Church above 120 were confirmed, the average having been twenty; in my church fifty-three, the average having been ten; in the Magdalene Chapel above sixty, the average in former years being under twenty; in Ballymacarret ninety-five, the average thirty: these only have been held, and the numbers preparing for confirmation in the other churches are in the same proportion. In my own church, which is, as you are well aware, in an out of the way place, my communicants average now above one hundred; in former years under fifty. The poor throng the church, whereas since it was opened I could scarcely get above twenty of them to attend. My prayer-meetings, which I had to give up, for want of attendants, are now well and largely attended; my classes are more than doubled—'the Lord has done great things for me, whereof I am indeed glad.' I find also an increased demand for Bibles and religious books everywhere, but especially among my own people.

In various ministers' houses here, and in several schools, there are prayer-meetings held by the young men and women, and by the boys also, which are well sustained and productive of good; and I have known men and boys to save up their pence for the purpose of purchasing tracts for circulation among their acquaintance. As to the physical manifestations, about which so much has been said, and at which so much offence has been taken, my view is this, they are divisible into two parts-

1. In some they have been caused by the sudden view of sin and danger given to the mind, which, as in the case of any strong and sudden emotion, has been overpowering to the frame, which has given way.

2. In other cases they have resulted from mere sympathy; persons witnessing these have, as will frequently happen, fainted from mere sympathy, without any deep mental emotion whatever. There is little doubt, I think, that a nervous epidemic existed, and that many were seized by it who were not present at any religious meeting, nor had any religious feeling whatever. I do not think that, as a rule, any bad bodily effects resulted, unless when injudicious treatment had been resorted to; for instance, frequent return to meetings of an exciting character, or a keeping up of the excitement on the frame by singing, praying, &c., while the person was in that state. I may also add, that there has been a drawing together of ministers and members of various Evangelical churches, as witnessed by the late meetings of the Evangelical Alliance held here, and by the prayer-meetings held here twice a week, as well as in most other parishes where the good work has gone on, conducted by ministers of various Evangelical churches.

In considering this glorious movement, we should, I think, remember, that it is only part of a great work going on at present in all parts of the world, in a variety of ways suited to the character and disposition of the people among whom it takes place. It is, I have no doubt, preparatory to the winding-up of the present dispensation, and is for the purpose of calling out God's people everywhere, and giving to those already called out, that spiritual comfort and refreshment, which will fit them to bear the dark days—for seducers will abound, and the love of many grow cold, wicked men grow worse and worse. Meantime, it is our clear and bounden duty to take advantage of the circumstances of the times to preach Christ's gospel everywhere, to redouble our exertions, and increase our prayer, that 'God would shortly accomplish the number of his elect, and hasten his kingdom, that we may have our perfect consummation and bliss, both in body and soul, in his eternal and everlasting glory.

Yours, ever truly,
CHARLES SEAVER.

The Rev. William Craig, minister of the First Presbyterian congregation of Dromara, in the county of Down, has also most fully replied to the queries which I addressed to him. Mr Craig has for many years presided over one of the largest congregations in Ulster. His letter is as follows:—

The Manse: Dromara, 10th November, 1859.

MY DEAR SIR,—I sit down to answer the queries contained in your letter, and I have no objection that you make use of my name in any way you please. The work is still going on over my entire congregation as prosperously as it ever did, and the most extensive and blessed change over the entire country is the delightful result.

1st. Formalism has been succeeded by earnestness and devoutness.

2nd. Family worship, ere the Revival commenced, was confined to a comparatively few families, now it is very general.

3rd. There is a very extensive and blessed Revival, of what I believe to be true piety; and many who had deserted the house of God, neglected the Saviour's dying command, and were like Gallio, caring for none of these things, are now in regular attendance on all the ordinances, and never absent from prayer-meetings.

4th. The fruits of the Spirit are happily manifest among all classes.

5th. Innumerable copies of God's word have been purchased lately, and we have Bible-classes in the evening, and on the Sabbath, all over the country.

6th. My elders, the teachers of our national schools, and the converts, are almost every night out holding prayer-meetings in my own congregation, and over the surrounding country—they never tire. Our collections for missions are greatly increased, and in some cases doubled.

I cannot give any special cases of power by the preached word, but the people attend more numerously, are apparently more attentive, and many have confessed they never went from proper motives, or heard God's word from right principles, until now; and, although I cannot give any special cases, I believe the preached word has produced blessed effects.

II. Social Results.

1st. Crimes greatly decreased.

2nd. There is no party spirit now—no Orange parades—no beating of drums—no exclamations, 'To hell with the Pope or King William', and on the part of the Protestants, no wickedness towards the Roman Catholics; but the Roman Catholics ridicule the Revival, and I fear, are embittered against it, and against the subjects of the Revival.

3rd. As to dishonesty, I cannot say from knowledge, I am certain the people are greatly improved on that point; and although I have heard of some instances of restitution, we have had no cases here that I have known or heard of.

4th. I believe there have been very many instances, where quarrels have been made up both in families and among neighbours, and the scriptural statement has been extensively verified, 'Behold these Christians here, they love one another.'

5th. The most remarkable and satisfactory evidence of the reality and blessed effects of the Revival, is to be seen in the sobriety and temperance of the people; we have almost given up our temperance and total abstinence addresses, they are not required *now;* many public-houses have closed, and many, very many more, will follow their example—some through inclination, and some through necessity; if they don't give up their trade, it will give them up.

6th. I do believe that impurity, which was remarkably prevalent, and was eating up religion, the crying sin of the age and of this county, is greatly decreased; and in my congregation I know several Magdalens, penitent and reformed. In a word, such a blessed change I never expected to see,—so unexpected, so sudden, so extensive, and producing such blessed results.

The communicants in all our congregations are greatly increased, in many cases one-third: some were in my own congregation; we had, on last occasion, 712 who sat down to the Lord's Supper—seven long tables full, 140 more than we have had for several years. I had at one time more than this, but not for the last fourteen years.

I have answered all your questions; you requested me to be brief, and so I have. I could have written a dozen of pages, giving you remarkable cases of conversions, but you have seen so many in the several accounts, that I have deemed it unnecessary. With my kind, Christian regards, ever believe me,

My dear Sir, respectfully and truly,
WM. CRAIG.

P. S.—I could not tell the exact number in my own church that has been brought under the influence of the Spirit, but I should suppose four or five hundred. In one townland alone, fifty-two-in some others, even more.

In support of the reality of the Irish Awakening, the following is the testimony of V. S. Darkin, Esq., Sub-Inspector of Factories, dated Lisburn, October 7th, 1859;—

My duties bring me in constant communication with the manufacturing population of Ireland. In the three months ending the 10th ult. I travelled between three and four thousand miles, to inspect Irish factories, and I was invariably told by masters and managers that drunkenness had greatly decreased among their workpeople—in fact, that they had become wholly changed. This applies more particularly to the rural districts, but I have been frequently told the same in Belfast. Early last June, Mr Davison, of Roughshane (a large employer of labour, an active magistrate, and brother to one of the members for Belfast), told me that usually four or five drunken cases were brought before him every Sunday morning, but that for the previous month he had not had one. I saw him again last week at his factory, when he told me he had not had a single drunken case since I was there in June, either on Sunday or on any other day. This week another magistrate, and perhaps a still larger employer (Mr McMaster of Gilford), made a similar statement to me; and the same morning an employer in another county, told me that his work-people had not only improved in sobriety, but in conscientious attention to their duties. I have also been repeatedly assured that some whisky-shops had been closed, and that others must close, for want of custom; while an intelligent officer of the constabulary told me he knew of twelve or fourteen prostitutes who had left their haunts, and who he believed had reformed their lives.

Ever since the resuscitation of Evangelical life, thirty years ago and upwards, both in the Irish Established, and Presbyterian Churches, the one throwing off its coldness and formalism, and the other extruding Arianism from its borders, and uniting its divided bands on the basis of the Confession and Catechisms of the Church of Scotland, which had been forsaken for a time, there has been a marked advance in the missionary spirit, and an increasing consecration of gold and silver to the cause of Christ.[9] The Awakening has greatly enlarged and intensified this liberality, and in many places, like the poor, yet living, and earnest Macedonian churches of old, Ulster Christians, though many of them poor, 'to their power, and beyond their power, are willing of themselves'. Thus, the Rev. James Spears, one of the Secretaries of the General Assembly's missions, writing on the 5th of November, says—'The Revival, so far, *has had a marked effect in augmenting the contributions of the people for missionary objects*. The collections taken two months ago show that in those portions of the Church, blessed by the outpouring of the Spirit, the hearts of the people have been moved to great liberality. Some congregations which used to send us £2 have given £10. Others, *twice or three* times the *ordinary sum*. This refers to the localities graciously visited; in other localities we see no great change.

On Tuesday, the 15th of November last, agreeably to an invitation addressed by the Moderator to all the ministers and congregations of the General Assembly, a day of thanksgiving was generally and devoutly observed throughout Ulster.

---

[9] The writer recollects the time when the Presbyterians of Ireland did not contribute more than £200 yearly to missions, and this was for the extension of the gospel in Ireland only. Now there are Foreign, Jewish, Colonial, and Home Missions, and the missionary income last year (1859) was £13,690. Besides, £60,000 has been raised within a few years for the Church and Manse Fund, and the stipend of ministers has been increased £6,000 per annum [*in toto*].

We shall conclude this chapter with two letters, one from the Rev. Dr Givan, Castlereagh, Belfast, and the other from the Hon. and Rev. Henry Ward, of Killinchy, Down.

Castlereagh, Nov. 21st, 1859.

My Dear Dr Weir,—You will, no doubt, think me remiss for not replying sooner to your kind note of last month; but just then it was our communion here, which, in consequence of the gracious work of Awakening still going on in this district, was an unusually solemn and interesting occasion. The number of communicants, which has been steadily on the increase for the last five years, exceeded by nearly one hundred any previous roll of membership. Since the communion, I have been engaged in several matters requiring much of my time, in addition to my ordinary duties, but conducing materially to the interests of the congregation.

The chief reason, however, of my not replying earlier is, that though I might be able to furnish you with interesting details of many individual cases of revival, yet I do not feel myself in a position to answer your queries as to the several effects of the Awakening. It appears to me that sufficient time has not yet elapsed to testify in a satisfactory manner those effects; neither is my experience in this respect sufficiently extensive to justify me in forwarding statistics of the social results compared with large towns, or even many of the country districts. There is, I conceive, very little of the iniquities embraced in five of the headings specified in your letter, that is, 'crime, party spirit, family strife, the social evil, and dishonesty'; the only one on which I can speak with correctness is 'intemperance', and with respect to the effect of the Revival in doing away with the fearful prevalence of this sin, I can speak, both from personal observation, and the experience of several members of my congregation, who are the advocates of temperance.

Now, the expressed experience of those persons coincides exactly with my own observation in the matter, and both convince me that the drinking habits of the people are decidedly and greatly on the decrease. All in this locality who have been reached by the Revival, seem to entertain an utter abhorrence of drunkenness. They eschew the evil themselves, and frown upon others who might be disposed to indulge, or in any way countenance it. Marketings and bargain-making, once so beneficial to the public-houses, are now, for the most part, concluded in other, and more suitable places. Those moral pest-houses are in a rapid decline, and dissolution quick and decisive must soon, in many cases, inevitably ensue. As matters even now stand, not a few of them are dragging out a decayed existence, being reduced to a mere beggarly array of empty barrels, bottles, and kindred *etceteras,* while the poor tavern-keeper is really an object for commiseration. There he is! poor man, he always looked stupid, nor did he look it more than he was, but now he seems perfectly doltish and vacant—his arms are folded, his air listless; his craft is clearly gone, and his household gods shivered around him. Oh, how it must cheer his heart when some desperado enters, some one who has been accustomed to defy God and despise man, and who is resolved to stand by Satan till the last, swearing though all should forsake him, he will not. That drunken desperado, the tavern-keeper, and their master before mentioned, now form in places not a few, the miserable wreck of a once jolly companionship. Truly, times are changed, and changing fast. When we consider this single item of reformation apart from all others—when we observe the seriousness that overspreads the surface of society—when we reflect on the religiousness that goes yet deeper down—when we see the real fruits of vital godliness, where, to say the least of it, extreme carelessness prevailed before—above all, when we find hundreds awakened, convinced of sin, and most, if not all, converted to God, surely we are bound in gratitude to acknowledge that God hath done great things for us, whereof we are glad.

A very striking case of Revival occurred here last week; space and time prevent me entering into the details, suffice it to say, it was the case of a man strong in body and stubborn in spirit, who had been living for years in gross sin: three months ago I observed him become weak in my church at the morning service, but took no further notice of him, except remarking him more frequently than formerly at our several meetings. Since then he has been struggling against convictions; impressions, as he himself expresses it, came and went: at length, one day last week, they returned with overwhelming power; he was completely overcome. I was sent for, and I never saw a man so ill in my life—no bodily disease I ever witnessed was so bad: his tongue was protruded, he foamed at the mouth, he could not speak, occasionally he uttered a wild roar, he laboured under a sort of unnatural panting.—I could only compare him to the poor demoniac, who was torn and prostrated by the spirit of evil when making the last fearful struggle before being ejected. He told me in the first interval of his agony, that he had felt as though his heart were being rent and torn out of him. A few days after he was able to say, calmly, coolly, and clearly, 'This was a glorious morning; when I rose early this day all things seemed new. If any man be in Christ Jesus, he is a new creature: old things are passed away, behold all things are become new.' That man is now clothed, and in his right mind, and at Jesus' feet, very humble, very contrite, very thankful, penitent for the past, and promising for the future. In haste, yours truly,

JOHN I. GIVAN.

The Hon. and Rev. H. Ward writes thus:—

You ask me about God's work of Revival in this place, and inquire concerning its progress. If some time ago, while labouring amidst much discouragement, it had been told me that, hereafter, I should see the heavens open, and the angels of God ascending and descending upon the people of my parish, I could more readily have anticipated the literal accomplishment of such an event, than of that of which, through the mercy of God, our eyes are now permitted to see, and our ears to hear.

That Jesus is in the midst of us, in power and manifestation, dwelling in the hearts of many delivered from sin and converted to God by his Spirit, is a truth which every day's experience more and more fully confirms. I have conferred with my fellow-labourer, and I agree with him that not one case, once regarded as hopeful, has as yet disappointed us. None have gone out from us who have at any time been received as of us.

You ask for fruits and their extent. What fruits would satisfy you? Would you consider the following as trustworthy witnesses for God in the heart and life, viz., hatred of sin and love of holiness, testifying of grace reigning within—love, joy, peace, exhibiting grace radiant without? If we are permitted to speak of these things as fruits meet for repentance, it must be manifest to all present amongst us, who have senses exercised to discern spiritual things, that in this neighbourhood there is a goodly number who, having experienced a saving change, are continuing steadfast and unmovable in the ways of the Lord.

As to extent, in former times we were most thankful to be able to count such monuments of mercy by tens, or even by twos; but now, blessed be God, they can be counted by hundreds. And this I am persuaded is an understatement rather than an exaggeration.

You inquire in respect to crime and drunkenness. In rural districts we have not the same facilities for procuring information upon these matters as in towns, neither do I consider them at best very reliable data upon which to form an opinion as to the moral influence of the Revival movement. Before coming to any conclusion in reference to this question from statistics furnished by police-courts, I think we should take into consideration that the casting out of the devil from the hearts of God's people is one thing, and the casting him out of the world is another: the work of Revival contemplates the former, but not the latter. And need we wonder if in the assault made upon the dominions of the wicked one, to make ready a people prepared for the Lord, that vice should grow rampant, and iniquity assume a bolder attitude of defiance than formerly? The roaring lion, disappointed of his prey, may be expected to rage the more furiously.

Nevertheless, I have reason to believe that all our converts are honestly striving to lead a godly and a Christian life: they hear and receive the word of God with a relish I never before witnessed; meetings for prayer are multiplying on every side, and although many of these meetings are conducted by persons but recently added to the church, the prayers of such for fervency and sobriety—for spiritual tone and thought—for variety and edification, are by no means inferior to those of others who have been longer under the teaching and discipline of the Spirit.

Not a few of those who formerly were content to spend their lives in ungodliness, and have as yet shown no signs of a converted state, seem now to be influenced by a better spirit; a higher standard of morality is now adopted; a deeper religious feeling pervades the community at large; a greater reverence for religious ordinances is more manifest than ever I remember before to have existed.

I have observed a discrepancy in the reports given of this work by those who have visited us. This may be in part accounted for by the object with which the visit of inspection is undertaken. Those who come to see signs and wonders only, whether it be to speculate and philosophize upon them, or to find occasion to speak evil of the work, not seeking Jesus, they do not find him; their eyes are holden, they would not know him if they saw him. But those who come seeking Jesus are not disappointed; they see him girt with his sword upon his thigh, and in his majesty riding prosperously.

HENRY WARD.

CHAPTER 28
URGENT NEED OF REVIVAL IN GREAT BRITAIN

Facts, Inferences, and Lessons.

WHILE we magnify and praise the holy name of him who has so greatly increased piety in our day, as contrasted with a dark and dismal past, and while we rejoice in the encouragements recently afforded of the growing willingness of the masses to attend to religious instruction, yet the lamentable fact remains that, both in the social and spiritual condition of millions of our population, there is much to deplore. Notwithstanding the efforts of social reformers and Christian philanthropists, crime is still rampant in the land. From a recent authentic statement of 'judicial statistics', it appears that, in England and Wales, the number of committals, in the year 1858, amounted to 139,457. 'It is', we are assured, 'from the neglected, uncared-for masses, that the habitual criminals spring, and to these must be added those who lapse into crime from drunkenness, idleness, and vicious indulgence.'

The gross total of judicial expenses for 1858 amounted to £2,381,054: this immense sum being paid by the nation for police, prisoners, prosecutions, and reformatories. The number of criminal classes at large is estimated at 135,000 persons, who live by the plunder and vices of the community. It has been estimated that the expense of these, at £25 each, added to the costs of police, prisons, &c., amounts to not less than ten millions sterling annually, which is more than one-third of the interest of the national debt. Is there any system of curative means to be found for such a state of things, independent of the leaven of a genuine apostolic Christianity, instinct with purifying life and power, pervading our home population?

Again, let it not be forgotten that the desecration of the Lord's day, and the total neglect of public worship, prevail to an extent truly alarming.

According to evidence (recently published) before the Lords' Select Committee on Church-rates, which sat towards the close of last session, and from calculations based upon accurate data, it appears that there are 7,546,948 actual church-going men of the Church of England, or 42 per cent of the gross population; and 4,466,266 *nominal churchmen, but practically of no church, or 25 per cent of the gross population.*

Again, we find from the same evidence, that the total number of worshipping *bona fide* Protestant Dissenters, including in the number Jews and Mormons, is 5,303,609, or 29 per cent of the gross population.

Further, there is an alarming picture presented of the irreligion in which large masses of the population are steeped. For example, in Southwark there are 68 per cent of the people who attend no place of worship; in Lambeth, 60.5; in Sheffield, 62; in Oldham, 61.5; in Gateshead, 60 ; in Preston, 59; in Brighton, 54; in the Tower Hamlets, 53.5; in Finsbury, 53; in Salford, 52; in Manchester, 51.5; in Bolton 51.5; in Stoke 51.5; in Westminster, 50; and in Coventry, 50. 'So that in all these places, except in the two last-named cities, the odds are on the side of those who absent themselves from every habitual service whatever.'

> Of thirty-four of the great towns of England, embracing an aggregate population of 3,933,467, 2,197,388, or 52.5 *per cent., are wholly non-worshipping.*
>
> The Rev. Dr Hume, the incumbent of a parish populous but poor, in Liverpool, and a witness before the Committee, expressed his con-

viction, founded upon long experience and observation, that the large masses of the population who attended no place of worship whatever, are in danger of being lost not only to the Church, but to religion altogether.

The population of the country, always on the increase, is becoming more and more a town population. In 1851, there were 9,000,000 living in towns, of 10,000 people and upwards, and only 8,000,000 living in smaller towns, in villages, and districts. Dr Hume apprehends that at the close of the present century 70 per cent of the gross population will be located in large towns; and therefore he adds, *if our large towns are left to themselves, practical heathenism must inevitably outgrow Christianity.*[10]

Are not such statistics as these very alarming? Is there any hopeful means of arresting this onward, downward tendency to the dominance of 'practical heathenism' in England but the gospel of Jesus Christ, accompanying with the quickening, converting, sanctifying energy of God, the Holy Ghost? Is not this the cause why the mining population of Cornwall have given up their 'heathenism', and, as a class, are a church-going and chapel-going people? Is it not this that has conserved Christianity in Wales, and that now is leavening afresh the masses there? And have we not seen that that class in Ulster *who attended no place of worship,* many of whom, as one correspondent says, *'had grown grey in the neglect of ordinances',* and from whom, as another correspondent has stated, 'the drunkards and criminals came', are *now,* because of a mighty spiritual Awakening, crowding to the house of God as devout worshippers and earnest hearers of that word which, in its power and love, always purifies? And what God has done thus in Belfast, in Ballymena, in Derry, and in other towns in Ireland,—among the men in the salt-mines at Carrickfergus, among weavers, farmers, labourers, artisans of every kind in Ulster,—can he not do in England? 'The Conversion of all England' is the theme of a noble and stirring tractate,[11] by one who knows what the gospel has done for Ulster, and who believes—and seeks to kindle a similar faith in all Christian hearts—that our English masses can and *shall*

[10] *The Times,* Nov. 5th, 1859.
[11] By the Rev. W. Arthur, M.A.

be evangelized, if the church of God be but true to her vocation of united, believing, persevering prayer, and earnest self-denying effort. He has faith and hope to *expect* a 'great Revival'—that the Divine breath shall come with the word of the Lord, and that the 'dry bones shall live' (*Ezek.* 37:10). May God grant his people so to believe—so to expect—so to pray! For with God all things are possible.

God himself is 'the worker most wanted'. And so let us cry,

> Come, Holy Spirit, come! We want something we have not—something more—something mightier—something we cannot create—something we cannot do—something diviner—a work done that is above us;—we want, O God, thee to work! *It is time.* We thought we could prevent men making void thy law by *our* working, by law-making, and penalty-making, and book-making, and school-making, and church-making, and minister-making, and Sabbath observance, and moral and social reformation: but our success has been partial and our failures great. 'It is time for *thee,* Lord, to work!' Ye who make the complaint adopt the appeal. Henceforth let there not be less work, but less of lawless work, and *more prayer.*[12]

Far be it from us to depreciate or deny the presence and power of the quickening Spirit in times past in our churches, in our Sunday, daily, and ragged schools, and in the pious pains of godly parents in training up their children for Christ. We adoringly recognize the Almighty Agent in the days that are past, in the thorough cleansing of hearts once foul, in the happy and peaceful death-beds of many who have been taken away from amongst our flocks, and schools, and families, and in the earnest and loving piety of many who are now members of Christ's visible church, who, through the power of the Spirit of God are daily adorning the doctrine of God our Saviour in all things.

But yet do not the most earnest of our ministers, teachers, and parents, long for a more abundant manifestation of Divine influence?

Do not we all want a fresh baptism of fire, that our hearts may glow and our lips may be purified? Have we not been prone to trust too much in our machinery and means? Have we not, also, been too ready to reckon up successes by secular and moral results, achieved by

[12] Rev. S. Martin, Westminster.

increasing congregations, as well as by additional annual revenues and resources, and by fresh ground occupied each succeeding year. What, if we have been proud of our preaching, of our skill, of our management, of our mechanism, of our triumphs over opposition, of the recognition of our usefulness by the press and the country? Have we given God *all* the glory? Or have we kept constantly and steadily in view the *highest* and *noblest* end of our operations, namely, the education of immortal spirits for a holy heaven and a blissful eternity?

And have we not sometimes grown weary *of* our work and warfare, as well as weary *in* it? Or, if most have been steadfast and persevering, yet, when the ranks were thinned by death or desertion, or withdrawment by the hand of Providence, have volunteers in plenty stepped forward to fill up the gaps in the battle line? While we have laboured, have we been tender, and pitiful, and forbearing to the froward ones under our charge? Or have we sometimes unbelievingly despaired of success, as if 'anything' was too hard for the Lord? Have we, indeed, felt that friends were nothing? an unmutilated Bible nothing, willing teachers and faithful preachers nothing, unless God's own Spirit should put breath upon the bones in the valley of vision, and cause them to stand on their feet, clothed not only with skin, but instinct with a life divine?

And what if we, who have been instructors of others, have not watched over our own vineyards, and cultivated personal piety to the uttermost? What, if ours has been too much the spirit of officialism, and formalism, or, at least, of lukewarmness, in the best of causes? What if we have not habitually risen to the height of the great argument as to the worth of souls, the urgent peril of their loss, the necessity of redeeming the time?

One thing is certain, that there are vast multitudes both in London and out of it, in great towns and rural districts, whom our instrumentalities, have *not* reached, but whose case is just as desperate as was that of those already rescued, and who must grow up in ignorance and vice, and perish at last in their guilt, unless a revived and extended Christianity supply the agents and the means necessary to their rescue. Each succeeding year, in the report of accelerated progress, is but a rebuke of the lethargic and imperfect past. Have we yet reached the true standard of liberality or zeal in the cause of Christ? Would many sanctuaries be embarrassed with debt, would there be found so frequent that 'scandalous maintenance' for the pastorate, which, as Matthew Henry says, leads to 'a scandalous ministry'—or could there be any inefficiency in our public instructors or our bands of voluntary teachers of the young, if the church of Christ were really and thoroughly revived? There is of gold and silver more than enough in the visible church for every kindred enterprise of Britain; but have we laid to heart—by the teaching of the Holy Spirit coming with a weighty and awakening power—that solemn statement, 'The silver is mine, and the gold is mine, saith the Lord?' If it please the great Head of the church to quicken and revive his people, we shall not want anything needful as to spirit, zeal, unity, liberality, consecration of talents, and prayerful energy, necessary to ensure a wondrously enlarged success.

We invite then, in conclusion, an intelligent and earnest attention to the great themes which we have so imperfectly dwelt upon. The outpouring of the Holy Ghost is the 'promise of the Father'; it is dispensed in answer to the prayer of faith by the enthroned Saviour as water upon the thirsty, and as floods upon the dry ground, out of his own inexhaustible fullness. We would stir up ourselves and all our fellow-workers in the Christian ministry, to a deeper sense of the need of an *abundant* supply of the Spirit of Jesus Christ, for our own souls, for our flocks, the true believers committed to our charge, as well as for those outcast classes of society for whose souls as yet no man has cared. We would urge the continuance of that *united* prayer, which we rejoice to believe is now so generally observed. 'Is there', says the Rev. C. H. Spurgeon,

> any limitation in the Spirit of God? Why should not the feeblest minister become the means of salvation to thousands? Is God's arm shortened? My brethren, when I bid you pray that God would make the ministry quick and powerful, like a two-edged sword, for the salvation of sinners, I am not setting you a hard, much less an impossible task. We have but to ask and to get. Before we cry, God will answer; and while we are yet speaking, he will hear. From this moment you may pray

more; from this moment God may bless the ministry more. From this hour other pulpits may become more full of life and vigour than before. From this moment the word of God may flow, and run, and rush, and get to itself an amazing and boundless victory. Only wrestle in prayer, meet together in your houses, go to your closets, be instant, be earnest in season and out of season, agonize for souls, and all that you have heard shall be forgotten in what you shall see; and all that others have told you shall be as nothing compared with what ye shall hear with your ears, and behold with your eyes in your own midst.

One blessed result will be an increase of personal piety; another, of liberty and delight in the Lord's service; a third, of greater sympathy and warm love among the scattered builders round the wall; and a fourth, that—unless we are indeed hindering the great Miracle-Worker by our unbelief—we shall assuredly, ere long, behold such spiritual results in Great Britain, as shall fill our hearts with thankful joy. And shall there not also be holy activity and earnest individual toil on the part of the members of the church of God? Christian fathers and mothers! with unconverted children on the brink of perdition, will you not begin to speak to your offspring about their souls' salvation, as well as speak and plead for them at the throne of grace? Christian brethren and sisters! are there not many with whom you come in daily contact, whom you know to be ungodly and under Divine wrath, yet whom you have not even once warned or entreated to flee from the coming storm of God's anger. Saved yourselves, and feeling that you are saved, will you not unceasingly labour to save others; and labour, too, in the confidence that the end is sure and the reward inconceivably glorious?

> Art thou content? Hast thou no higher aim,
> Than just to gain admittance at that door;
> In faintest characters to trace thy name
> Among the list of those who die no more?
>
> Saved from the wreck, reach out a saving hand—
> Thousands are sinking 'neath the waves of sin;
> Stay not thine efforts till God bids thee land—
> Thy task accomplish'd, He will steer thee in.

Dost thou not know, that in thy diadem,
The souls which owe their heaven-sent light to thee
Shall form, each one, a bright, immortal gem,
Gracing thy brow through all eternity?

THE END